MW00364119

CONVERSATIONS

with

Eritrean
Political Prisoners

Dan Connell

The Red Sea Press, Inc.
Publishers & Distributors of Third World Books

P.O. Box 1892 P.O. Box 48

Trenton, NJ 08607 Asmara, ERITREA

The Red Sea Press, Inc.
Publishers & Distributors of Third World Books

P.O. Box 1892 P.O. Box 48
Trenton, NJ 08607 Asmara, ERITREA

Book design: Sam Saverance
Cover design: Debbie Hird

Cataloging-in-Publication Data is available from Library of Congress

ISBN: 1-56902-234-8 (hardcover)
ISBN: 1-56902-235-6 (Paperback)

When confronted with criticism, it is not useful to think only in terms of digging up trenches and launching counter-offensives. Criticism should be accepted with an open heart and an environment of tolerance. No person or institution has a monopoly on wisdom and foresight.

Petros Solomon, Tsigenai, June 11, 2001

Table of Contents

Acknowledgements

Those to whom I – and the readers of this volume – owe the greatest debt are the people whose words grace these pages: the political prisoners with whom I had these conversations shortly before they disappeared. They did not stop giving of themselves for the sake of their nation until the moment they were silenced.

We also owe a debt to the many others languishing with them – some for more than a decade – whose words go unheard because there was no one there with a tape recorder or a notebook before they were taken. My hope is that this book plays some small role in keeping their memories and their messages alive, however contrary or contradictory they may be. In this very diversity lies true freedom.

Thanks to Judy and Sib Wright for providing me a quiet retreat on the icy, wind-swept northern coast of Cape Ann to organize and edit much of this material; to Simmons College Dean Diane Raymond for funds to cover manuscript preparation; to Simmons student Charollee Thompson for deciphering and transcribing these conversations; and to Simmons Communications Department Chair Jim Corcoran for advising and supporting me through the process.

Special thanks, too, to my wife and partner Debbie Hird for her unflagging personal and professional support. And her optimism.

Introduction

For nearly nine months in 2001, the Eritrean people – both inside the country and out – experienced the most open, extensive debate over the conduct of leadership and the content of public policy in the history of the nation. This came to an abrupt halt on September 18 and 19 when the Isaias Afwerki government arrested eleven of its most prominent critics and shut down the private press, a key venue for the expression of critical opinions.

This book revisits that debate through a series of private conversations I had with five of the eleven arrested critics – top government officials and former liberation movement leaders identified with what became known as the Group of 15 (G-15)[1] – shortly before they disappeared into the Eritrean gulag. Since then, none has been seen, heard or accounted for. Nor has any been charged with a crime – not just the five whose voices are reproduced here, often touted as the "ringleaders," but the other six, as well. (Three of the original fifteen were out of the country at the time of the crackdown, and one recanted.) One of those incarcerated in 2001 is thought to have died of what government officials, speaking off-the-record, claim were "natural causes," but there has been no official confirmation or explanation of who this is or of what happened. No outside observer has had access to any of them since they were taken prisoner.

As these conversations reveal, the speakers knew precisely what was in store for them – their arrest and indefinite detention – though they hoped for a public outcry, if not for them personally, at least for the issues they put forward. This is why they published their "open letters" to members of the ruling People's Front for Democracy and Justice (PFDJ) in May 2001 and to the Eritrean people that August. And it is why they spoke with me in the months leading up to their detention. They wanted to be understood for what they were doing and saying, whether or not it helped their "case," and they wanted the debate over Eritrea's future to continue.

---

[1] The G-15 is the designation for those who signed the May 2001 "Open Letter to the PFDJ" that is reproduced in the Appendix.

As do I.

Significant segments of these conversations – and my initial impetus for conducting them – derive from my effort to understand the roots of Eritrea's post-independence political crisis within the context of the singular history of the Eritrean People's Liberation Front (EPLF). The more I learned about the structure and operations of the clandestine political party that guided the Front – the Eritrean People's Revolutionary Party (EPRP), usually referred to simply as the People's Party – the more I became convinced that its organizational and political practices set the tone and direction for the postwar transition.

It is not merely that an armed political movement – the EPLF – had difficulty adapting to the exigencies of postwar civilian governance, as has so often been the case with such transitions. Rather, it is that the secret "vanguard" of that armed force clung to the patterns and perquisites of its unaccountable power and could not – would not – act otherwise. It is my view that this legacy presents the primary obstacle to the transition to democracy in Eritrea today.

Is there a new, secret party operating inside the EPLF's successor, the PFDJ? Possibly.

But whether it is set up as a "vanguard" organization or not – with leadership tiers, a system of branches and cells, periodic clandestine congresses and so on – is beside the point. What has become obvious since the 1998-2000 border war with Ethiopia is that the formal structures of power in Eritrea – the Council of Ministers (the cabinet), the National Assembly, the judiciary, even the Executive Committee and Central Council of the PFDJ – are window-dressing for a system of carefully circumscribed one-man rule.

All significant decisions in Eritrea today are made behind closed doors. Precisely which doors and who sits behind them at what points needs to be elaborated, but the question of how such a system operates can best be understood by looking at the soil out of which it grew.

The People's Front – as both the EPLF and the PFDJ are informally known (*shaebia* in Arabic, *hizbowi gumbar* in Tigrinya) – arose in perilous times. In the armed movement created in the 1960s to free the country from foreign rule – the Eritrean Liberation Front (ELF) – one's political preferences, even one's regional or ethnic origin, were enough to get you killed. In those days, secrecy was another word for survival.

Haile Wold'ensae's March 2000 narrative on the birth of the People's Party under these conditions opens this volume. And it makes compelling reading. How, one wonders, could it have been any different for this new political movement? If these initiatives had not been carried out in the deepest secrecy, would any of the protagonists have lived to tell the tale? Yet Haile's description of the organization-within-an-organization among the secondary school students in Asmara out of which he, Isaias and other prominent EPRP and EPLF leaders came to the ELF is also telling. This was their modus operandi from the outset – layers within layers within layers.

Necessary then? Probably.

Necessary now? That is the question that lies behind the current political crisis.

What the president and his supporters argue today is that Eritrea is so much at risk from so many directions, within and without, that its leadership cannot be laid open to challenge or even to unmediated observation and public assessment. And that neither the Eritrean people nor most of the men and women who helped to liberate them only a decade ago can be trusted without stringent controls. No one can but those at the top. Not yet. "The time is not right," say President Isaias and his aides.

But a survey of past practice – how Isaias came to this point and what he and his closest supporters said and did along the way – suggests that, for them, there has never been such a time. Nor will there likely be one on the future. A reading of this history is essential to grasp what is happening today and why. This volume is a stab in that direction, even as it focuses attention on the final days of freedom for a cadre of heroes and patriots without whom there would not be an independent Eritrea at all.

The Roots of Autocracy

The political organization that rules Eritrea today, the EPLF/PFDJ, was created out of a deeply divided society and a corrupted national movement – the ELF of the 1960s. The EPLF, along with a reconstructed version of the ELF, rode a rising tide of opposition from within a highly politicized student and workers movement in the 1970s, drawing on both Eritrea's own rich history of protest and on the revolutionary nationalist currents then sweeping the world, especially the Middle East. The formation of a secret marxist-leninist party within the EPLF was an outgrowth of these circumstances and was perhaps as inevitable as it was appropriate for its time, as both Haile Wold'ensae and Mahmoud Sherifo argue here.[2]

This party played a crucial role in the unification of the nationalist movement under a political leadership that turned the war into a struggle not just for a politically independent Eritrea but for a socially and economically "liberated" one – a new country whose society was to be transformed on a more egalitarian, inclusive basis, even as it was freed from external rule.

But at what cost?

Hearing Haile tell his abbreviated tale of the "anarchists" in the *menqa* incident in 1973-74 and the "rightist" deviation (*yamin*) that came

---

[2] The new ELF was also led by a secret organization, the Eritrean Labor Party.

close on its heels in 1974-75, one sees them now not as aberrations but as omens. The early EPLF's response to dissent – the summary execution of the ringleaders of both groups – aped the absolutist approach to the resolution of political differences in the old ELF, even as it presaged the response to differences in post-independence Eritrea: When there are challenges, silence them. Where there is opposition, smash it. Above all, be decisive – and don't look back.

I have tried in the Appendix to chart the fate of many of those who joined Isaias in launching the party that guided the liberation movement. As the reader will see, only two of the founders, apart from Isaias, remain near the center of power in 2004, whatever their actual influence – Foreign Minister Ali Said Abdella and PFDJ secretary Alamin Mohammed Said. Two more remain free and active, if marginalized – Ahmed Tahir Baduri (Eritrea's representative to the UN) and Mohammed Ali Omaru (Eritrea's ambassador to Kenya). That is all.

Or consider another trajectory. Of the five military and political figures who came together in 1970 to form the faction that Isaias rode to leadership of the new front – known as PLF 2 – only one other (Asmorem Gherezgiher[3]) remains alive and active within the PFDJ today. Tewolde Iyob was executed in the menqa, together with Isaias's high school friend and comrade Mussie Tesfamichael. Solomon Woldemariam, the head of internal security and one of Tewolde's accusers, was himself executed in the later crackdown on the "rightist" group, yamin. The fifth from among these early Isaias allies, Mesfin Hagos, is a member of the G-15 and is now in exile in Europe.

I lack the information to fully unpack the EPLF's political history. Nor is this the place for it. But I highlight these events and trends because they hold important secrets that need to come out, if we are to understand current events. I urge those with direct knowledge of those times to share them.

Similarly, the political upheavals within EPLF in the mid-1980s cry out for examination and assessment, particularly the "three-privileges campaign" that Haile, Petros and Berhane refer to in their conversations here. This tactic – the discrediting of rival political leaders by appealing over their heads to mid-level cadres in the manner of China's Cultural Revolution (which Isaias witnessed firsthand in 1968) – reverberates in the PFDJ's anti-G-15 campaigns in January and August 2001 that form the backdrop for the conversations in this volume and that set up the September 2001 arrests. It is an Isaias staple, and it reeks of demagoguery.

That period – the mid-1980s – represents a crucial turning point in the trajectory of the EPRP/EPLF in which Isaias made a bid to marginal-

---

[3] Asmorem Gherezgiher was a member of the EPLF Central Committee but never served on party leadership bodies. He served most of his time in EPLF in military capacities. After independence, he was assigned to the Customs office. He was moved to logistics in the Ministry of Defense in late 2000.

ize the political core of the movement's founding leadership and then diluted it through the militarization of party and front decision-making bodies, packing the party Central Committee and the front's Political Bureau with military men unswervingly loyal to him.[4]

The "three-privileges campaign," which set the stage for this reorganization, was a moral crusade in which Isaias appealed to second-tier cadres to heap shame on their leaders for drinking, womanizing, and using their positions to secure material advantages. He then brought three generals into both the party CC and the EPLF's Political Bureau.

More than a decade later, the political struggle that arose during the renewed war with Ethiopia was in many ways a rerun of these earlier conflicts over the style and substance of Isaias's leadership. (See the conversation with Petros and Berhane on August 2, 2001). Going into it, he still lacked complete control. There were a number veterans in the leadership apart from those hand-picked by Isaias who retained political influence – Haile, Sherifo and Petros, among them – and the structure of the movement itself, with its legacy of group decision-making and its tradition of criticism-self-criticism, provided limited checks and balances. One can find numerous precursors of Isaias's penchant for despotic rule, but I would argue that it was not until this war and its immediate aftermath that he was finally able to rise to a position where he could exercise it unchecked – where, in effect, his dictatorship was fully consolidated.

Several trends contended within the EPLF in the last years of the independence war as the leadership discussed plans for the transition to civilian life. Participants in these debates say that questions abounded on the postwar role of the Front, the framework for the establishment of political parties, the appropriate pace and direction of democracy-building, and more. By the same token, those who questioned Isaias on specific policy issues or command decisions during this period did so from an unconsolidated organizational and political framework – nothing one could call a self-consciously democratic trend or caucus – and often they did so from what today seem surprising, even contradictory, quarters.

In the late 1980s, for example, a group of intellectuals associated with the Department of Political Guidance came together to develop a newspaper – *Harbenya* (The Patriot) – that was to carry both in-depth reportage and lively debates over the pressing social and political issues of the day. Among those involved were Mohamed al-Qeisi, Kidane Solomon, Semere Solomon, Alemseged Tesfay and Zemhret Yohannes. The

---

[4] See "Enough! A Critique of Eritrea's Post-Liberation Politics" on the Web at http://allafrica.com/stories/200311060876.html and in the introductory essays from which I drew for this paper in *Taking on the Superpowers: Collected Articles on the Eritrean Revolution (1976-83), vol. 1* (Red Sea Press, 2003), and *Building a New Nation: Collected Articles on the Eritrean Revolution (1984-2002), vol. 2* (Red Sea Press, 2004).

experiment lasted a year and was reportedly quite popular among the forces before it was shut down and its participants dispersed by the department's top officials – Alamin Mohamed Said and Haile Wold'ensae.

Isaias took formal control of the EPLF at its second congress in 1987, when he replaced Romedan Mohamed Nur as the Front's secretary general, though as party head Isaias had always been the key figure within the EPLF. He then froze the People's Party (known by this time as the Eritrean Socialist Party, but essentially the same organization as that which had "guided" the Front from its earliest days). This positioned him both to assume the presidency in the postwar transition and to make the state the dominant institutional apparatus in an independent Eritrea, subordinating both the Front and what remained of the party. (See "Inside the EPLF: The Origins of the 'People's Party' & its Role in the Liberation of Eritrea" in the Appendix.)

Prior to the EPLF's third congress in 1994, when it changed its name to the PFDJ, Isaias convinced many veterans to step aside from the leadership in order to bring what he called "new blood" into the political movement. (One of these veterans no longer needed was Romedan.) Afterward, however, Isaias rarely used the Front's newly elected bodies to decide issues. Instead, the PFDJ's nineteen-member executive committee spent most of its time discussing how to implement policies determined elsewhere. In this respect, the Front mimicked the EPLF's operational forms during the liberation struggle, when the clandestine People's Party had run the organization – setting its priorities in advance of larger meetings, preparing candidate slates for elections, and so on. But there was a singular difference in this new period: There was no organized party providing the guidance – no collective body, however limited, however secret, operating behind the scenes. There was only the president and his personally selected advisors.

The same was true of the state. Though the new government had the appearance of a separation of powers – an executive office with a cabinet of ministers, an interim parliament (pending the first national elections) and a nominally independent judiciary – it was an illusion. The cabinet did not provide a forum for serious debate or decision-making. It, too, served mainly as a clearinghouse to determine how policies hammered out elsewhere would be put into practice. Even the military remained under the president's personal control, as Isaias leapfrogged his own defense ministry to exercise direct command over the theater-operation generals, whom he had brought with him from the EPRP.

Throughout the 1990s, Isaias expanded and strengthened the President's Office with specialized departments on economic and political policy that duplicated (and effectively out-ranked) similar cabinet ministries. He staffed these departments with loyal individuals who reported to no one but him. Ministerial portfolios were frequently shuffled to keep rivals from developing power bases of their own. When ministers or other government officials contested new appointments or criticized policies, they were routinely "frozen" – removed from their posts but kept on salary and prevented from taking other jobs, inside or out of government. This process, known as *midiskal*, was derived from the Chinese practice of taking offending government or party officials out of circulation for long periods while they are either rehabilitated or rendered mute. It was applied to dozens of EPLF veterans through the first decade of Eritrea's independence when they ran afoul of the president. This erosion of accountability and the trend toward one-man rule came to a head during and immediately after the border war with Ethiopia in 1998-2000.

Nevertheless, the political arena was contested throughout this period. As Isaias maneuvered to define and control the apparatus of the state in Asmara, so also were the regions reorganized and regional assemblies elected. Though there were no national elections and though Isaias retained absolute control over the national legislature, even determining whether or not it would meet, it began to take on a life of its own in the late 1990s, setting up committees and commissions to draft policies on the crucial issues of the day – the conduct of the war, the framework for the establishment of political parties and the convening of the first national elections, for example.

Meanwhile, the year-long mobilization for the 1993 referendum on Eritrea's political status brought thousands of people into the political process for the first time. Following close on this was a highly-participatory, three-year constitution-making process that produced a legal foundation for the articulation, exercise and future contestation of basic civil and human rights. Much has been made of Isaias's refusal to implement the Constitution since it was ratified in 1997, but it has also to be said that the document has flaws, notably the lopsided power it invests in the executive and the many loopholes it contains for suspending the rights it enshrines on the basis of "national security." Still, the manner in which it was produced, involving tens of thousands of Eritreans at home and abroad in discussions of what rights they held dear and what they wanted from their newly created state, added value well beyond the document itself or the specific articles it contained. And it fed the dream held by many liberation era veterans and others outside the EPLF that Eritrea was on the road, however rocky, toward the development of a popular democracy that would operate transparently within a clearly defined legal framework and that differences that were "untimely" then would eventually have an institutional arena in which to be taken up and struggled through.

Up against this dream was the vision held by those at the center of power that the people could not be trusted to rule themselves, especially in this unsettled regional environment where enemies and spies might manipulate them against their interests. What was needed under these conditions was "guided democracy" in which an enlightened few would make the key decisions about Eritrea's future and involve the general population (and the rest of the movement) in these decisions largely by mobilizing them to participate in their implementation.

Throughout the 1990s, the country followed two paths at once – one toward shared participation in the very definition of the New Eritrea, as well as in its reconstruction, development and rule; the other toward increasingly centralized executive power that stripped the rest of the population of any *agency* in the process – providing them tangible material benefits but as objects, not subjects, of their collective destiny. Renewed war brought these contradictions to a head – and decisively resolved them in favor of the latter path. The 2001 crackdown was thus a political move that placed the winners – mainly but not only Isaias – in a position of unchallenged power by disposing of the main individuals from within his movement who continued to contest this vision. Thus, the war provided both context and impetus for a coup from above.

War and its Discontents

Throughout 1996 and 1997, relations between Eritrea and Ethiopia grew steadily more strained over economic and political issues – terms of trade, access to the ports, currency regimes, and more. They were further aggravated by a series of Ethiopian incursions into Eritrean territory and by the November 1997 publication in Tigray of new maps that claimed significant areas of Eritrea. Later, both sides would cite such issues to demonstrate that the war was the other side's fault, but these were triggers, not causes, for a confrontation whose origins lay deeper in the contentious experience of the two ruling political movements – the EPLF/PFDJ in Eritrea and the Tigray People's Liberation Front (TPLF), operating within a coalition that it dominated, the Ethiopian People's Revolutionary Democratic Front (EPRDF)[5] – and in the tendency they had to deal with each other as secretive political movements, rather than as states. The upshot was a war whose cost to both countries will be felt for generations.[6]

Eritrea survived with its governing structure intact and its borders largely re-affirmed, allowing the leadership to claim victory, but the price was astounding, not only in lives lost and material resources expended (or destroyed), but in the intangibles that had always distinguished Eritrea – its remarkable spirit and its strong national consensus. The conflict also squandered the country's reservoir of international good will and foreclosed the possibility of integrated regional development.

In the aftermath of this terrible war, the questions for Eritrea's leaders were many: Could this crisis have been foreseen? If anticipated,

---

[5] The TPLF, in turn, was until recently led by a clandestine party, the Marxist-Leninist League of Tigray, mimicking the onion-like organ-izational structure in Eritrea.

[6] This account draws heavily on an essay I wrote for the Prologue to Section Eight (covering the period from 1998 to 2002) in Connell, *Building a New Nation*.

Introduction

could open conflict have been avoided? Once underway, could it have been brought to a halt sooner? If not, could Eritrea have prevented the devastating losses that came with the last round of fighting? And what had happened to this visionary popular liberation movement that it was now so thoroughly out of touch with its surroundings that it neither saw this conflict coming, nor grasped the nature and dimensions of the challenge as it was unfolding? What blinkered vision prevented the Eritrean leadership from recognizing that this was not the TPLF of the mid-1980s but rather a Tigrayan-led Ethiopia with enormous human and material resources, a considerable edge in the international sphere, and an experience of guerrilla warfare that would produce a very different battlefield strategy than its predecessor's?

Discrete diplomatic efforts failed to defuse this crisis in 1997-98. After a series of armed incidents during which several Eritrean officials were killed near the disputed village of Badme, the Eritrean army rolled into the area with a large mechanized force and took the village and its environs. Shortly afterward, Ethiopia, claiming it had been invaded, declared "total war" on Eritrea and mobilized its armed forces for a full-scale assault.[7]

Three rounds of combat in 1998 - 2000 produced tens of thousands of casualties. This was accompanied by a mass Ethiopian expulsion of Eritreans and Ethiopians of Eritrean origin, creating a severe social crisis on top of that caused by the war itself. The last round of fighting, launched in May 2000, started with an Ethiopian surprise attack after a forced march over mountains that Eritrean strategists thought were impassable for such an army. When Eritrean defenses were overrun, the Ethiopians quickly occupied nearly one-fourth of the country, displacing some 600,000 civilians and inflicting enormous damage to Eritrea's infrastructure. The Eritreans retreated to defensible positions, as they had done during the liberation war in 1978, and halted the advance. Ethiopia agreed to a ceasefire in mid-June, and fighting ended.

On December 12, 2000, Eritrea and Ethiopia signed a Comprehensive Peace Agreement in Algiers, assisted by mediators from the U.S., the European Union, and the Organization of African Unity. Under its terms, a twenty-five-kilometer-wide Temporary Security Zone was established within Eritrea to be patrolled by UN peacekeeping forces, while an international Boundary Commission, whose members were approved in advance by both sides, delimited the contested border. A separate commission was to investigate civilian compensation claims, and there was to be a comprehensive report on the causes of the conflict.

The Boundary Commission issued its findings in April 2002, giving a little to each side but confirming that Badme was in Eritrea. Both parties initially accepted the outcome, but Ethiopia voiced continuing

---

[7] For an account of the early stages of the war, see my article "Against More Odds: The Second Siege of Eritrea," *Eritrean Studies Review* (Spring, 1999), reprinted in Connell, *Building a New Nation*.

objections over Badme, which had become the symbolic rationale for the war itself. As a result of Ethiopia's refusal to abide by the arbitrated outcome – and the absence of international pressure to make it do so – the actual demarcation has yet to take place.

Throughout the conflict, members of Eritrea's leadership were raising questions about the war – how Eritrea got drawn into it, how it was waged, how to get out of it. But such debates took place on an informal basis among individuals in the top echelons of the state and party leadership – not during official meetings – and they were for the most part hostile and accusatory with little semblance of the consensus-building dialogue of the liberation-war era.

The first contentious issue was the four-point peace plan forwarded by U.S. and Rwandan mediators in June 1998, which Isaias accepted one day and rejected the next over what appeared to be inconsequential details, as Haile Wold'ensae describes in his August 13, 2001, conversation. This proposal, as with others that arose and were rejected over the next twenty-four months, would have given Eritrea far better terms at far less cost than those it was forced to swallow after the third round of fighting, yet those who urged acceptance then are today condemned as "defeatists" or worse.

Tensions came to a head in the third round of fighting, as the Ethiopians steamrolled through Eritrean defenses at Barentu. The tantalizing but indistinct reference made to these events in the G-15's response to PFDJ secretary Al-Amin Mohammed Said in an August 11, 2001, press release (reproduced in the Appendix) implies that Isaias issued an order that would have decisively affected Eritrea and that would shock the public if revealed, but the authors do not spell out their charges. Whatever happened, it is clear that there was a serious confrontation between Isaias and other military and political leaders during this crisis.

Haile Wold'ensae says in his August 13, 2001, conversation that amidst the chaos, the issue of Isaias stepping down arose as one among many military and political options, but he insists that there was never a group position that could be interpreted as an effort to bring it about. For their part, the president's supporters argue that these officials not only pushed the idea but that they passed an offer to remove Isaias to Ethiopian officials through American and Italian intermediaries, making this a full-fledged coup plot.

This unsubstantiated charge is the basis for insinuations that Isaias's critics are "traitors." Unfortunately, the details of what transpired during those terrible days are known only to those who were there – most of whom are now in prison. Absent a trial or a public inquiry, it is impossible to know the truth, as is the case with so much of what currently roils the Eritrean community.

In any event, major differences within the leadership resurfaced during a closed session of the PFDJ Central Council in August 2000, barely two months after the ceasefire with Ethiopia was reached. They erupted again in a raucous session of the National Assembly in September, also closed to the public (and the media), at which Isaias came under withering criticism for his performance during the war and for his resistance to the democratization process prior to and after the fighting. Before this meeting was over, the president was forced to accept the establishment of separate commissions to assess the political, military and diplomatic experience during the war and to set the guidelines for multiparty national elections. However, neither the PFDJ Central Council nor the National Assembly met again until early 2002, as Isaias refused to call the bodies back into session until his critics were purged. Meanwhile, the crisis accelerated.

Silencing Criticism

Haile met with the president in November 2000 to present his views on the situation and on the need for institutional forums to debate them, but he was severely reprimanded for his efforts. This was the last time he had a face-to-face session with Isaias. This meeting took place a month after thirteen prominent Eritrean professionals met in Berlin to draft a letter to Isaias – later leaked to the Internet – criticizing the trend toward one-man rule and calling for the disbanding of the special courts, the implementation of the Constitution and other moves toward political democratization. (This group became known as the G-13.) Eleven of the group met the president in December, but they, too, were sharply censured for their initiative, which Isaias rejected out of hand.

The president and his supporters opened their counteroffensive the following month, in January 2001. Acting through the PFDJ central office, they organized seminars for mid-level political cadres and second-tier government officials to discredit his attackers, most of whom were cabinet ministers, generals or other high-level officials to which those in the assemblage reported, in a reprise of the 1980s "three privileges" campaign – only this time on political grounds. For those excluded from these sessions – Isaias's critics – the writing was on the wall.

Like the cabinet, the National Assembly played no initiating role in policy or legislation during the post-independence transition – at least not until after the second war with Ethiopia. When it tried to do so in September 2000, the president simply refused to call it back into session until he had changed its membership and cowed the dissidents. Even members of the judiciary were moved about to meet presidential needs – and when that was not sufficient, Isaias set up a system of personally appointed "special courts" to hear sensitive cases.

This was government by highly concentrated personal authority even within the executive branch of the state and the highest councils of the political movement. The people with the most access to the president were either those in the PFDJ's central office or those in the president's own office, plus the top echelons of the army. But it all came down to a single individual – Isaias – who, like the Wizard of Oz, pulled all the

11

strings from behind a curtain of opaque but absolute authority. The result was a system of informal and structurally unaccountable power – a far cry from the collective leadership of the earlier era.

The tensions within the EPLF/PFDJ leadership came to a head over the first eight months of 2001, as the power struggle inside the movement spilled into public view, but Isaias had already outflanked his critics.

The challengers coalesced around Haile Wold'ensae and other EPLF commanders and political leaders who had been with Isaias since the 1960s and early 1970s. However, they were unable to convince more than nineteen members of the central council to sign their names to a letter to the president protesting his closure of political debate, as many closet critics feared repercussions and declined to put their careers (and perhaps their lives) on the line over these issues. In May 2001, with rumors swirling about Asmara and within the diaspora of unresolved internal divisions and with Isaias unwilling to engage his critics directly, the group, now down to fifteen (the G-15), put their critique on the Internet in an "Open Letter to the PFDJ."

Eritrea's nascent private press picked up the controversy with vigor, running news stories and lengthy interviews with prominent government critics on the hot-button issues of the day, often accompanied by highly opinionated (and at times inflammatory) commentaries. Many Asmarinos started their mornings by reading two, three, or more newspapers to pick up the latest gibes and jabs. With the added dimension of the Internet, these publications reached Eritreans throughout the world.

A July 2001 conference of the Eritrean Studies Association, held for the first time in Eritrea, drew hundreds of overseas Eritrean scholars and activists. It, too, became a venue for the debate, with many panels taking up the hottest controversies and with the informal hallway discussions dominated by them. At one forum on legal and constitutional issues, Teame Beyene, the chief justice of Eritrea's High Court, blasted Isaias for interfering with the judiciary and maintaining highly secretive special courts. Teame warned that if manpower and material shortages were not ameliorated and interference halted, "there will be something amiss in the development of democracy in Eritrea."[8]

PFDJ political affairs specialist and close presidential advisor Yemane Gebreab responded from the floor by outlining the government's position that such courts had a role to play then and would be integrated into the judicial system with the implementation of the Constitution. This unusual exchange led many of those present to think

---

[8] Set up in 1996 to deal with high-level corruption, the special courts were staffed by presidential appointees – mostly military officers – with no legal training, and they were not required to adhere to established judicial procedure or due process. They had the power to overturn the decisions of other courts, but there was no appeal from their decisions. Teame's paper was titled "The Eritrean Judiciary: Toddling (Struggling) for Independence."

a milestone had been reached, opening up the possibility of public debates on disputed policy issues, but Teame was ousted from his post shortly after the conference, and no more such exchanges took place. Apart from this encounter, however, the government and the party were studiously silent. Few doubted what this presaged.

The first to be arrested, perhaps because of the volatility of his constituency, was University of Asmara Student Union president Semere Kesete, the valedictorian of the senior class. Semere had publicly criticized the president of the university and the government over the mandatory summer work program. He spoke for students who were demanding larger allowances and other benefits for work on state projects. For this, he was carted off to prison (though he later escaped), and the offending students were forcibly rounded up and bussed to a blistering hot work camp in the Danakil desert, where several died before the summer was over. Parents who protested were roughed up; a few were detained. As this was taking place, the PFDJ central office convened another round of seminars for the party's mid-level cadres in the town of Embatkala – pointedly excluding those in what was now called "the opposition" – to prepare them for the coming crackdown.

The main blow came in September 2001, following al-Qaeda's attacks in New York and Washington and the Bush administration's declaration of a global "war on terrorism." With the world's attention thus diverted, Isaias ordered the arrest of the G-15, the closure of the country's entire private press, and the detention of the offending media's leading editors and reporters. Days later, two Eritreans who had translated press clippings for the American embassy were also taken prisoner, sparking a controversy with Washington that has yet to be resolved.

In the months that followed, there were many less-publicized arrests – several respected elders who had sought to mediate on behalf of the detainees, more journalists associated with both the private press and the state media, mid-level officials critical of the leadership, businessmen and other civilian critics, and others. Some were held for short periods and discharged. Others – like the G-15 and the journalists – were held indefinitely with no charges leveled and no visitors allowed. A few who were taken and released described mistreatment verging on torture – detainees were forced to kneel for long periods with arms and legs shackled, beaten with fists and blunt instruments and kept awake for days on end before and during interrogations – but there were no known executions. Still, the impact was immediate and pervasive.

As no clear red lines had been drawn, it was impossible to know precisely where or when one was crossing them. There was an arrest here, an arrest there, then a sudden release – sometimes without even an interrogation. What had the person done? One could not be sure. People began to act and speak with great restraint. Conversations in public places became muted. Few would raise or respond to a political topic on the phone. Rumors flew that all Internet communication was monitored. Who knew what was accurate, and what was not? Which was precisely the point.

And the arrests continue.

Government and party officials still claim there are no political prisoners in Eritrea, that the various detainees are "criminals." But no charges have been brought against any of those arrested – the G-15 or others – and no trials have been conducted to back up these allegations, not even sham trials before the super-secret "special courts." In fact, the government/party has done little more than broadcast unsubstantiated accusations and engage in character assassination to shore up its internal constituency, while stonewalling the international community in the expectation it would lose interest.

The ritualized nature of the occasional American protests over this sweeping crackdown may have something to do with the fact that Eritrea, reversing a decades-old policy of self-reliance and non-alignment, signed onto President Bush's "coalition of the willing" to invade and occupy Iraq in 2003.

The core members of the G-15, comprised largely of the five whom I interviewed for this book, have not been charged with a crime, nor ever provided with a hearing of any kind, but they have been systematically pilloried as traitors willing to trade sovereignty for security, willing to compromise with the hated *woyane* [TPLF] at any cost, and working through the U.S. Central Intelligence Agency to bring this about. These are damning, if also far-fetched, suggestions for men who have given so much for so long to liberate this country. But what of the other ten, whose voices are not heard here?

Are all the G-15 dissidents cowards and traitors – dangers to the state? Is this true of former Minister of Information, Minister of Education and ambassador to Germany Beraki Ghebreslassie, the EPLF veteran who built the movement's education system? Of Brigadier General Estifanos Seyoum, the soft-spoken University of Wisconsin graduate who helped shape the movement's postwar economic policy but who questioned the PFDJ's misuse of funds and its failure to pay taxes? Of Astier Feshatsion, the veteran fighter and postwar regional administrator who presented a powerful paper at the 1999 National Union of Eritrean Women anniversary conference on "The Role and Impact of Eritrean Women During the Liberation Struggle" – doing so in the midst of the war she is charged with subverting? Of the former Eritrean ambassador to Ethiopia and to the UN, Haile Menkerios, one of the intellectual heavyweights of the liberation movement, now in exile and working for Kofi Annan at the UN? Of the popular war hero, former defense minister and governor of Debub Mesfin Hagos, now also in exile? Of former ambassador to Nigeria Adhanom Ghebremariam? Or of PFDJ Central Council members Hamid Himid, Saleh Kekya, Mohammed Berhan Blata (who recanted before the crackdown) or Germano Nati – perhaps less well-known but no less devoted throughout their adult lives to liberating their nation? What charges await them publicly for criticizing the autocratic behavior of their president and former army commander? And who will speak for them in the meantime?

This collection is only part of the record of this crackdown and of the reversal of the democratization process at the start of this decade. The full account would have to include interviews the G-15 gave to the Eritrean media, most of which were published in Tigrinya, as well as other documents produced by both sides during the lead-up to the arrests in September 2001. It would need to include accounts of the January and August 2001 PFDJ seminars in which the party laid out to its members the things they were accusing the G-15 of in speeches relying on written treatises that reportedly went on for up to three hours. And it would need to reach beyond these fifteen women and men to the hundreds more who have been detained, some for years on end, for raising their voices against this regime as far back as the early 1990s.

On the issue of the EPRP and its demise at the end of the liberation war, there is also a paper Isaias wrote for a discussion in the early 1990s, and, there are extensive minutes of party meetings throughout the organization's existence, the transcripts of which are thought to be in the President's Office.

But most important for the historical record, for future generations, and for sorting out who is truly to blame for what would be the verbal accounts of what transpired during the last war, especially during the third round, in some form of open hearings that drew testimony from all those involved.

Crimes have been committed – by those who control the state now. Whatever took place during the war, the treatment of those who raised questions about it afterward contradicts not only international human rights law, but the Eritrean Constitution and the values for which this revolution was fought. Some form of hearings need to be held both to get at the truth of what happened and to hold accountable those who committed actual crimes – crimes not only against individuals but against the nation itself.

The Conversations

The first of the conversations reproduced here – a lengthy one with Haile Wold'ensae – took place in early 2000, as I was fine-tuning the manuscript of my book *Rethinking Revolution* shortly before its publication. I had become aware of a gathering storm within the Eritrean movement's leadership and went to see Haile, a long-time confidant, in part to ask him about it. However, the main focus of that interview was the role of the People's Party in the early EPLF and how the party's legacy affected the post-independence political arena, for I intended to end that study with reflections on the future role of parties in Eritrea and the other countries I was looking at then.

I had spent nearly four years researching the changing roles and relationships among post-cold war social and political movements in

Eritrea, South Africa, Palestine and Nicaragua – countries or countries in-the-making where the leading nationalist forces drew on revolutionary marxist and national liberation traditions for their inspiration. I was especially interested to see how the rise of new social movements affected these highly centralized political organizations – could they harness this new energy without suffocating it, and could they open themselves to a creative tension that undermined their social control even as it expanded and strengthened their base?

The existence of the secret People's Party had been confirmed at the PFDJ's founding congress in 1994, but nothing had been said officially about it since. With the PFDJ at the end of what had been initially characterized as a four-year transition from independence to constitutional government – inexplicably delayed after the Constitution's ratification in 1997 and then repeatedly pushed back after the outbreak of war in 1998 – the issue of what form a party or parties would take in the new Eritrea seemed to be back on the agenda. I wanted to know what lessons had been taken from the experience of the liberation front, the party that had guided it, the amorphous mass movement that grew out of it, and the experience of other nationalist movements in crafting a newly democratic political arena.

I had posed similar questions to other leading PFDJ figures – among them, youth union head Mohedin Shengeb (who has since fled the country), women's union leader Luul Gebreab, PFDJ political affairs head Yemane Gebreab and acting Minister of Information Zemhret Yohannes. Their positions differed on what sort of party would emerge from the PFDJ after the war – or whether several different parties might, representing competing programs for how to develop the new nation – but the debate itself was a live one and, so far as I understood it, not yet settled.

My questions to Haile in March 2000 at his office in the Ministry of Foreign Affairs triggered a lengthy rumination on how and why the People's Party had come into being. The more I heard, the more I became convinced that this experience was crucial to an understanding of the divisions that were developing within the movement at that time, though still largely out of the public spotlight. There was yet no hint of an internal "opposition," organized or not, but there were rumblings of discontent over the conduct of the war and the anemic efforts to negotiate an end to it, and it was becoming ever more clear that these debates masked a power struggle over how and by whom such decisions were being made – whatever their outcome.

Over the next year, I worked on a paper that pulled together the strands I had picked up on the party's history for the July 2001 ESA conference in Asmara. But by the time the paper was presented, the political environment within Eritrea had changed. The third round of fighting with Ethiopia in May-June 2000 not only radically altered the military and political situation, it surfaced the deep disagreements within the

Eritrean leadership and set in motion the development of a loosely networked but as yet unorganized opposition.

Haile had been demoted from Foreign Minister to Minister of Trade and Industry. We met in his office on March 1 to discuss party history and the accelerating contemporary crisis. By this time he was deeply disillusioned and aware that the machinery of the party was being mobilized against him and the others who had criticized the president and his conduct at closed door sessions of the party and the parliament. That conversation, for which the tape has been lost, is briefly summarized in this volume from hand-written notes.

The presentation of my paper on the People's Party at the July ESA conference had the twin effects of further isolating me from the current leadership and opening new avenues for research into the movement's past, as several of the key participants in the party's formation came to me with suggestions that there were holes in my account which they could fill. Among them was Mahmoud Sherifo, previously viewed as the country's unofficial vice president but by then on the outs with Isaias and recently ousted from his post as Minister of Local Government for publicizing a draft party law that restricted the role of the PFDJ. I interviewed him shortly after the ESA conference, together with Alemseged Tesfai who was researching a book on party history and who served as my translator. That conversation is reproduced here. Due to time constraints imposed by the coincidence of a funeral that Sherifo needed to attend, the exchange focused almost exclusively on the party and not on the current political situation.

A few days latter, I met Petros Solomon and Berhane Gebreghzabhier to discuss party origins and postwar politics within the EPLF. I had known Petros since 1976 – on the frontlines and in other, more secure circumstances – as a courageous, creative and selfless patriot. He was a military commander who for a time headed the front's security operations. He commanded the forces in the 1977 fight for Massawa, which I observed up close, and in other major battles. And he was on the party CC and the Front's political bureau through most of the 1970s and 1980s. After independence, he served as Minister of Defense and then as Minister of Foreign Affairs. His early questioning of Isaias's decision-making led to his demotion to Minister of Marine Resources, where he excelled at efforts to promote economic self-sufficiency. Almost anything he took on, he did well, and he inspired intense loyalty among those who worked with him.

Major General Berhane Gebreghzabhier was the Chief of the Eritrean National Reserve, when he was fired in early 2001 for criticizing Isaias's leadership. He, too, had been a member of the party CC and the Front's political bureau since the mid-1970s, and he was a key figure in developing the EPLF's military strategy during and after the liberation war.

On the same day I met these two men, I spoke with another former liberation front commander and war-time political leader, General Ogbe

Abraha, about his early role in the People's Party. Ogbe had served as the head of the EPLF's Economic Commission at independence and went on to serve as the Minister of Trade and Industry, the Minister of Labor and Social Affairs and the Chief of Staff of the Eritrean Defense Forces. In 2001, he was under a cloud after being accused (falsely, he insisted) of involvement in a scandal in the PFDJ-controlled Red Sea Trading Corporation. Ogbe had publicly called for an investigation to clear his name, charging that he was being smeared for political reasons. As he had to cut this conversation short, I returned five days later to talk about his experiences with Isaias in the postwar period in an effort to understand how party and front founders could end up in such determined opposition three decades later.

I met with Haile again on August 13, three days after PFDJ secretary Al-Amin Mohammed Said used the state press to attack the G-15 in a lengthy interview that was printed in all the government newspapers and reported on at length on the state-run radio and television networks. [See Appendix.] Haile elaborated on the plans underway to discredit and imprison the G-15.

The last recorded conversation I had with any of these soon-to-be political prisoners took place on August 23 with Petros, who was by then visibly tormented by the direction events were taking. He paced through much of the discussion, which ranged from the current crisis and what he thought would be his imminent court-martial to the conduct of the recent war with Ethiopia. He was extremely angry – both at Isaias's misleadership and at his own failure to protest sooner. In the midst of this emotional exchange, however, he was lucid in his insistence that freedom of expression was "one of the most important pillars within a society" and that now, even if too late and perhaps to no avail, he had to stand up for it. He also insisted that the recent war with Ethiopia could have ended far sooner and at considerably less cost under different leadership.

When I met Haile for the last time in early September, without a tape running, he mentioned that he expected that the dissenters would be taken prisoner very soon. However, our discussion centered mainly on his effort to straighten out the party chronology that appears in the Appendix. That conversation is summarized from notes.

I left Eritrea shortly after that meeting and was not in the country on September 18 and 19 when eleven of the fifteen, including all five interviewed here, were snatched from their homes and taken to an undisclosed location for what turned into indefinite detention. I returned several times – most recently in September 2002 – but I had no access to the detainees, despite asking for it, and I, like everyone else, have had no news since then of their condition or their status. They are, for all practical purposes, part of Eritrea's growing ranks of the "disappeared."

Chronology of the Crackdown

2000

January	PFDJ Central Council (CC) urges the President to implement the Constitution and conduct multiparty elections; Isaias refuses.
February	After privately criticizing Isaias's handling of the war, former army Chief of Staff Gen. Ogbe Abraha is ousted as Minister of Labor and Human Welfare and banned from other positions.
May	A crisis of command erupts in the third round of fighting with Ethiopia; a fierce argument over strategy among Isaias and top military and political commanders is the basis for later accusations of treason.
August	PFDJ CC debates war and peace, implementation of Constitution, parameters and timing of elections; Isaias comes under heavy criticism but declines to respond.
	Foreign Minister Haile Wold'ensae — a leading Isaias critic — is demoted to Minister of Trade and Industry.
September	National Assembly debates Isaias's handling of the war and the political transition and establishes sets up commissions to assess experience and define rules for multiparty elections, which are set for December 2001.
October	Thirteen prominent Eritrean academics and professionals send letter to Isaias (the "Berlin manifesto") criticizing one-man rule and calling for a debate on the war, implementation of the Constitution, abolition of special courts, and other reforms.
November	Former chief administrator in the President's Office and Minister of Transport and Communications

	Seleh Kekya — an Isaias critic — is "frozen" after refusing post as mayor of Assab.
December	Eleven Berlin letter signers meet with Isaias; their proposals are dismissed and the signers are censured.
	Haile Wold'ensae meets privately with Isaias to voice criticisms and is severely reprimanded.

2001

January	PFDJ central office circulates paper on "Woyane's Third Offensive and the Political Campaign that Followed It" and initiates campaign among mid-level cadre to discredit Isaias's critics.
	Maj. Gen. Berhane Gebreghzabhier — an Isaias critic — is relieved of duty and "frozen."
February	Nineteen PFDJ leaders petition Isaias for emergency PFDJ CC meeting to resolve differences; Isaias rejects request.
	Over Isaias's objections, the Party Commission makes public its recommendations for open, multiparty elections.
	The report is squelched.
March	An unsigned letter is sent to all PFDJ CC members ordering them to drop calls for an emergency meeting.
April	Party Commission chair Mahmoud Ahmed Sherifo (informal "vice president") is sacked as Minister of Local Government and "frozen."
	"A Comprehensive Manifesto for Reform" is published in the private press under the pen name Tesfay Sherif. It critiques PFDJ practices and the conduct of the war and calls for implementation of the Constitution, empowerment of the National Assembly, and sweeping changes in foreign and domestic policy.
May	Former Minister of Information, Minister of Education and ambassador to Germany Berakhi Gebreselassie — an Isaias critic — is recalled and "frozen."
	Fifteen of seventy-five PFDJ CC members (the "G-15") post an "Open Letter to the PFDJ" on the Internet, calling Isaias's actions "illegal and unconstitutional" and demanding a meeting on issues.

June

G-15 member Mesfin Hagos (former Defense Minister, current Debub governor) gives interview to private press supporting calls for reform.

G-15 members Haile Wold'ensae and Petros Solomon (former Minister of Foreign Affairs, Defense and Fisheries) — are stripped of posts and "frozen." Both give press interviews calling for implementation of the Constitution and other reforms.

July

Eritrean Studies Association holds conference in Asmara where political debates are widely covered by the private press.

University of Asmara Student Union president Semere Kesete is arrested after criticizing the government's summer work program for university students.

August

Hundreds of protesting students are forcibly dispatched to summer work camp at Wi'a (Dankalia), where two die of heat stroke.

The University of Asmara Student Union is forcibly disbanded and replaced by a PFDJ-controlled youth union chapter.

G-15 member Brig. Gen. Estifanos Seyoum is relieved of his post in the Finance Ministry and "frozen" after revealing irregularities in tax payments by PFDJ-owned businesses.

High Court Justice Teame Beyene is fired and "frozen" for publicly criticizing Isaias's judicial interference at the ESA conference.

The G-15 publish an "Open Letter to the Eritrean People" in the private press, with a detailed reform agenda ranging from war and peace issues to economic and social policy.

PFDJ Secretary Alamin Mohammed Said provides a scathing critique of the G-15 to the state press, saying the front and the government's patience has run out, terming the critics "defeatists," and accusing the dissidents of "anti-people and anti-state agitation" [see Appendix for text].

The G-15 issue a response titled "In Lieu of Defamation, Better to Argue with Facts" [see Appendix for text].

PFDJ central office organizes 15-day party seminars to prepare members for the coming crackdown.

September   Eleven of the G-15 are arrested (one recants; three, including Mesfin Hagos, are outside Eritrea and go into exile).

Private press is shut down, and nine journalists are arrested.

More arrests follow; all public political debate ends.

October   Two Eritrean employees at U.S. embassy are arrested on unspecified charges of aiding the G-15.

2002

January   National Assembly, purged of reformists and meeting for the first time in eighteen months, ratifies the president's agenda; dissidents are denounced as "treasonous;" political parties are termed "premature;" elections are promised, but traitors are disqualified.

More arrests.

2003

No PFDJ congress.
No other political parties permitted.
No independent press.
No national elections.
No charges brought against the country's political prisoners.
More arrests.

2004

No PFDJ congress.
No other political parties permitted.
No independent press.
No national elections.
No charges brought against the country's political prisoners.
More arrests.

CONVERSATIONS

A Conversation with
Haile "Drue" Wold'ensae

March 13, 2000

This conversation took place in Haile's office in Asmara. At this time, he held the post of Minister of Foreign Affairs and was the lead actor in negotiations to end the costly border war with Ethiopia. It was not until after a third and final round of fighting in May-June 2000 that OAU-sponsored negotiations produced a temporary ceasefire. A formal Cessation of Hostilities agreement was reached that December.

I called Haile the morning of March 13 to ask for a quick interview before I was to leave the country. He was extremely busy with war-and-peace issues and said that he had only thirty minutes. When we sat together and I told him what I wanted to talk about – party history – he warmed up gradually. Once he started talking, he became more and more animated. Finally, he stopped to ask his secretary to hold all calls. We talked for nearly four hours.

This was the first time he and I discussed the party as a party, though we had had numerous conversations since the mid-1970s on the politics of the liberation front that sketched the operations, structure and ideology of the EPRP without actually naming it. Brief highlights from this interview appeared in the final chapter of my book, Rethinking Revolution: New Strategies for Democracy and Social Justice *(completed in the spring of 2001 but not published until 2002).*

I also used the notes from this conversation to draft a paper for the July 2001 Eritrean Studies Association conference in Asmara. I revised this with input from other former EPRP/EPLF leaders – including conversations reproduced in this volume – for publication in the Review of African Political Economy *in November. [See Appendix.]*

This conversation opened a window into the party and its legacy that led me to explore the issue in much greater depth over the next two years and to pursue the interviews that make up much of the rest of this volume. Though it precedes the crackdown on the government's critics and the arrest of those given voice here by nearly eighteen months, I reproduce it in full.

Connell: I want to talk with you about the role of the People's Party during the liberation struggle, and the need for political leadership in the future.

This is a transition time, as I understand it, with a broad political movement, the PFDJ, whose main task is to draw the population into the political process and create conditions in which a national political arena exists and not competing regional ethnic or other centers, as has been the case nearly everywhere else.

What I'm looking for are some reflections on the role of the People's Party in the past, and some thinking about the future role of a party or parties. Part of my concern is that there is an absence of a clear political focus now – the PFDJ is a very broad, very amorphous movement.

In its day, the People's Party had several roles. One was that it re-molded the members of the EPLF; it developed them as cadres of a new political culture. It made the EPLF a better EPLF. I'm struck with the similarities to the situation I found in South Africa while researching my last book [*Rethinking Revolution*], where the role of the Communist Party has been to make the ANC a "better ANC," though at some point the SACP will break off on its own as an independent political force.

But in 1987, when Isaias became the official head of the EPLF, he stopped using the party for this or any other distinctive role, and it began to wind down in importance until it more or less disappeared.

Can you tell me more of the details of how the party came about in the first place, what importance it had in unifying the movement, and why it came to an end?

It's my impression that it was consolidated in 1972. Or did it go back to the mid-'60s, when you first were organizing inside the ELF?

Haile: It came together in 1974.

But if we talk about its inception, I think we can go to the mid-'60s, when there was this idea of the need for a political core. First of all there was this student movement…

Connell: There were lots of left ideas coming from outside. You had Cuba and China having some influence. And Syria.

Haile: Yes. But the most important thing affecting the Eritrean libera-tion struggle was the bankruptcy of the leaders of the ELF. It was the problems within the ELF that created the necessity for a democratic organization inside ELF.

There was a crisis in the movement at that time, particularly in the use of this so-called Algerian experience as a model for the Eritrean revolution.

Connell: The alliance of the five regions – the war-lordism of the move-ment.

Haile: Yes.

Connell: I talked about this period with Isaias some years ago. He described what it was like then in Kassala and in the field.

He said that no one talked about Eritrea. They only talked about their regions. The problem wasn't ideology so much. It was who could be a genuine nationalist. And ideology enabled the nationalism to develop.

Haile: As I have said, there was this revolutionary fervor in the '60s in the student movement. But the political situation in the ELF was short of a national agenda. This gave impetus to the search for a political organization.

Usually I prefer to interpret it in such a way, although there were these revolutionary ideas in the student movement. More than that, it was the bankruptcy of the national program and the national politicians in the ELF, which accelerated the need for materializing a concrete political organization within the liberation struggle.

We did not join the ELF individually. We had a student movement in Eritrea, so we were organized, and we joined the front as a student organization, not individually.

Connell: In Asmara or Addis?

Haile: We had the organization here in Asmara in high school, and we went to university in Addis. In fact we contacted the ELF while we were twelfth-grade students prior to going to Addis.

The link was short-lived because there were imprisonments, and then we had to go to Addis for our university.

Then ELF sent somebody to revitalize the link. But we had our own organization.

Connell: Did it have a name?

Haile: No, we called it the student movement in general.

But when we went to the university, there was a hot discussion, because we felt it should not be linked to students alone. We had to incorporate people from other walks of life. This meant mainly workers from telecommunications because there was a core group there.

We had our own organizational structure at that time.

Connell: This was '65?

Haile: Yes, 1965.

We had a so-called executive committee, where Isaias and myself were called the screening committee for recruitment of new members.

Connell: Were there other people on the executive committee who I would know today?

Haile: For example, Tesfai Gebreselassie, who is the Minister of Energy....

[silence]

Haile: I was lost somewhere.

The point that I was trying to say is that the driving force was first of all the internal situation of the ELF.

Isaias went in September 1966. I went three months later at the end of December.

Isaias already wrote a letter from Kassala, which I did not get.

So when I went to Kassala the first thing Isaias told us was that this was a complete mess.

There is no national leadership. It is short of national programs.

Whatever idea we had about the ELF – because it was only the expression of our wish for the continuation of an armed struggle for the political movement that was already in Eritrea. So we had created an image for ourselves. But ELF was found to be short of our expectations.

So the first thing when I went there in Kassala, when I knocked on the door – in fact, Isaias was the one who opened the gate – and the first thing he told me was that I have to shut up my mouth, and that he's going to tell me a lot of things. So I have simply had to register to myself – to make no comment, no proposals of whatever we're thinking of, no disclosing of any programs we've had until we talked separately.

I was shocked, I tell you.

What happened to this guy? Why is he so afraid? I couldn't imagine.

He said, "Did you receive my letter?"

I said, "No."

"This thing is completely opposed to what we were thinking, and we cannot talk about it here."

So I said, "We have to go to a restaurant. Then you have to tell me everything about the problems with the leadership."

As I told you, we were creating an image of the ELF because that was our expression.

ELF started in the western lowlands and from 1961 there were not many highlanders or intellectuals joining the front. At this time, Ethiopia was using religious propaganda – saying these were Arab people, Muslim people and what not. And Israel was training commando units to fight the ELF, and most of the commando people were recruited mainly from the highlands, particularly those illiterate people – telling them that Israel is the best, the strongest country, the best fighters and so forth.

Therefore, we used to hear of some wrong doings of the ELF, but we preferred to interpret it as being the making of some individuals within the ELF, and that the ELF has to recruit people even short of national programs. Therefore, this is a temporary phenomenon.

But the problem was with the leadership. That was the main point.

From that time on, we knew that we have to devise some strategy. So the idea of a clandestine organization within the ELF was the order of the day.

When you look at this now, it may seem very simple. But this was a very dark moment for us. And therefore we had to commit ourselves to look for a hard, dangerous and clandestine organization with all risks – but to commit ourselves to be dedicated.

Even to differentiate – this is a very important question now – to differentiate between those nationalists who could be committed to have a long-term strategy and those nationalists who are only emotional.

That is why we thought there is a need for a clandestine organization at the beginning, or a small core group, which would mobilize around the nationalists but not on a broad basis.

So we had to make a special commitment. And we said, this is a very dangerous endeavor.

Connell: How many were you? A small number?

Haile: A very small number.

Connell: Like six or eight?

Haile: Not even. If for those six, seven, eight people, we have to differentiate.

To some of them, we had to talk on a national basis. But we had to have a very small group. In fact for the beginning, we were three of us – myself, Isaias, and Mussie.

Connell: Mussie?

Haile: Mussie Tesfamikael. He was with us. He was sacrificed in the PLF in 1973.

So you know what we did? We said: This is a very dangerous move, and therefore we have to make an oath. And we have to sign it with our blood.

Connell: Wow!

Haile: Well, you could be very emotional at that time.

Here is an E [rolling up his right sleeve]. It is for "Eritrea."

Even if these challenges are difficult, we have to carve this E – the three of us.

Connell: Isaias still has this, too?

Haile: Yes. This was 1967, most probably February, before he left for China after that.

At that time China wanted to help the Eritrean struggle. But they knew that the leadership was....[he claps dismissively].

So – while the ELF was asking for arms, money, and what not – they made a condition. First, they want to take the political commissars from each of the five divisions for a political-military training to China.

That was the time when the fifth division had not yet been organized. But it was on the....

I don't want to talk about that now because that raises a lot of issues. Because it was created by the competition between the two rivals in the High Council.

The ELF had the High Council. The president was Idris Mohamed Adem. He was the Speaker of the Eritrean Parliament during the federal period.

But the two main actors were Osman Saleh Sabbe who took the responsibility for external relations and Idris Ghalaudios who took the responsibility for military affairs.

The competition was between these two. Idris Mohamed Adem was a symbolic figure. He was not an intellectual as such. Therefore the competition was between these other two.[1]

By the way this Ghalaudios is one of the commission members of the commission for the referendum.

It's important to mention some of these things.

Connell: You 're going to go over the half hour.

Haile: It looks like that, yes. Because I want you to have this history.

The idea of borrowing the experience of the Algerian revolution and dividing the army into zones – or divisions, as we call them – when I say divisions, I mean zones – was an excuse to create power bases for these mainly two competing figures in the High Council.

The first one was the Barka zone. It was supposed to be the power base for Idris Mohamed Adem, because he's from Barka – the president of the High Council.

---

[1] Idris Mohammed Adem died in Saudi Arabia in 2003 without ever visiting independent Eritrea.

The second one was this Sahel, Senhit zone – the Keren area. Idris Ghalaudios is from that area, and the second division or zone was supposed to be the power base for him.

The third zone comprised the highland area of Akele Guzai, where there are the Saho. That was given for the Sahos, but they did not have a prominent figure in the High Council. They had one in the Revolutionary Command, which was in Kassala – the link between the High Council and the divisions. There was an eleven-man Revolutionary Command, we called it.

The fourth was the zone of Massawa and Dankalia – Semhar and Dankalia. And that was supposed to be the power base of Osman Saleh Sabbe because he was from there.

Before the fifth division was formed, the Revolutionary Command in Kassala was the go-between for the High Council, which was usually in Syria or in other Arab countries.

So whatever the High Council gets for support – money, ammunition and what not – was supposed to go to the Revolutionary Command in Kassala, who were supposed to divide it among the divisions.

But there was a discrimination. And the third division – which did not have a prominent person in the High Council – did not get an equal share among the other three. For them, operating in the highlands in the Akele Guzai area, it was very difficult because the enemy has all these forces there. And if they were attacked, they had to run either to the areas of the first division in Barka or to Semhar, the fourth division.

Now, as Isaias told you, nobody in these four divisions thought about Eritrea in general. We used to call them the generalissimos. Everyone wanted to have his own fiefdom.

And whenever there were military operations against the government, nobody from one division wanted to help the other divisions.

So the enemy used this divide and rule. There would be a military operation on one zone, and the others relaxed. Even to the extent that every division would not allow fighters from the other division to go around their area. Even they started to forbid people to buy things from shops in a different area. Except to make it a transit area to go to the Sudan, maybe. And then, you know, both Osman Saleh Sabbe and Idris Ghalaudios had a long vision of having power bases.

Because the first division is in Barka, and it is geographically linked with the second division, of Semhar and Sahel, they made alliances. Particularly the first division – Mohamed Adem was symbolic – so mainly it was the military affairs head, Ghalaudios, who was able to manipulate this to create an alliance between them to his own advantage. And this triggered a suspicion in Osman Sabbe. Because he was left with one division.

So there were all kinds of stories, which would seem very trivial, but the ELF worked in that kind of mentality.

31

Sabbe had some original links with the Saho in his family tree, and therefore he started to create an alliance between the third and the fourth divisions, because the third division had no prominent figure on the High Council. He used to send supplies via the Red Sea – from Saudi or Yemen or somewhere – which was hidden from the Revolutionary Command and the High Council.

In 1967, both the third and the fourth divisions made an alliance, even to the extent that there were conferences about having a joint command. That was a message to Idris Ghalaudios, who wanted to have the same kind of satellite division – because the third division was a satellite. This was not an alliance in the proper sense.

So the number five [division] was the child of Idris Ghalaudios. He was not satisfied with the alliance of the first and the second. He also wanted to have a satellite – like the third being a satellite to the fourth. Because he was the one responsible for political and military affairs, he was the one who engineered to have a fifth division. He had an opportunity, because now what was left was the Hamasien area, because the third division was supposed to work in Akele Guzai and Serai. And Hamasien had proximity to Senhit as well.

So he wanted to have a fifth division, and he had the justification that the only area where we don't have a division is this one. But if you have to have a division in Hamasien, who is going to be the head of it will be the most important thing.

He had his own candidate – a man from Hamasien. But he was from Anseba, and Anseba is Senhit. And he said: So far the Christians don't have a division. So this was done under the umbrella of giving the Christians a division for the Hamasien area.

The third division – which did not have a prominent personality and because of the problems of the war – was to some extent tolerant toward the highlanders in order to survive. It was supposed to be the force of the Saho, but alone the Saho would not compete with the others. At the same time, it would be very difficult also to face the enemy. So it had to tolerate Christians and the highland Muslims – the Jiberti – from Akele Guzai and Serai. So prior to the formation of the fifth division, any Christian or any highlander would prefer to go to the third division rather than the others because he was not accepted in the others.

There, also, he was discriminated against, but at least in order to make it a competent division, there was some degree of tolerance. At least the so-called Saho leaders want to use the highlanders – Christians and the Jiberti – to strengthen the division.

Everybody asks you, if you join the ELF at that time, in the '60s: Where are you from? If you are from Semhar, the only way you can join the ELF is to go to the fourth division. And the same for the others. So it was a very canny idea to create the fifth division.

Because the fifth division is supposed to be the one for the Christians and for the highland area of Hamasien, there should be a candidate from that area – mainly, a Christian. But to be from the Hamasien area would be more justifiable. And because most of the Christians and the highlanders were joining the third division, that was the pool for the candidate.

But, by a coincidence, one of those veterans in the third division, a Christian called Tsegai Gebremedhin had been in the Sudanese Army prior to joining the ELF. He was a special case, because many Eritreans who joined the ELF from the Sudanese army were from the lowlands and were Muslims.

He was a veteran in the third division, and there was no quarrel about him. He was militarily strong, very capable, and there was no dispute about him being the first veteran. He was a good leader who had proved it from his performance in the third division.

Therefore, for the fifth division, if there was going to be a Christian leader – because they were saying this was to be a Christian division – it was supposed to be him, so there was no way to bring another one when this fellow was there.

But Idris Ghalaudios made a conspiracy. He started to propagate that the Revolutionary Command in Kassala thought that he was to be a target, and this provoked him to flee. This succeeded because any Christian at that time had no guarantee.

Even we were not taking medicines, even anti-malarials. Anything they give us, you pretend as if you are taking it, but you never know – it could be a poison. Even in battles, you prefer to guard yourself mainly from bullets that come through behind, rather than from the front.

So there was a rumor going inside that Tsegai Gebremedhin would be a target for elimination because they wanted him to flee.

And they knew because he used to live in the Sudan, he was in the army, he had a wife in Gedaref, that he could go. There were many from the highlands when they quarreled and they suspected the leadership is going to take some action against them, they escaped to Sudan and stayed there.

They made a rumor that because he was asking for some equality in the third division, that there is some danger. They actually put out such kinds of rumors to reach him.

Nobody was guaranteed acceptance. He knew it could happen at any time. So when he went for a leave, he went to Kassala and then to Gedaref to his area, where he stayed.

So, at that time, they had created all these circumstances, and they said because Tsegai has left the ELF, now there is a candidate called Woldai Khasai who is from Anseba, very close to the Senhit area, and who is also in the third division. So that's how the fifth division was in the making while we were there.

The first thing we said was: This is a very dangerous move from the ELF leadership – to create a division under the name of the Christians, we polarize these divisions on religious and regional basis.

Connell: They weren't saying Tigrinya-speakers – they were saying Christians?

Haile: Christians. Christians, they were saying.

They were saying that because the Christians had felt that they are second class in the ELF, now we are giving them the right to have their own division.

But the assistant commander was from us. We wanted to make sure that this Woldai would not create his own fiefdom. And many of the first combatants were from the area of the second division and some from the first division in Barka. Even those highlanders were very few.

So he wanted the fifth division to be a satellite to the second division. And there was the alliance with the first division.

Connell: Back to the party?

Haile: Yes, back to the party.

We said that giving a division to the Christians would only make the problem worse. Because the Christians have been experiencing a lot of harassment from the other divisions, under Woldai Kahsai they would only think of creating a Christian force, and that was it.

But we said, No. We don't have to come to this track of the ELF.

They were saying to every Christian to join this expedition. But we said [to ourselves], No. We have to be in the different divisions, try to work with other nationalists from other areas. We don't have to concentrate into the fifth division. So, even before I went to Kassala, there was this quarrel between Woldai and Isaias.

Now, Woldai knew that Idris Ghalaudios was creating this division to be a satellite to the second division. But, he said, we will make this our own division, and we will show them. In a very short time, this division will be the strongest division of the ELF. We will go and recruit from the highlands, and we will succeed because we know how to do that.

Even prior to my coming there, Isaias had said to him that is not how we should work. We don't have to go into their trap. We should use the fifth division to recruit many people from the highlands to give us some strength in bargaining for the equality [within ELF] and for reforms and for change.

But Woldai said, No. Now they have chosen me as the commander of this. Every Christian in the highlands should come and join our division and make this very strong.

So there was a problem from the very beginning.

And then Woldai Kahsai would say, I don't like this organization of yours. Because he knew we had our organization in Asmara, in the cities in Eritrea, and in Addis. He used to say, I don't like this organized group. Let everybody join me. We will be strong in a very short time. We will show them our strength. And through that strength, we will realize our equality.

So, there was a quarrel from the very beginning.

Before the fifth division started to be organized, we had to suffer a lot. Not only from the ELF leadership, but from the leadership of the fifth division itself. In fact, at that time, while it was at its inception, this new element, the external element – the Chinese request for a political-military training camp – came up.

But the fifth division – Woldai Kahsai was the commander who was nominated – but still it was not organized.

The Chinese told them that they want five commissars, the political commissars of each of those divisions. The fifth division was only in its inception – there was no political commissar – but they told them, we have to have a political commissar from the fifth division. That was a time when the leadership was…

Connell: They were watching this very closely.

Haile: Oh, yes.

The Chinese said: We will not give you ammunition, money, before we train these people.

And for the ELF, it was an open agenda to say that the fifth division is for the Christian; and therefore we have to bring one Christian.

Connell: Woldai probably wanted to get Isaias out.

Haile: That is possible. So he was chosen.

But, you know, in February when we were in Kassala, we said at first that Isaias should not be one of those five people who was going to China, because usually, under the pretext of some training or sending some message, they take people and eliminate them. When the three of us heard this, we said, now they are saying that Isaias is going to China, but we don't know whether he's going to reach China or not.

But then we said, in case they are doing it in order to satisfy the Chinese, it would be an opportunity for us to build an external link with progressive forces outside. Not only as an exposure but as an invest-ment for this external link. Because external relations are dominated by the ELF leadership.

And so we agreed that I should go to the fifth division to be a link to our clandestine organizations inside Eritrea and in Ethiopia. I would be the link. Isaias would be going outside. We were not sure – 50/50, we said at that time, he might not go.

And we preferred the third one, Mussie, to stay in Kassala because we have already started a magazine. There was no Tigrinya literature in ELF at that time, so we started a journal, or a newspaper. We named it, "The Renaissance of the Youth." We used to write it on a typewriter, on a stencil. And therefore, we said, he will take care of that newspaper. He will be a link in Kassala.

We were very frank among ourselves, the three of us, to say: Because Mussie was very emotional, he would not survive going inside. In fact, we thought he could spoil our strategy because he was not very balanced. He was more emotional.

Connell: What do you mean?

Haile: Even before, while we were in the high school, Mussie was very dedicated. But because he was very emotional, when we organized that clandestine organization, we said he is committed, but he cannot work in the clandestine organization, he would be dangerous. So we said, he will be outside that. We will not tell him. But we will allow him to participate without being inside.

So even he went with me to Kassala. I did not go alone. And he never knew we had that clandestine organization, a link with the ELF. We would simply say that we hear something about the ELF...

Only when I crossed the border of Eritrea and Sudan, going to Kassala, I told him, Okay, we have this clandestine organization. But because of your character, your emotion, your anarchist tendencies, we felt it would be dangerous to the clandestine organization and to you. But we never hid anything from you.

So that was one of the reasons why we wanted him to stay there.

Connell: But by this time you did bring him in?

Haile: Yes, yes, yes. But let me tell you the necessary context.

We felt that, like what we have done with Mussie before, there will be people who would not be *insiders* because it is a very dangerous environment. And then – I will tell you – and this is very important – Woldai now was saying that he is a general, another general, and that every Christian should come from the other divisions – particularly from the third division.

We were opposed to that, so already there was a rift. But we wanted to exploit the friction between Woldai Kahsai and the Revolutionary Command in Kassala to our advantage.

Every division has its own area. And therefore whatever money is collected will go to that division. And then, the cities – for example, for the second division, Keren is the capital city. And because it is a big town, there will be a lot of money-contributions that will go to the second division. And any – they used to call it *fedayin*, terrorist – for example, in that area. Every division had its own *fedayin* group, which would take military action – liquidation of the enemy, something like that.

When the fifth division was named to work on Hamasien, the capital of Hamasien was the same as the country – Asmara – so now there was a friction between the fifth division and the Revolutionary Command. Because the Revolutionary Command now says: No, Asmara is the capital of Eritrea, and therefore it must be under my jurisdiction.

And Woldai said: Well, Asmara is the capital of Hamasien, and therefore it must be mine.

So what is important at that time – we used to quarrel.

When we were talking about what we are doing, what is the strategy...

The strategy of the ELF is on where do we find food! It is not how to progress the revolution or to attack enemies, because the main strategy of the leaders of the units was that if we work in that area, maybe there will be another unit and therefore will be too many, the food will be too short for us.

So the strategy of the leaders of the ELF was based on operating where you find enough food so that there are no other units who are competing with you. But they never talked about what are we going to do to mobilize the people, to attack the enemy.

So, where is your area was important because you get money from that and do some *fedayin* works there. So this was a problem between the fifth division and the Revolutionary Command in Kassala.

The Revolutionary Command said: No, Asmara is the capital of Eritrea and therefore it must be under direct jurisdiction. So they said they will form this *fedayin* group of the Revolutionary Command – its own *fedayin* group which will do *fedayin* works and at the same time, collect money. Because money to be collected from Asmara would be very great. So now we said: They know we have this clandestine organization in Asmara and in Ethiopia, in Addis Ababa, so we will use that.

I teased them, saying: Well, you are correct, Asmara is the capital city of Eritrea, and it [the Asmara population] has extensions in Addis Ababa and in other cities of Ethiopia, and we are the ones that have organized it.

They know it. And therefore I made myself a candidate for the Revolutionary Command in Kassala – to be their man, to link them with the clandestine organization in Asmara and other cities.

They knew I am one of those, and therefore they made a special program to train me on the *fedayin* activities on the border between Sudan and Eritrea.

At that time, Woldai was sent to the same area of the Sudan because they said there were some arms which were coming across the Red Sea, and we had to receive this portion – the portion of the division. At that time I used that opportunity to make a conspiracy.

There were some people who were trained in Syria. They gave me a special training to be a *fedayin* so that I will go to the fifth division but be a link to the Revolutionary Command.

While Woldai was out, and still the fighters were not organized, I had to go inside Asmara and Addis. So the Revolutionary Command thinks it has now recruited me against Woldai. (Woldai doesn't know I have gone to Asmara and Addis. He went to bring the arms.) I had to go inside to tell our clandestine organization what the situation looks like. And to inform them that now we are trying to use the fifth division, not the way Woldai wants it, but in a clandestine way, and to have the clandestine organization as our base.

There could be some problem. We might not get supplies from the Revolutionary Command in Kassala. And therefore for all kinds of medicines – because of the war wounds and what not – the internal organization, the clandestine organization had to prepare for medicines, for clothes, for all kinds of logistics.

So I went there. At that time, Tesfai Gebreselassie was still one of the executive members of the clandestine organization inside. He was still in Addis. The other prominent leader was Kidane Kiflu, who later the Revolutionary Command killed in Kassala, one of the two guys they killed there in 1969. But he was inside when I went there.

I told them everything.

When Isaias left to China, I took that training for a short time – I think it was a week – and by March I was inside. I met those people and told them about the problem inside the fifth division.

There were three clandestine activities in the fifth division at that time. One was the deputy commander who was supposed to make the fifth division a satellite of the second division. He had his own men. He would not allow it to be an independent division.

Then there is Woldai, trying to make it a Christian division.

And we are inside, exploiting the difference between Woldai and the Revolutionary Command in Kassala. That was the only organized clandestine organization. The others were emotional individuals. But ours was an organized group, a revolutionary organization – we had the left orientation.

With our clandestine organization in Asmara and in Addis, we thought the Ethiopian government would be looking for us, and therefore we said we have to have a camouflage. So we created another broad-based Eritrean association, which will deal with social and culture affairs as a camouflage for us.

There were many of our friends in this – who were nationalists, for that matter – but we had this clandestine internal one and we had another broad-based one as a camouflage – a cooperative – to deal with social problems and what not.

We called it an Eritrean Association of the Youth – a cooperative, in Tigrinya – because we were students and we could solve some problems together, cultural problems. We used the cultural element as a unifying force. We used drama to preserve our culture and develop the language.

So the Eritreans were deceived because they thought that was the only clandestine organization. The government was deceived because they thought they know about this – but they didn't know about our other activities. So, even at that time, we had an organization within an organization.

So I met these internal organizations. I told them everything, everything. That our strategy was to persevere until such time that we can organize people on a national level with other members of the other divisions but having that central core group whose base would be that clandestine organization.

And we told them anyone who came from the city would not be able to tolerate the situation in the ELF. He would simply react and it would spoil our project.

So I told them, nobody should join now from the city. Prepare yourself for any difficulties that you might encounter, so that we can be relying on you for all kinds of support.

But we will try to use this fifth division to recruit peasants from the highlands, because these peasants are not educated and therefore they will not be much questioning the political line. They are in a better position to adjust themselves, because it is a very difficult condition at that time. These are the ones whom we can rely on for the time being.

So we will try to recruit from the peasants who can tolerate these things, who will not be much questioning about this democracy and the political line, and who can survive these hardships, the physical hardships.

No one should come from that clandestine internal organization – unless he is exposed and the government wants to catch him. That is the only thing. Otherwise, we have another agenda and a long-term strategy. There was no need for them to come.

And then I made a lot of coordination and told them I would now also deceive Woldai to look as if I would be a loyal person of him. And in order to have a link with the city, with the internal group, I would make myself a candidate of Woldai to be in the *fedayin* group for the fifth division – in order to get access to the inside.

We made all kinds of arrangements – codes and what not. And then, when I returned back, still the fifth division was organizing its

39

army, so I went to Barka and I met them and then I proposed myself to be in the *fedayin*. I discussed this with Woldai that the Revolutionary Command wants Asmara to be under their control. This is not right. It must be under the fifth division, and I know the inside of everything. And therefore I will be the *fedayin* from the fifth division, to have the link with the internal organization.

He had already made a lot of calculations himself. Well, he told me, the ELF now has the support of – at that time, they used to call it, artillery. This was the first time the ELF got 60 mm mortars. And there was one 60 mm mortar for every division. So there was a new 60 mm mortar for the fifth division, and of course because the Revolutionary Command did not want the fifth division to be an independent division, they had come with an officer, who was trained in Iraq, who was to be responsible for the artillery.

At that time there was only the one mortar but they were thinking there would be more. The officer had been trained in Iraq for two years, but all he had was one mortar.

And now, Woldai told me, there is one mortar. And there will be more coming. They have sent this officer from the other areas. They want to control us. Now I want you to be the artillery chief because you are an engineering student, and you are the only one from the Christians who could easily be trained so that later you will take his position and you will train others and whenever there is new artillery coming, you will be the one who is responsible for that in order for us Christians to command our own artillery.

This was a typical ELF intrigue. Because let alone this mortar – which was supposed to be superior artillery – the machine gun was the heaviest we had. You know in the ELF they want to keep you from any activity, they will assign you to this machine gun.

If you are assigned to a machine gun, you never move from it. You never contact other people. Even when people are eating, they have to come to your place to eat with you.

And now he's telling me that because we want to control ourselves, we have to take over this mortar, and you have to do it.

He did not want me to be in the *fedayin* because he is afraid of us – that we are organized, and we have not accepted his way of thinking. We are not interested in making the division a Christian division. And we had told some highlanders in the third division to remain there.

Connell: He knew that?

Haile: Yes, he knew that.

At the first moment, we thought he could understand us and go with our thinking, so we had exposed ourselves to some extent. And therefore, he told me, you are dangerous.

Now I have to use the same logic to convince him. So I said, there is nothing ingenious about this mortar. I can make a table. If you know the distance, what would be the angle, I can make a table that anybody can use. You have to guess the distance and then you know the angle.

Each of us is having a hidden agenda.

Connell: You were an engineering student? Along with Isaias?

Haile: Isaias was not an engineering student; he was in science. I was in engineering.

Connell: Was Isaias in touch with you when he was in China?

Haile: No. He was not around. The training was supposed to be six months, but it took longer. Maybe eight months, I'm not sure.

And we don't know whether he is alive or not. There was no communication at all, no nothing.

Okay. So I tried arguing, bringing all kinds of excuses, but he refused. I had to stick with that mortar. No way to move.

But he has organized a *fedayin* group of the fifth division. And he didn't know that I had somebody from our core group, or clandestine organization, inside it.

Now this is a long story because from the very beginning, all the conflicts inside ELF boiled down into the fifth division.

The fifth division almost ended just as it was beginning, and it led to the boiling of all the contradictions inside the ELF from each side, from all the actors.

As a fifth division, we organized ourselves in April that we had to move ourselves to Hamasien.

All the contradictions exploded in the fifth division because from the very beginning the deputy commander has to make sure that the fifth division does not become independent. And therefore, he did not want a healthy communication of the fifth division with the highlanders. Otherwise, there will be a lot of recruits and it will be out of control. So he had to bring some kind of contradiction within us, to create a friction between the fifth division and the population in Hamasien. He has to work on this from day one.

Woldai had to make sure that it becomes a strong organization from day one.

And from day one we had to work to make sure that our internal clandestine organization was set up properly so as not to be jeopardized.

So there was ambition from everybody.

And then the Revolutionary Command in Kassala, because of the distance, wanted to make sure by sending so-called prominent people to make sure its interests were realized there. That is why, in a very short time, everything came to a boil.

And that is why there came the necessity for creating the clandestine organization. And more than that, it has to go beyond the national program.

So, all the challenges in the ELF necessitated to have an ideology that could match or challenge all the different parts – not only the ELF, even narrow national feelings have to be fought. And therefore, there is the need for a philosophy, a need for an ideology, as a tool to be used to fight all these challenges.

I would prefer to say the need for a revolutionary party – although it had some theoretical background because we were exposed to leftist thinking – came mainly from the intrigue and conflict within the ELF, which made us feel that there must be a particular ideology that would fight all kinds of things, even nationalists who were short-sighted – narrow nationalists. We had to fight it.

So I think, from my experience, although we had some exposure of leftist thinking, it was not mature. I would consider it on an emotional plane or state before we joined the ELF. But the reality created an incentive to look for an outlook that would deliver a solution for all these kinds of problems.

Isaias, when he went to China also – the intentions of China were from the very beginning to have an ideological training. Immediately, out of those five, only the two – Isaias and Romedan (Romedan was representing the fourth division) – have to look at the Chinese experience as something that Eritrea can benefit from. Trying to analyze our problems with the experience of China on one hand – and with the political orientation, ideological orientation – to see whether those things could be a solution to the conflicts we were facing in the Eritrean revolution.

So for them, it was an exposure on one hand; at the same time, it was enlightening to see that the Chinese revolution had gone through a lot of problems, maybe similar problems to some extent. And they thought this was, at minimum, a similar and, at best, if not a model, at least some possible solutions for the conflict problems.

So that was the time when they decided also to have this inside group, because the Chinese were giving them all this ideological strategy.

Connell: This is just Romedan and Isaias, or the whole five?

Haile: No, the other three were not interested in the studies. They wouldn't eat the meat of the pig. All kinds of things, they would not do.

They were saying that the ELF has sent us in order for the Chinese to be able to send us arms. Otherwise we don't have to study these things. Simply, we have to listen and forget it.

The others were not interested in the experience of Chinese. They were saying that these are Communists. There was a clear difference between these three and Isaias and Romedan. That is why there was a confidence built between Isaias and Romedan. They met there. They did not know each other before.

Connell: Romedan obviously came there with some of the same ideas.

Haile: Yes, because he was in Cairo. He was an intellectual. But the others were representing the reactionary groups inside the ELF.

Connell: So you have these two. You're busy organizing and strengthening the contacts of the clandestine organization?

Haile: Which I failed to some extent, because I was assigned to this artillery.

And later, maybe by June or July '67, there was some problem inside Addis, and the government of Ethiopia knew about some of the members of the internal clandestine organization, so they have to escape.

So, Kidane Kiflu, Tesfai Gebreselassie – who is Minister of Energy now – they have to escape. And because they knew we had this new fifth division in highlands, in Hamasien, they came, and they wanted to contact me – to give them guidance where to go.

They knew about Woldai; they knew about the complications of the ELF. And when they came, he met them. When they asked about me, he said I was somewhere with the mortar, and he told them they have to stay there. But they know that in the fifth division there are all these kinds of problems, so they preferred to go to Kassala.

He tried to convince them to stay there, because he didn't want people to go to Kassala. They would be a link to that clandestine organization, so he wanted to make sure to control them. He wanted them there.

But they said they are going to Kassala, and one of our people in the *fedayin* group met them and told them the area I was around, so they had to pass that area. At this time, I was around Filfil. You remember that area?

Connell: Yes.

Haile: This guy told them that they should go there.

But Woldai sent a message to our artillery unit – we called it that, with only one mortar! – telling me of the possibility of an enemy offensive from Merera, on the mountain. And because the other fighters were not competent, I had to go myself and make a reconnaissance. This was on the same day the others were coming.

So when Woldai sent this message to me, I asked, why is he saying this? Does he want me to be a victim of some offensive? The artillery unit is a small unit, with only one mortar, and he wants me to go up this long, high mountain with this? Why? There is something fishy about this.

[Meanwhile], one of these *fedayin* told them they have to go to this area and ask for Haile. They did this. But when they asked about me, they were told that I was on the mountain – that I was on duty, and they could not find me now.

Since they know about all these tricks, they said they would stay some hours. So they went here and there for some time, and then at last they came to me.

There was not any offensive, so I came back and found them. For me, it was a surprise. How come, I asked them, you did not send me a message? When they told me what had happened, I knew this was a trick by Woldai.

First, I told them, you don't have to go to Kassala because Kassala would be another prison by the Revolutionary Command. Instead, you should go to Port Sudan. From there, you can go straight to Khartoum because at least there you would be free to follow the developments and to do something, whatever you can do. Because there are a lot of problems here, let us handle them, and you can be our contact with the outside world.

After this, Woldai told them to go to Kassala, but they went to Khartoum instead. Immediately, they made a link to the Communist Party of Sudan, and they continued to watch everything from there.

At this time, with the complexity of the situation, you cannot even trust some of your colleagues, even so-called comrades in arms. And therefore, a clandestine organization and a clear political line or ideology was a necessity that was created by the problems that were inside the Eritrean revolution.

But Romedan and Isaias, while they were in China, where they taught them all these things – they said, the Eritrean revolution can only succeed if it can form a political party. And the Chinese gave them lessons on how to form a party.

For them, it was very interesting.

Connell: Was it only the two of them who got these lessons, or did they give this to everybody?

Haile: They gave it to everybody, but the others were saying...

Connell: The others weren't listening.

Haile: The others weren't interested. But let me tell you how, on the question of a party, the ELF tried to sabotage it.

They knew there would be a problem. They said that when sending people to China, they would be ideologically charged. With the other three, they were confident that they would not have an ear for these things. But with Isaias and Romedan, they expected problems.

At that time, it was the Cultural Revolution. The Red Book. That was in 1967.

So, during their studies, these five people were trying to relate the experience of China to the problems in Eritrea. How could those ideological means that the Chinese revolutionaries were using be a help to Eritreans to address their problems inside. And there was a discussion with their lecturers.

Isaias and Romedan started to expose the problems within the ELF in order to find some solutions related to the experience of the Chinese revolution – the Kuomintang, the Chinese Communist Party and what not.

The other three people started to say, "You are exposing some things against the ELF – watch out."

When they took their meals together and they were cutting some fruits and such things, these three would take their knives and make threatening gestures, saying, "You are entertaining ideas that are opposed to the ELF. This is what will happen to you when you get back."

And then the Chinese lecturers were able to identify this.

They might have taken Isaias and Romedan aside, but they did not do so, since the others were relying on Arab translators but Isaias was speaking English.

This also helped him to quickly understand Arabic. When they went, he didn't have a word of Arabic. He learned it there.

Connell: He learned ping-pong, too.

Haile: Yes, also ping-pong.

But let me tell you one incident there – the intervention of the high council. It was Osman Saleh Sabbe who was the one responsible for external relations. He created this relationship with China. Now, Idris Ghalaudios was thinking that because there was the prospect of a lot of arms from China, he did not want to leave this domain to Sabbe. Because it would affect their power base – the balance of power among the divisions.

So almost from the beginning – most probably these other three had contacts with him, too – he was asking the Chinese what are they doing and how long are the students staying and so on. Then he came to China to visit the Eritrean students and at the same time to establish a relationship with the Chinese government.

When he went there, it was the Cultural Revolution and the Red Book and so on, and he heard slogans that it would be spread throughout the Horn of Africa.

He was very keen to win their support, so he told them: "These are your disciples who will expand the Red Book and make the whole Horn of Africa and the Red Sea area red with your teachings. I will give them all the responsibility – because at that time they were studying on party formation and what not – these are the ones who are going to form a party and spread the ideology of the Red Book."

And the Chinese were convinced. They believed this.

Isaias and Romedan were surprised. This was a dilemma for them. They knew this guy was playing a trick, and that the other three people were telling him that these guys were discussing what they think were the problems of Eritrean revolution and how they would be solved, that they were entertaining the ideology – genuinely studying the ideology, genuinely studying the formation of a political party.

This was the trick of ELF. They were very shrewd.

Connell: Well, it was the same trick you were trying on Woldai. [Laughter.] But you'd think the Chinese would be smarter.

Haile: They should have been. They should have been.

But I just wanted to tell you that all the intrigues were there. And then, of course, Isaias and Romedan started to take notes on how to form a party and so on. So these are the first elements of the formation of a party.

After he left – of course they know what he was discussing with the other three – they told the Chinese that this guy is not going to allow them to establish a party. Let alone establish a party, he was not going to let them do any political work. It was a drama.

In fact, he was one of the engineers of all the problems in the ELF. But he was smart enough to look however they wanted him to look like. So this was another problem for Isaias and Romedan. Because now he was going to cheat them, while he would not allow them to work inside. Already the Chinese had been deceived, so this was a great challenge for them.

So after they finished, they were discussing this, and they started to think of people who would go for the second round. They were telling the Chinese that in order to make use of these courses they will nominate capable people. And they gave them a list, including myself. This is what they told me later.

So when they finished the course, they flew to Damascus, Syria. When they reached there, it was Idris Ghalaudios who received them and told them that he was playing a trick with the Chinese: "No red book, no party, no ideology. We want only to exploit it in order to get arms and money."

And then he said, "Since you are going to go via Saudi [Arabia], and it would be very dangerous if you had any kind of Communist materials, your books, any materials you have, even some of your clothes, we will send it by air to Khartoum. You have to go via Jidda, and then you will get your books and what not in Sudan."

Up to now, they have not seen their books.

But you know what they did, when he told them such things? They knew it, of course. They went to the Chinese ambassador in Damascus, and they told him what Idris Ghalaudios had told them. They informed the Chinese that he had been deceiving them, that he was not going to allow them to work and therefore to take care in the future.

Now, I went into so many details to give you a feeling and a picture of how even to have an intact organization, you had to have an inside organization.

Before they returned from China, as I have told you, all the conflicts, all the problems, exploded in the field.

Many of the highlanders were killed.

The problem inside was of such magnitude that it had an overspill effect on the other divisions as well.

And the ELF couldn't go as it used to go, with that explosion, though they wanted to keep it as it was. Because at that time in 1967, the Ethiopian government launched many offensives, one at a time. And villages and villages were burned. Their cattle and their property were lost…

Connell: This was the time of the first refugee camps in Sudan.

Haile: A lot of people escaped – in thousands.

Connell: Also, the U.S. experience in Vietnam, with strategic hamlets and such, was being transferred here.

Haile: Do you remember I said what was the strategy of the ELF? It was food.

So, they were going from village to village to get food, and some of the villagers who were poor, some of the women, were giving food to the fighters even when their children were crying because of the poverty they had.

But when the enemy launched its offenses, one of the mistakes that the ELF made was that there was no support from the other divisions.

Because the enemy concentrated at first on Barka, for example. And the others were relaxing while villages were burned.

The worst thing was that the fighters of that same division would stay in the villages and when the enemy came, they fired but escaped before the civilians could get out. And the enemy was using this as an excuse to burn villages, to kill people in mass.

So the first protests came from the mothers. This is very important. The mothers were saying: "We were feeding the fighters while leaving our children hungry. But when the enemy came, rather than at least not be inside to give a pretext for the enemy to burn the village, the worst thing the ELF fighters were doing was they stayed in the villages, they fired some shots, and then escaped. And they wouldn't even try to do some fighting so the elderly, the children, and the mothers to get out."

So they said, "Why are we feeding these people, leaving our children hungry? And then they escape before the children, before the old men, before the mothers?"

So there was a protest. They said, "This is wrong. While we are being victims of the Ethiopian aggression, the other fighters in the other divisions are relaxing. Then, the enemy will go to the other divisions and do the same thing, with no support from the others."

The issue was not just challenging the enemy, but at least to give a chance to the villagers to escape. So what they said – the mothers – was: "From now on we will not give food to the fighters because they escape before the old men, the children, and so on."

And of course a lot of people went to the Sudan and they were saying that the fighters had not performed well. There was no support.

So this idea of divisions was one of the big weaknesses of the ELF. That was why many were killed and many villages burned. That was why people went to Sudan and became refugees. Everybody became vocal because of this.

And this helped the nationalists in each of the divisions to say: "Yes, this is what we were opposing – dividing the army along religious and tribal, or regional, basis. That is the weakness of ELF."

And they were saying: "The leadership is staying outside, and they don't know the real problems. They are not experienced in the problems of the fighters and the people. Therefore, leadership must be inside the field."

There were three slogans we were trying to promote: First of all, unity of the fighters – the end of these divisions. The enemy was attacking each area one at a time, and this was very difficult for the fighters and the people.

Second, the leadership is not inside. They are in the hotels in Khartoum in a high condition, and the others are in Kassala, and therefore it must be inside.

The third thing was that human rights and the rights of the people were not guaranteed in the ELF.

ELF was contacting the people only to gather money, not to organize them, not to politicize them, and at the same time not to respect their rights. Because there were a lot of approaches against the civilians, against the population.

So these three issues were the mobilizing slogans, which received the support from the fighters and the people in general. So this bad situation helped also.

And in the fifth division, many highlanders were killed. Only a few of us escaped, because at that time we had gone to Kassala.

But this enabling environment gave it a chance to be questioned.

And the one who killed many highlanders of the fifth division was the deputy commander himself.

Everybody was saying that he had killed a lot of fighters, so the leadership was forced to give a direction that there is a big investigation committee. Which did not work, of course. And they said that since they were going to form a committee to investigate these things, the deputy commander will be in prison for the time being.

So these three slogans were the mobilizing tools for a rectification movement. And it was at this time that Isaias, Romedan, and the others came back.

It was this situation, in fact, that helped them survive – because things had already exploded.

Isaias went with the fifth division when he came, and Romedan went to the fourth – as political commissars. For the fourth division, the leader was Omaro – Mohammed Ali Omaro – who is now [2000} our ambassador in Nairobi.

So, this idea of forming a party was short-circuited.

The problem became widespread. There was a chance to mobilize on a broad base on these three slogans I have told you – unity of the army, leadership in the field, human rights and the right of organization of the population.

So, for the time being, these issues became very critical, and it was not giving a breathing space. And because there was an opportunist group who saw that the ELF cannot go on as it has been doing. And there is this sort of revolution within the revolution. And therefore to give lip service to these slogans but highjack it.

So there was a genuine movement, and a sham movement to use the resentment the fighters had to hijack the reform movement.

And these two outlooks, these two lines, at the end of the day, materialized into the so-called democratic organizations in the ELF – the Labor Party in the ELF and the Socialist Party, the People's Party, in EPLF.

Connell: What was it called in EPLF? I thought it was the Eritrean People's Revolutionary Party.

Haile: Previously, it was called so. Later, it was called Eritrean Socialist Party.

Connell: When was that – in the '80s?

Haile: At the first congress.

Connell: You had two congresses – in '76 and '86?

Haile: '76 and '87.

Connell: Before the EPLF's congress each time.

Haile: So, up to '76, it was called Eritrean People's Revolutionary Party. Or maybe it was at the second congress we changed the name.

Connell: So, from '68 to '71, what was going on with the party?

Haile: Then there was this whole situation. It was so preoccupying.

And there was an opportunity to work on a mass basis, a broad basis, on those three things. So that movement united the three divisions – the third, fourth and fifth divisions – but the second and the first were sabotaging that unity.

So there was a unity of those three divisions. They elected a leadership, inside the field.

Connell: What year?

Haile: 1968.

There was a twelve-man leadership elected by the fighters. And – at that time, of course – there were some who joined this group not because of democratic convictions but because of some problems with leaders in the first and second divisions.

And therefore the tactic was that this is a process, and from the very beginning, one should not vote for democratic leaders alone. Therefore, there were people who were elected in that provisional leadership from some of those reactionary elements. And it was one of the mistakes that were made.

The reactionary forces in the first and second, and in the Revolutionary Command and the High Command, found a Trojan horse inside this unity. And there were a lot of intrigues in the Unified Force, as we called them. The others were still the first and second division.

It was united, it elected its leadership, and it was a hope for the population and for the fighters. Even fighters in the first division and second division started to look for this new arrangement and started to escape from those first and second divisions to join.

And in its short life, there was, of course, also the enemy. It was a dangerous time. And the enemy tried an offensive.

But this United Force challenged that offensive and defended people in their villages, and therefore it became a savior – and popular.

One of the leaders of the two – the commander of the second division – when the United Force started to become popular among the people, among the fighters even within his division and the others, it was a challenge for them. It was almost making them naked of their colors.

And because the United Force repelled an Ethiopian offensive and downed one aircraft – it was very strange at that time for an Eritrean force to do this – there was a lot of pressure from the fighters in the second division. So, in order not to allow these fighters to look for the United Force as an alternative that has done a lot of heroic things, he designed to attack an [Ethiopian] army barracks in Halhal.

Of course, it was a very small army in that camp. But there was no secret – the enemy knew. I am not sure, I have forgotten the numbers, but I could say that the enemy was a third of the number of the fighters, one-to-three. But they knew that he was attacking. They went outside their camp, into their trenches, and they defeated him. He himself was wounded, and he died on his way to Kassala.

He did that in order to create sort of a heroic activity in order to sabotage this sentiment of uniting the fighters. But he failed, and fighters kept leaving the first and second divisions.

At first, they [ELF leaders] wanted to attack the United Force, but they could not, so they tried another way: intrigue with some of the leaders in the United Force, because there were already measures taken in the United Force by the democratic element in the leadership – organizing people, giving political education to the fighters – which were dangerous for them.

So, they had to make an unholy alliance with their likes in the first and second divisions. And then the first division and second divisions made a call that they are ready for a unity. That was the Adobha congress in 1969.

When they found out that they cannot control the sentiment of the fighters in the United Force, then they prefer to call for a unity – making intrigues.

And it was Idris Ghalaudios who came to the field and engineered all these intrigues, so as to kill the democratic force in the Adobha conference.

And that is what happened.

51

Connell: Sounds like an ambush.

Haile: No, No.

They preferred to raise this slogan of unity, but make all kinds of intrigues with some of the leaders inside the United Force. That's why I said there was a Trojan Horse inside the United Force.

And so, when they came to Adobha, they had a lot of intrigues – about the number of the representatives, the way of deciding things and what not. There was an intrigue made with those inside.

And in Adobha, they dominated it. The reactionaries dominated it.

Immediately, they began to take actions. They killed a lot.

And therefore before organizing itself, the democratic force had to face the question of escaping.

Many people escaped to the Sudan.

Isaias had to escape to Ala with some of the fighters, and that is why there was no coordination of the establishment of the alternative.

And the situation was worse than it was before – worse than during the period of the divisions. But it was very difficult to have confidence between even those who have been fighting together.

That is why there were three groups, which went out of ELF.

The idea of a political party was there also. But the period in '68 and '69 did not give us breathing space.

So when there was this PLF first group, PLF second group – the Allah group and the Dankalia group – Isaias was there and Romedan was there.

Connell: Romedan was in Dankalia? Did he come across from Yemen?

Haile: Yes.

So, while there were these two groups, there was a clandestine discussion about the party, and it was established on April 4, 1971, while its members were involved in two groups.

Still there were problems about the two groups themselves. There was no confidence among each other. There were maybe negative experiences from the previous situation.

What was the most unifying factor was the declaration of a civil war by the ELF. Then many secondary issues have to be overlooked.

And because it was a question of survival, it created a conducive climate for the democratic element and groups within the two to work for a better unity on the front level, using the party as a core.

Connell: And "Our Struggle and its Goals" – did that come from this core?[2]

Haile: From the Isaias group.

Connell: So that represented the public face – the front, not the party – although the party was interacting in everything a bit.

Haile: Even within the first group, people were not ready to accept the ideology, but at least this.

So, again, on the Ala front, this small core had formed. Isaias made the same thing with that very small group in the Ala group.

Connell: Well, because we don't have very much more time – it's almost five o'clock – can you summarize the importance of the party as it pulled the EPLF together?

What I understand to be one of its strongest roles was to create a democratic space among those who were in it – to have very open discussions of issues – and to re-mold people so that they were able to transform the EPLF culture, the political culture.

Nation-building often means that one dominant ethnic group absorbs everybody into itself. But what you've got here now is a national culture coming out of a political organization, the EPLF, which is a very different kind of project.

Haile: Which we couldn't even imagine in the '60s and '70s.

Connell: What else would you say was its primary achievement? The first thing would be to unify the front.

Haile: National unity was one of the most important, because that was the most challenged aspect in the ELF.

National unity. And then bringing youngsters from the different ethnic groups, working together in the most difficult situation of survival. And having an ideology that could give some light at the end of that dark tunnel was very important.

Political and organizational work was so important.

Because we were inside that process, it was sometimes difficult to explain them or give them some expression. But it made miracles. It made people commit themselves. It made each and every individual

---

[2] "Our Struggle and its Goals," produced in 1971 outside Asmara, was the Isaias faction's early manifesto. A summary appeared in the first issue of the EPLF's official organ *Vanguard* in January 1973. It is reprinted in footnotes to *Against All Odds* (chapter 5) and *Rethinking Revolution* (chapter 1).

think of himself as part of the whole organization, and even in difficult situations not to lose his bearings, and to work as if the whole organization – as if he is using the energy and muscle of the whole organization.

That was manifested even in the military field, and in all challenging situations.

Each individual was trying to face challenges without questioning his other colleagues. He wouldn't look backward.

And addressing the basic issues in the society in order to transform them – particularly, from the beginning, trying to address the woman-issue. The organization tried to convince the mother. By convincing the mother, the whole society was convinced.

Connell: In the research I did for my book [*Rethinking Revolution*], it was clear that the failure in Nicaragua [in 1990] and the disaster in Palestine [in the 1990s] was partly because they didn't effectively mobilize women. The Palestinians had the challenge of unifying a dispersed nation, too, and they never did that either.

Haile: Not only that.

They never had even a small base inside their territories where they launched their struggle. Because having outside bases, there was a lot of intervention.

All the countries – the Arab countries – wanted their own stooge group. Let alone different philosophies, even one philosophy – the Ba'ath itself – had to have the Syrian trend and the Iraqi trend.

And because all the other countries support them – and the support was so much – that made them very relaxed.

Connell: So they didn't have to depend on their own people and weren't accountable to them.

But what about the role of the party in Eritrea now? The country doesn't have one. Does it need one?

Haile: It doesn't have one. As you have said, it is a broad-based front or movement.

Well, it has its own merits in the sense that we're in this transitional period when petty things could try to polarize the society when it's still young enough to be affected by them.

It becomes a sort of luxury at this particular moment, when there is this challenge of reconstruction and the forces of the national unity itself are still in a process to stand on a sound basis. There is a need for a broad-based movement on this transitional period.

But, I think – this is my personal view – this will be healthy and constructive transition, as long as it allows free discussion of different political opinions within that same movement. Meaning, as long as it cultivates a political culture of tolerance for different political views on whatever level – on policy, on orientation, on assessment, on everything.

That could be a healthy transition and a background for an articulated political pluralism in the future.

Connell: Is it doing this?

Haile: Always, there is a danger.

There is a need for this broad-based movement. Otherwise, there is the danger of unnecessary polarization, which will hamper the process of reconstruction and the laying down the necessary groundwork, including institutions, for democracy. And, mainly, the political culture.

But one has to watch out.

There must be the seeds already in this broad-based movement that would guarantee a smooth transition to the period of political pluralism. Otherwise, if there is a case of suffocation in this process, then naturally there will be reactive and destructive options.

I am not well versed with the experience in Nicaragua. The situation could be different. But even the experience of Algeria should be studied properly. Because I feel there was created a gap between the leadership – which had gone through all that experience and which acts with new issues as it used to do before – and the new generation.

The old generation forgot that this new generation of youths is not tempered in the same way the old generation was tempered. For it, there are a lot of different agendas that the old generation took for granted. And therefore, when there were crises, there was a gap between the old guard and the new movement.

I want to study the Algerian experience itself, because there are elements that one can profit from – the different experiences.

So, as I have said, there is a need for a broad-based movement in the transition period. The timescale could be controversial, but this broad-based movement should be the breeding ground for the seeds, and at the same time should be a leveling process.

And this should be a phase where there must be laid the basis, particularly the institutional basis, that would guarantee the democratic transformation of the society in general, but at the same time, have the elements for a healthy, political pluralism.

Connell: Do you think this is happening now – that those seeds are being planted, that political opinions are being developed, shared and tested within the movement?

Haile: If I don't say they are yet, then it means I am frustrated.

For example, now there is this challenge of the *woyane*. It should not be a pretext to suffocate us, to hide our weaknesses under the guise of not allowing the *woyanes* to exploit them.

Connell: Every revolutionary movement in history has all faced such challenges. One of the Nicaraguan problems was that during the *contra* war, the government co-opted all the mass organizations to fight the war, and dismantled a lot of the political infrastructure. And I think the party lost contact with its base.

They alienated women, for example. They postponed work on gender issues after opening the door. And, in 1991, after they lost power, not many women were left.

I was in Nicaragua in '96 to watch the election, and it was amazing how many women's organizations around the country were working for women at the grassroots – but not for the party. That party could have had those women organizing for it, if it had been genuine about resolving those women's issues, but instead they hired a public relations firm in Costa Rica to run a campaign targeted at the media.

Haile: That's what I meant, for example, when I brought this issue of the experience of Algeria. That's because the leadership had lost its link with its base.

Of course, in our case, to some extent, this broader conflict could be taken as a blessing in disguise – giving shock to this broad-based movement to look at itself in the mirror. At the same time, to allow many of the youths into that stream with the old combatants.

It could have positive and negative aspects, because when we were shocked, we have to ask, what do we expect about this new generation? Are they stream-lined? Would they feel part of the old guard? What are their expectations? Can we satisfy, or at least *seem* to try to satisfy, their expectations? Do we know their expectations?

Connell: Well, you might know the answers if you had a party out there.

One of the things that occurs to me is that you will have much stronger nationalism after they've gone through this experience, but it's not a nationalism with the same political content as before. There's no party working in the army, in the trenches.

And, in fact, there are many problems in the trenches – you've got many women coming out and saying they were mistreated, for example. There's not the discipline there was before either.

Maybe, given this challenge, and the work that's been done to consolidate the nation – maybe it's time to start thinking about a party again.

Haile: But always, I have been trying to say…

Connell: It doesn't have to be a secret party.

Haile: No. All the experience that we have gone through, I have been trying to say, there is the need for a core group to be a dynamo.

Connell: That's what I'm talking about.

Haile: But not allow itself to be diluted in such a way that things would not be effective.

Whether you call this a party or something else, whether it is clandestine or not, there is always the need for a core group, not to lose bearings and always to be exemplary.

Connell: Shengeb and I were talking about this the other day. He says the same thing.

Within NUEYS [the National Union of Eritrean Youth and Students], they have 20,000 people that are the ones that get their highest level of education. He says you can't make 120,000 people all move in the same direction when they come from all over. Some come just for sports. You always have to have a core group.

I think, in some ways, you have the extraordinary good fortune here to have a very dynamic youth coming up. Maybe it will change things.

Haile: It will not be easy.

I'm trying to learn to accept the reality that it cannot be the same as it was.

Connell: I hope this is a small question, and then I'll give you a rest. What exactly was your role in the party?

I remember when we talked about politics in the '70s and '80s, you were running around the cadre school and doing all sorts of political things. That was basically the development of the party, though it was not openly called that.

Haile: Actually, there was a crisis in the party in 1971.

It's not an easy question, because the formation itself was from individuals from both the first and the second PLF groups. There were problems mainly in the first group – the Dankalia group – with those who were watching the democratic element in the first group and envying the particular relationships they had with democratic elements in the second one.

And therefore, there was a kind of rivalry – it is not easy to say that – but some sort of trying to sabotage the alliance, to discredit democratic elements like Romedan inside the first group.

And sometimes that had an effect on the thinking of the ordinary fighters in the second group to be "allergic" to some of them. And it had influence on that party. Because that party was not organizationally organic. And therefore, at some point, it almost was paralyzed.

Connell: We're not talking about *menqa* yet. This is early.

Haile: Early. Early. From '72 to the end of '74, maybe, the party was only in name. Functionally, it was dead.

Connell: Was the *menqa* affair in '73 part of this?

Haile: In fact, one of the main problems of that crisis was that the party was already dead.

In '71, when it was formed, there was no organic link. The members were in two different groups. The contradiction between us and the ELF was very sharp, and there was a war with them.

When the ELF declared their intention to liquidate us [in 1972], this created an atmosphere to build some confidence, to concentrate on how much we needed each other. And this threat created an opportune moment to strengthen our unity.

But the problem within the party had gone to that extent that it was not easy to remedy. So, first, then it became the other way around. You have to create confidence on the front level in order to build confidence for revitalizing the party. And when it was revitalized, Isaias was the Secretary General and Romedan was the Assistant Secretary General.

But by 1975, the armed struggle entered a new phase, and it was decided that there should be a party leadership outside the front leadership. So, myself and Alamin were nominated to be the Secretary and the Assistant Secretary for the party, while head of the political department of the front.

Connell: In 1975. And what happened at the '76 congress – the first party congress?

Haile: At that time, we had the Polit-Bureau of the front and the Central Committee of the party in an organized way. And, again, we were to become the ideological department – the cadre school and what not would be under our guidance.

Connell: You and Alamin?

Haile: Yes. Then, in the first front congress in January '77, Alamin was assigned to foreign relations. Therefore, it was me who was leading the party.

We had the Central Committee, and Isaias was the Chairman. But I was leading the party on a day-to-day basis, and we tried to differentiate the front and the party work.

Connell: Isaias was the chair of the Central Committee of the party.

Haile: Yes. But I had taken the responsibility for running the party.

Connell: Did that change in '86 for you?

Haile: Well, we tried to make it more collective. Already by '86 there were problems.

It expanded so much that there were a lot of problems, particularly in the recruiting. The party organizations – the cells and what not – started to be far distant from the center. There started to crop up unhealthy ways of recruitment – friendship – not using valid criteria.

And of course we were thinking that the majority of the front members were a little bit incompetent to be party members. But out on the primary organizations of the party, there were a lot of problems.

People avoided competent people but recruited from friendship or other criteria. And therefore, the primary cell particularly started to degenerate and – rather than lead the front – started to be problem for the front activities themselves. Because there were competent people from the front who were not recruited in the party, but there were unhealthy elements recruited in the party. And, therefore, it became a problem – let alone to the party, even to the front.

Their level of consciousness, their level of commitment, was short of some of the front leaders. So, at one time, the Central Committee realized this and felt that it has to intervene in this process of the selection and what not, to even investigate some of the recruitment procedures.

Connell: This is around '85, '86?

Haile: Yes.

Connell: So what happened at the '86 congress – the second party congress?

Haile: Well, it started to be diluted and to create problems, and therefore the Central Committee started to question the validity of the primary organizations.

Because we were able to see committed people from the front, whereas some unhealthy elements made the primary organizations a safe haven to protect their weaknesses

Connell: And when you say primary, you mean the party organization?

Haile: The party organizations – the elementary organizations – the grassroots cells.

Connell: I see.

Haile: That was one part.

And the other part was that there was a lot of ideological weight. Definitely, of course, it was not at a far distance from the practical war, but there were a lot of ideological discussions, sometimes which were not very practical.

There were many issues – the question of the Soviet Union, the socialist camp, and what not. All these things came, and again came the question of realistic and unrealistic objectives themselves. As I said there was a lot of ideological weight – I was talking about the communist society, the withering of the state, and all these things.

Connell: I remember.

Haile: So we wanted to be very practical. Our experience itself helped a lot. We wanted to be pragmatic.

And therefore, we have to define an achievable program, a realistic program, rather than become idealists.

So we started to shed away some of our naivety to become very practical, to look at the world with a reasonable expectation – to be practical. And, of course, not to sacrifice our national interests to ideal philosophical issues. To be very practical.

So we started to look at the primary organizations of the party – what are the best ones, which are the best elements?

But this clandestinity itself had its own problems. Because, we said, if these people were to be exposed among the front fighters – who do not know that these people are party members – and if we were to expose them, maybe it will be very ridiculous. From their commitment, from their discipline, from their outlook, from anything. It had become a hidden place for another element.

So we started to question: We had to make it clandestine at first – there was a reason for it – because there was a hostile external environment in the ELF areas and all around us. It had to be clandestine then, and it served its purpose. Later, of course, it became a hindrance because it was no longer the club of the best ones.

There was a dilemma: Do we make it open, and then evaluate every individual and every cell in front of the fighters and the people, which can only rectify the party? Or, are we now convinced with all the stream-lining, the pragmatism, and setting achievable objectives – do we find now that there is any gap between the achievable objectives of the party and the programs of the front?

We were convinced now that these are coming closer and closer and closer, and it almost became impossible to try to make a lot of difference. So why should not the party become the party of the mass? Why not bridge the gap between the programs of the party and the programs of the front?

That is why we met in '89. But in '87, it had already started.

Connell: So, in '86, at the congress of the party, you had not made this decision yet?

Haile: No, we had not made the decision, but it was almost clear now that we had to do something. It was a process.

But in '87, we were convinced that we cannot go the way we were going. In fact, we made an exercise.

In 1985 or '86 – now I am forgetting, I am becoming old, I think – we started to revise our political educational material for the front. In that exercise, we were trying to bring closer the objectives of the front and the party. So, it is an exercise that was preparing to make the party synonymous to the front.

We were also saying that this clandestinity of the party had created a problem. Because, even on the front, we said, when we see that the majority of the front fighters were committed to the objectives of the party, but they were not members.

More than that, because of this clandestinity, although we had party cells and branches in our mass organizations, among the people, we felt this has crippled us, not to have enough say from the people. So there must be done something.

So at the end of the day, in '89, we said, we are now entering a new phase. It is almost consuming – the liberation struggle. And therefore, the broad-based movement should replace the party in order to allow not only the front members but all the population to channel its resources, to work for the objectives of the party, which has now become generally most of the objectives of the front.

Of course, I'd like to say that it was not an easy decision. Maybe for two reasons.

One, there were elements who said that this would be diluting it, and it would be a wrong decision – that the party would be already gone if a time comes when we feel that there is a need for such kind of organization. It will be irreversible.

Others might have thought that they were looking for the party as a privilege, and therefore dissolving the party would bring each and every member of the party in front of the whole front and the whole population, to prove himself whether or not he is committed or not.

I mean, there are so many reasons – some of them are overt, some are covert – but there are all these things. So, I think myself that it was not possible to continue that way.

But was there a possibility of the transition that we could devise in such a way that every member of the party could have felt part of this decision? Maybe there could have been a transition devised in such a way as to convince everybody that we are now entering a new phase, with different kinds of challenges, and the need for organizing the population on a mass basis, and that a clandestine organization would not be in a position to handle the challenges.

It would be a point of creating differences, because many of the front fighters started to realize that there is a clandestine organization. And the worst thing – people started to find out there are some elements in that clandestine organization which cannot compete with them on their capacity, their determination, and what not.

Connell: And as you say, there's one decision as to whether to have a clandestine party, and there's another decision on whether to have a party at all. They are not the same.

The question is: Is there a way of making this transition without it being irreversible?

Haile: No. But there was a question.

The question was that: At this moment we are entering a new phase. It was '89. In fact, it was almost '90 when it was "freezed," let me say.

Connell: And who decided?

Haile: The Central Committee.

But there were discussions before that within the Central Committee, with all the intervening. There were a lot of problems. Almost there was exposure. Many people were in the front and didn't know about it.

Could we have a political party with a different organizational system to make it a mass party? That was the question: Why not the whole front to become the whole party?

But still the front itself was narrow when you look at the society in general and the phase we are entering – the independence period. The facts would be different. And of course with different remnants of the ELF and what not, we saw the need for a broad-based movement.

Why should we try to change the party into a broad-based party, when we have the front, which is a broad-based movement? That was the choice. Because we thought that even the front was not enough.

Connell: And that is what the PFDJ said it was going to do – create this new political environment for mass participation.

Haile: Yes.

Connell: Then how do you make the transition to parties?

Presumably, parties come – there's no reason to lay-out blueprints – but one would assume that having created a political culture in which people are thinking about the nation, parties would emerge out of debates over its future. Is that happening?

Haile: The need for this transitional period, for this broad-based movement, definitely was there, and that is what we are doing. But to look at the long future, I am not comfortable whether we have laid a sound basis, first and foremost, to guarantee a democratic atmosphere for political pluralism.

I think we are a little bit slow, even though time is on our side. And therefore, there could be spontaneous difficulties.

Second, have we cultivated a culture of tolerance – a culture of bringing your opinions freely, even within the broad-based movement?

We could have used the mass media, for example.

At one time, there was a chance for that, but it was short-lived. Now when you see these independent papers, they are trash. They are not addressing issues of national interest. Some of them are bringing things in order to be sensational. So you see, because alternative news and opinions have not been using our mass media, then you see kind of trash news.

Connell: It seems to me that the state media could play a leading role in this – have panel discussions, publish contrasting views side by side, show the public what is meant by responsible debate by doing it – set the example – but they are completely afraid to try.

Haile: Even at one time, every minister of the government was supposed to have an accountable official of the government who was supposed to invite seminars so that people can assess the policy and the performance – openly accepting shortcomings.

It was a good start.

Connell: When was this?

Haile: '93, '94, even up to '95.

Every minister was supposed to discuss about his ministry's work – the problems and complaints for the people to hear.

For example, when I was the Minister of Finance and Economy, we had organized an association of translators, who work for the merchants and so forth, for the customs procedures and declarations. They developed sort of a confidence to air their views, even to criticize. But if you only have such meetings officially once in a blue moon, nothing changes.

I think there was a time when this was starting to happen, but always there were those who resisted, and this policy was stopped. I think this was a mistake.

What I was trying to impress on the others was that the strength of a political party is not on how many people it has in absolute numbers. The main strength is on how much it can mobilize the people and make them feel that the objectives of the party are their objectives. That is the secret of building a political movement.

It is not how many units you have, how many people you have. If you can mobilize the people and make them feel that what you want to realize as objectives are their objectives, then you have the capability to build a political organization.

If they are going to feel that these are their objectives, it must address their own concrete issues that have bearing on their daily lives. Otherwise, it becomes just noise. You can talk, you can talk, you can talk. But it has to be intermingled with their daily lives.

Now, look at what the People's Front is doing.

To take people from different walks of life, who have different interests, who have different expectations, who have different experiences in life – particularly on the daily life – to bring old women, household women, with an engineer, with a student, with a laborer – what is the common agenda? Maybe you have some political agenda yourself, but you will have difficulty to motivate them.

If you can mobilize the engineers, for example, in a special way, and ask them: What are the challenges of the town planning, what are the shortages of housing, the problems of real estate developers and what not. Then, this would be an incentive for them. They think they have done something for the country. That it is something that one can evaluate.

Connell: Isn't this something for mass organizations, which you need to have much more of? Different organizations that the party then works with independently? But you only have three – and not independent.

Haile: Those mass organizations are supposed to be the limbs of the movement, but there is a need for more – and different organizations.

They have to be separated into different groups according to common interests and what makes them feel that they are addressing their common issues.

Connell: But the PFDJ is now organized on a geographical basis – in neighborhood organizations – whoever lives there is in the same cell?

Haile: Before in the front, in the party, there was one thing – whether you resist enemy attacks or not. And everybody is part of that. Everybody contributes to that.

Now we are in a different situation.

Why should you have a Sunday meeting in order to accommodate the different walks of life, for example?

Those employees – government or private – can spare their time only on Saturday or Sunday. But for a housewife? It would be better to have meetings with her equals in the afternoon of the working day. But on Sundays, she has a lot of social obligations.

Do you think she would be interested in such kinds of meetings? It doesn't come to their real life.

So on the organizational aspect, on the agendas for discussion, I myself am not comfortable. I know this is not working. We have to change. There is a need for a complete change. Everything must be directly related with their daily life.

Before, everything was related to their daily life. What we were teaching in the cadre school was making miracles. When they came to the cadre school, they considered it was a privilege, because they had an obligation to do. And it was a multiplying factor for their commitment.

Now we have to devise a different thing.

Maybe it is easy to criticize, to evaluate, because I am in the government, in the Ministry of Foreign Affairs, going here and there. Maybe I have the luxury to comment on these things. But I feel it. I feel it.

You know there are professionals – they think the government is not opening avenues to enable them to channel their best contribution.

All the government institutions – they don't have enough expertise.

You could form committees of these professionals with relevant skills and tell them to come with ideas and proposals. They will compete themselves to show what they can do, and they can contribute a lot. But you cannot raise such questions now. You cannot make such new organizations.

One of the main problems, I think, is that people have become – I don't know – a little bit defensive. And they will not allow criticism.

We used to have this criticism/self-criticism – in the party and in the front – on two levels. We had used it all our lives, all our lives.

I am afraid now that we are losing what we developed before.

A Conversation with
Haile "Drue" Wold'ensae

March 1, 2001

When I met Haile this time, he was deeply disillusioned and anticipating moves against him by the President.

The big policy debates had erupted in the PFDJ Central Council and the National Assembly, with Isaias coming under criticism and challenge. Both bodies had been effectively shut down. Direct personal approaches to the President had been rebuffed. Private petitions for meetings to discuss these and other issues had been spurned. And a round of secret PFDJ seminars had just been conducted to discredit those leaders who had raised questions about Isaias's autocratic and, at times, dysfunctional leadership.

I do not have a tape of this conversation, so I am reconstructing the gist of it from hand-written notes taken at the time. We met in his office in the Ministry of Trade and Industry, to which he had been recently demoted from Foreign Affairs as a result of his dissent.

Haile closed the door and turned to me even before I sat down to say: "The revolution has been hijacked."

There had been signs of this way back in the mid-1980s, he said, but he had ignored them. As he saw it now, the turning point came in the early 1990s with the formation of the new state, the dissolution of the party, and the transformation of the EPLF – under Isaias's personal control – into the PFDJ. This was, in retrospect, when he ought to have acted.

He said that one mistake he particularly regretted was not protesting when Isaias ordered Romedan's name taken off the list for PFDJ leadership in a conference in 1993, while party leaders were preparing for the 1994 congress at which the EPLF was to be rechristened the PFDJ. Instead, he and others sought to soften the impact by asking Romedan to stand up and voluntarily withdraw. "But," he said, "this was a lie and a bitter one."

When Isaias proposed that the old guard move on and make room for the next generation – except himself – Haile said that he knew this was a bid to consolidate his personal power, but that he and others were thinking: "The country is liberated. We've done what we set out to do. Why pick a fight now?"

"This was another mistake," he added.

"Now," said Haile, "this group is controlling the front and the state – over the Cabinet of Ministers and over party structures – and it is crushing all dissent, even threatening to arrest party founders, such as myself.

"It is only a matter of time now."

A Conversation with
Mahmoud Sherifo

August 1, 2001

This conversation took place shortly after I presented my paper on the origins of the Eritrean People's Revolutionary Party at the Eritrean Studies Association conference in Asmara in July 2001. It was conducted at Sherifo's invitation in order to correct what he perceived to be mistakes of emphasis in the paper – mainly the singular focus on Isaias as the driving force in the conception and construction of the People's Party.

Sherifo and I had known each other for many years but had never done a formal interview, in part due to my lack of Tigrinya and to his limited command of English. EPLF veteran Alemseged Tesfay agreed to translate this interview for me, as he was also then engaged in research into the origins and structure of the EPRP for his ongoing historical work on Eritrean nationalism.

The interview was conducted in Sherifo's office in the Ministry of Local Government, though he had been stripped of his post as minister earlier in the year after he disobeyed Isaias's orders to vet a National Assembly commission report on guidelines for a new party law with the President's office before releasing it to the public.

This commission – whose members included EPLF veterans Haile Wold'ensae, Ahmed Tahir Baduri, Tesfai Gebreselassie, Musa Naib and Fawzia Hasim – set requirements for social and geographical diversity and insisted that at least 85 percent of members be residents of Eritrea. This reflected the EPLF/PFDJ's long-standing commitment to proscribe ethnic or religious-based parties. But they also recommended that parties not be permitted to own and operate large-scale economic enterprises in order to level the political playing field – a policy that would have enormous implications for the PFDJ, then (and now) far the largest player in the country's anemic economy.

Unfortunately, we were not able to get into this issue as the conversation was cut short by the need for both men to attend a funeral. In the weeks following this, with Sherifo evicted from his office and under constant surveillance, it was impossible to arrange a follow-up.

Sherifo started the conversation with a discussion of the political chaos within the ELF that created the need for a highly-unified core to reconstruct and lead the liberation movement, and he wound it up with a list of the dozen or so individuals who met in April 1971 to launch it.

Sherifo: The discussions that led to the establishment of the party came as a result of the failures that were consistently coming up within the ELF. In the 1960s, the leftist-marxist line of thinking had found its way into the thinking of various people within Eritrea. At the same time, leftist-marxist thinking was rife throughout the world. Therefore, one has to take into consideration this very broad leftist-marxist leaning, these tendencies, that existed in the world and in Eritrea.

Within the ELF itself, the desire to see the end of the divisions of the five zones, the transfer of the leadership from outside to inside putting a stop to regionalist tendencies and divisions, and the merging of the ELF army into one united army – all these were discussions that were taking place before the establishment of the party – before the establishment of a core for the party, in a very general and a very loose way amongst various countries.

This led to the establishment of the United Forces – the three divisions. Uniting the three separate zones – the third, the fourth and the fifth – was a step forward because it showed that the army of the ELF could be united into one front. The leadership also was established in the field, as opposed to outside, and the rights of people started to be protected. In the one-year life of this particular unity of the three forces, or the three zones, this was a very positive step forward in the history of ELF.

Then came the Congress at Adobha, which opposed all the progress that was made. The reason for this – because the decisions at Adobha completely negated the unity of the three forces – is because, though the three forces were united, there was no real core that could pull it together and make it sustainable.

Because there was no core to organize and make this sustainable, the forces of reaction, of backwardness and division, used the slogan of "unity" to go against the advances made by the unity of the three forces, the three zones, and they actually succeeded in completely negating – not only negating but dismantling – the advances, the gains, made by the unity of the three forces.

The people who did this were the leadership in Kassala, the leadership outside. Because they were more organized then the three – because they had more of a core inside them – they were able to gain power and imprison people, kill people.

And after Adobha, the ELF itself briefly split.

Connell: In my paper, I described one element of the democratic forces, starting in '66, with Isaias, Mussie, and others. Who else was involved then?

Sherifo: In '66, Isaias, Mussie and Drue may have been "democratic" people, as far as individuals, but they were not even in the field.

Connell: No, they were in Kassala. So who was there?

Sherifo: In '67, Drue was with me in the fifth division. He was in the field for a while, but then he left to Kassala and then from there he went back to Yemen. And Isaias was in China. So they were not the core in the field. If Isaias had any real influence in the party, in the organization of the party, then it came after he came back from China.

Connell: So where were you at this time? When did you join?

Sherifo: In '66. Drue and I were together here in the student organization, but he joined the organization about six or seven months before me.

Connell: Where you in Addis?

Sherifo: No.

Connell: You came direct from Asmara. And Isaias came from Addis and went to China. So what happened in the field?

Sherifo: It [the crisis in the ELF field units] was at this point a general reaction, a general opposition, to the forces of division – the leadership. You cannot really talk about this individual or that. Some of them because they had more enlightenment and because they had other ideas that were opposed to what was being done. And some people were being faced by very practical problems that they wanted to surmount.

At the beginning it was a whole range of people opposing, and you could not single out one or two people and say so-and-so influenced such and such. It was very difficult at that time.

In the creation of the unity of the three zones, it's possible that in the fifth division Abraham Tewolde and Isaias had a role. In the fourth division, Romedan and [Mohamed Ali] Omaro had a good role. In the third division, Mohamed Ahmed Abdu and Mohamed Ibrahim Ali were instrumental. And the cadres like myself, who revolved around these people – you could say they played a major role.

There was no real core – no real organization – to solidify this desire to unite. There was just a general hatred of what was happening, a general opposition that created this unity of the three forces.

Although we made this unity, and as a force we went to Adobha to face the two [other] forces, the president – the leader of the unity of the three zones – and the secretary went over to the other side. So it was *this* kind of unity; there was no real core to unite us.

Connell: I have written about the influence of China on Romedan and Isaias. I know Ibrahim Afa also went to Cuba, and there were other outside influences that had some shaping effect.

Sherifo: Let's wait. We are now in '69 in Adobha. Ibrahim Afa may have been in Cuba at this time. He was not in the field. We are talking about what's happening in the field. Let's bring the whole thing in the field first and then talk about what's happening outside.

After the failure of the Adobha Congress came the reprisals, the imprisonment, and so on and so forth. And now comes the breaking up of the ELF. The story of the break-up is too long, and I think you know it. You can find it elsewhere. We'll leave that aside.

Many people escaped, ran away to Sudan. Some people were already in Sudan; some people were elsewhere. And the people who assembled in Sudan went over to Aden – some by plane and some by sea – and assembled in Aden.

Connell: And you were one?

Sherifo: Yes. We came to Aden. And Aden was, of course, a government that was leftist.

When we got there, all the cadres that assembled there started to talk about the reasons for the failure of our attempts at changing the way the ELF was going. We came to the conclusion that the main reason why we were consistently facing this problem was that there was no unity. The democratic forces were not really pulling together, getting organized and forming a very strong core.

But after this period of discussion, there were no conclusive steps taken towards the actual establishment of this much-needed core. So it was in this state of affairs that we went to Dankalia, that we crossed over to Eritrea.

Because we had not taken this conclusive step, when we went into Dankalia and met in Sedoha Ela and had a Congress, we established a leadership and an organization, but still a split came about – another split. Even in the newly established ELF-Popular Front, the ELF-PLF.

Because this core was not created, another split come about.

Connell: This came when?

Sherifo: In July or August, 1970.

Connell: That was the alliance of the three?

Sherifo: No. This was the establishment of the PLF, what we call the PLF 1.

There was an argument over whether we should stay in Dankalia or not, because life was very, very difficult there. So three of the members of the leadership, newly appointed, split, took most of the troops, and went away – just left there.

Connell: And went where? To Sudan?

Sherifo: No, they came here [to the Eritrean highlands]. It was people like Papayo, Abu Tiara and others who went away. Most of the traditional people. And they took a lot of their people and just ran away. This was bombshell number two. After the failure of the unity-of-the-three, this was the second bombshell for the core.

The people who were left behind reopened the discussion that was left unfinished in Aden. Now, we said, we have been faced with all these splits and failures because the democratic forces are not really uniting to form a democratic core. So we started discussing ways and means of really establishing this core.

The people who were discussing this were Ibrahim Afa, Mesfin Hagos, Ma'asho Embai, Ali Said Abdella, Hasan Mohamed Amir. (He died later – he was martyred.) Abu Bakr Mohammed Hassan. (He was martyred also.)

Connell: Romedan was not there?

Sherifo: No, he was outside. He was fighting against "Ama," the central command of the ELF.

Connell: Which group was he with?

Sherifo: Romedan had not been in Adobha. He was not in the Congress. But he was elected one of the thirty-eight leaders of the Congress. When the split happened, Romedan was still outside. But he was campaigning against the ELF leadership.

Connell: He wasn't in the field?

Sherifo: No, but he was campaigning against the ELF in a different way.

So, we agreed, while still in Dankalia, that we had to have a party. The only way to organize this core was to form a party. This agreement

73

came about as a result of the discussions in Aden and in Dankalia and because of the failures I've just described.

Connell: Also in Aden was the Arab Nationalist Movement – the PFLP was there, the Popular Front for the Liberation of Bahrain, and others. There were many parties that took a name very similar to what we have emerging in Eritrea – the Popular Front for the Liberation of Eritrea, if you read the EPLF in a different sequence. There's a common strain; you see this in the names.

Sherifo: That was when leftism was a very popular thing throughout the world. You know, Black Panthers in America...

Connell: But in Aden there was a specific strain of leftism – the ANM – the Arab Nationalist Movement. What influence did that have on the EPLF?

Sherifo: Not a direct influence. But because we were seeing films and so on, and we heard all this talk about Arab radicalism, the PFLP, all these leftist things, the general feel was there. But a direct Arab nationalist influence in the party was not a factor. Even in Aden, most of the Arab nationalists were marxist by orientation.

Connell: So films and all this leftist material – from the Soviet Union and elsewhere?

Sherifo: When we were in Aden, because there were these [North] Koreans and so on and so forth, all these marxists – Chinese and so on – we used to get films from them and watch films and read things. And therefore, there was a general influence.

Besides, even [George] Habash and [Naif] Hawetmeh and even the Yemenis themselves, the parties, were marxist-leaning. And therefore there was this general feel. But you cannot call it a direct influence on the course of party formation here.

Toward the end of 1970, the beginning of 1971, these forces moved from Dankalia to what we call the Red Sea region here – towards Semhar and Northern Dankalia. Somehow Romedan and Omaro – who were both outside – came, and Isaias and what became the PLF 2 also came, so we settled in the same general area.

So it happened that Romedan and Isaias – who had been together outside in China – had this good relationship between them. Not only that, but Isaias also had good relations with me from our base in the fifth division. And so we started to talk.

Because Romedan and Isaias agreed with the opinion of the people who were still in the field to unite and form a party, they talked amongst themselves. And Romedan and Isaias came to an agreement, more or less, that they should form this core.

Because this general agreement was reached amongst the cadres, both coming from outside and the second Isaias-led Ala group, we agreed to meet in this April meeting that you asked about earlier. That was on the fourth of April, 1971, and it was held in Gedem, near the big mountain of Hirgigo, near to Massawa.

The people in the meeting were: Isaias, Romedan, Mesfin Hagos, Omaro, Abu Bakr Mohammed Hassan, Ibrahim Afa, Hasan Mohamed Amir, Ali Said Abdella, Ahmed Tahir Baduri, Ahmed al-Qeisi.

Ahmed Tahir Baduri and Ahmed al-Qeisi were newly arrived from Syria, but because they knew and had connections with Abu Bakr Mohammed Hassan and Ali Said Abdella, they were both included, and they agreed in general on the principles of the establishment of the party and what its ideology should be. And myself. Maybe there was one more.

These are the people who assembled.

A Conversation with Petros Solomon and Berhane Gebreghzabhier

August 2, 2001

This conversation took place in Petros Solomon's family home on Martyrs Boulevard in Asmara, across from the Nyala Hotel. I had met Petros in July 1976 on my first visit to the field with EPLF. We had spoken often since then.

I will never forget interviewing Petros on the battlefield in Massawa in December 1977, hours after the failure of the front to capture one of the last major Ethiopian strongholds in the country in what was a key turning point in the war. This marked the first stages of the fourteen-year Soviet intervention that forced the liberation movement into retreat, then stalemate for nearly a decade. Petros was visibly saddened, taking the loss of Eritrean life under his command personally – and he provided me with figures for EPLF casualties, one of the rare times the front did so. But he was already sorting through strategic and tactical options for the next confrontation, as was his (and most EPLF commanders') wont.

During the stalemate years I met him in a command bunker in Nakfa and in "guest houses" and underground offices in the Sahel. In the early 1990s, after the final victory, I interviewed him in his capacity as Minister of Defense (1992-1994), then as Foreign Minister (1994-1997), and later as the Minister of Fisheries (1997-2001). The most recent encounter had come during a visit with my wife, Debbie Hird, in February 1999 in the midst of the second round of fighting with Ethiopia.

Always, Petros was both passionate about his work and candid about his own and the country's strengths and weaknesses. He was a patriot and a pragmatist. He thrived on results and was equally impatient with bureaucracy and with others' egos, especially if they blocked effective action for attainable objectives. Yet he also had a quick wit and a sparkling, playful sense of humor. It was inevitable he would clash with Isaias.

I had met but never formally interviewed Berhane, who joined us for this conversation and whom I met again at his house in Asmara later in the month to talk further, though that time without a tape recorder.

An early member of both the EPLF and the People's Party, Berhane had been inducted into the party Central Committee in 1976 and remained part of the organization's inner core throughout the rest of its existence.

Conversations

As I loaded my first cassette tape, we chatted about the fruitless efforts of security officials, acting on direct presidential orders, to uncover corruption in the Ministry of Fisheries in Massawa in an attempt to discredit Petros and of the chaotic and opaque character of the government's and the PFDJ's spending practices – conditions which Petros had long criticized.

At this point, I turned on the machine and let the conversation drift a bit before turning to the subject of the People's Party and its role in the liberation struggle.

Petros: There is a lot of spending now. If this is really a corruption inspection, then everything has to be inspected. Somebody should be responsible for all the spending in this country, and I am quite sure it is not the Parliament. The Parliament has never discussed these issues.

All the government should be scrutinized for what has been going on: How are things administered? How is money collected? How is money disbursed?

Connell: There is no published national budget. Is that correct? There hasn't been since the formation of the government?

Petros: No. A budget that is discussed and ratified by the Parliament or the Cabinet? I think there have been one or two exercises in the Cabinet that were not fully implemented. And most of the time it didn't work, because they have two sections in the budget – the Recurring Budget and the Capital Budget.

The Recurring Budget is the salaries and the expendables. That's where people concentrate. The Capital Budget has been discussed many times, but it doesn't work, it doesn't function.

It's not a rational way of decision-making that we have, with ministries studying strategies, presenting them to Parliament, and then the government informing Parliament about the resources, materials, treasury, and all that, and then allowing the budget – or allowing money – to be spent in the most rational way for the country of Eritrea.

The discussion has been there one or two times, I think, but with no results.

Connell: But some of the international donors are starting to complain now about the lack of transparency on these financial issues.

Petros: As far as I know, there has never been a budget discussion in the Parliament. Maybe on some issues only.

Berhane: There was no budget law. There was no discussion about budgetary issues – in the sense of a budget for planning – no transparency,

78

how the plan was to be implemented and assessed, the real sense of budgetary working. So there was not a single fiscal budget.

Connell: Okay, I'm going to take a leap back into the party history, though the contemporary situation is important. They are obviously related, but I want to get the history first in order to understand what's happening now.

Did things work the same way in the EPLF, back in the '70s? Did you have a budget then? Who controlled the money? You had departments; you had a Political Bureau running the front. Did you ever discuss money?

Berhane: Sure. In the '70s, there was no known source for money, nothing we could count on. We may have money collected from the mass organizations and sometimes a limited donation from certain organizations – either NGOs or governments – but we knew the actual amount, at least in the Polit-Bureau. And we knew the allocation – that such and such money was allocated to certain departments, such and such money goes to arms-buying. We knew, actually. There was a discussion.

Petros: I think this must have stopped at a very early stage. These things might have been happening in 1983, 1984, maximum

Berhane: Maybe '85, '86.

Petros: After that, I don't think there was this kind of knowledge, even in the meetings. Back then, there was money. In fact, there was a lot of money that was coming from nobody-knows-where that was used for purchasing weapons, which we needed.

We don't know how it came. We don't care how it came. But we had the ammunitions that we needed coming from China at that time. In fact, there was quite a large amount.

Connell: This is in the mid-'80s?

Berhane: At least 1984, 1985.

Petros: Late '80s. So I think it's not just a situation where this tradition just came overnight; it gradually ended up to what it is in the 1990s.

Connell: Who knew where the money came from, in the 80's, and where it was going – only Isaias?

Petros: Well, donations were known. Aid was known. That's all.

Connell: But in the party itself, in the Central Committee of the party, which was eleven or twelve people then?

Berhane: I think so.

Connell: And this was the Political Bureau of the EPLF? The Central Committee of the party was almost the same as the front's Polit-Bureau, except for Mohammed Said-Barre?

Berhane: The second term, from 1987 to independence, the Central Committee of the party and the Polit-Bureau of the front, they were meeting together almost, for four or five days at a time. They were the same.

Connell: Mohammed Said-Barre was on the Polit-Bureau then, wasn't he?

Berhane: Yes. He was not elected to the Central Committee of the party after 1987.

Connell: And was there anybody on the Central Committee of the party who wasn't on the Polit-Bureau?

Berhane: No. Yes. I was a Central Committee of the party, but was not a Polit-Bureau member.

Petros: There were others, too.

Berhane: There was Haile "China." Tekle Habteselassie. Salle Hurui. The Polit-Bureau in 1987 was reduced to nine members.

Connell: So eight of them were CC from the party, and then there was Mohammed Said-Barre. And he was a member of the party but not of the Central Committee.

Sherifo said to me yesterday that the decision was never taken to dissolve the party; that there was a meeting in Af Abet where the issue of freezing the activities of the cells was discussed, but that the Central Committee of the party continued to meet without the party; that it was basically the same as the Polit-Bureau of the EPLF all the way up until 1994; and that the decision to shut down the party was taken by Isaias alone. Is this approximately correct? Or do you have any different memories?

Petros: Yes. Actually, we didn't decide to finish the party. We discussed the nature of the problems that we had at that time. One was that it became meaningless because many people who were not members of the party were for so long involved in the EPLF, it was difficult not to make them members of the party. Because the criteria of the party were based on clearly leftist political thinking.

Connell: Is this still true even in the late '80s?

Petros: The criteria were written there. Somebody is classified as "democratic." At the democratic there were three levels: democratic A, B, C. Below that there was "nationalist." Below that there was ... not even nationalist.

Berhane: Not active.

Petros: Something like that. So somebody, you follow him at that stage. When you say he is nationalist, it means EPLF. Then you put in some work, and he becomes democratic – first level, second level. He becomes a member of the party, something like that. So it became meaningless. EPLF politics and party politics at one time became the same.

We were going for "nationalist" in everything – looking for nationalist heroes in our stories, creating nationalism as such, enforcing it with our political manuals, books, propaganda. We stopped talking about Lenin, and Drue started to talk about Segeneiti and all those Eritreans who fought against the Italians, and – you know – nationalism, per se.

And then the cell leaders were abusing it also for their own personal vendettas. They would let somebody not become a party member for many years, even when he was a good performer. So a decision was taken that for such people the Central Committee has to decide when they are becoming members or not, and not the local cell or the local committee.

So, the ideology was bankrupt. East Europe was gone. Marxism had changed its form totally, and there was no model to look at. The ideology became meaningless. The organization itself had many problems.

So we said we should transform it into something that can help us continue this struggle for national independence. I think some ideas about social justice were discussed. We said, what is social justice? We have to define it. We have to study it. And let's do that.

But until such a time, the activities of the party at the lower levels are meaningless. This was, I think, what we decided – Berhane can correct me – this is what I remember about that discussion.

Berhane: And as you said in your paper [at the ESA conference], the party played a very important vanguard role, as far as I remember, from late '75. It was very organized from cell to Central Committee structure, and the members were not big enough to create problems. And they were actually vanguard in this sense in every aspect. But as time went on and the membership became bigger and bigger, especially the problem of recruiting became problematic. Some non-party members were more active than party members, and the secrets were leaking. Some were knowing in one way or another.

So also started the problem, as Petros said, the problem of ideology. We were supporting the Soviet Union despite their involvement in Ethiopia. But after a long discussion, we actually condemned them in the second Unity Congress in 1987. So with this problem, we met in Afabet, as you said, in late '88 or early '89 and said that this problem is becoming – the party issue became very problematic. We cannot separate who is party members and non-party members in their activities. Everybody is paying his blood – is sacrificing.

It is true that at the beginning we had to have an organized unity to lead in the right direction, but now it is becoming very hard to distinguish between party and non-party members – all are sacrificing. Therefore, we have to freeze party activities and study how to resolve this problem in the future. So, after '89, that was the decision of the Central Committee meeting in Afabet.

After that, after '89 -'90, we didn't have any meeting concerning this issue. After independence it continued like that. Immediately after independence, '90 – '91, there was no party meeting, not even a party members meeting.

There was no discussion as to how we should solve the problem, even though people were asking, "Why don't we meet, why don't we discuss?"

Then, the answer was: "Meetings will not solve problems. This is a sense of losing direction, something irrelevant to the issues we face now."

Connell: Wait, wait. Who is giving this answer?

Berhane: This is the President. Because questions were raised in different meetings – not of the party, but in the front.

Connell: So he's saying – say this again please – that meetings will not help?

Berhane: Yes. Meetings will not solve problems. What happened to us after independence was that questions were raised by many members and in some instances, Isaias said, "It is not because we're not meeting; it is because of a sense of losing direction from all of us."

So we didn't discuss how to resolve this party issue. We could have discussed it at the Third Congress – that the role of the party was such and such but the problem became like this. Now we are dissolving it, or if there is an alternative to this issue, we can discuss it. And we could have diffused it even with the non-party members, but we could have discussed it with them. But we didn't discuss it.

Connell: Was it forbidden to discuss?

Berhane: No, it was not forbidden. We actually lost a sense of direction immediately after independence.

Connell: Those three years after the war are so interesting, because this is where there is a rupture with the political culture of the struggle. And when you wake up, all of a sudden it is a presidential structure; all the power is in one office.

Berhane: That's the problem.

Petros: I wouldn't accept this analysis of "losing direction." Because the question comes: Who lost direction? What do we mean by losing direction? That was the official explanation, as you said.

I think he [Isaias] was saying that because he wanted to come with an alternative idea. Because he didn't want to accept the reality of the situation at independence. Because after independence, immediately, there was a demand for the fighters for some money. And then a demand for something to give to their parents. And then a demand about clothing and things like that. And all these demands were driving him crazy. So he called this "losing a sense of direction" – concentration on individual needs rather than the country's needs, trying to get rich quickly.

When people focused on their own individual needs, he was interpreting it as loss of direction. He was interpreting it as "nation-first" is being lost and "individual-first" is coming. So, literally he was saying, "It's wrong to do that, because we cannot afford it."

So the way I see it, people did not lose direction. It was natural after independence for people to come and ask for the betterment of their livelihood. And had we seen it as not a loss of direction but a natural, legitimate demand based on need rather than ideology, then we would have been able to respond to what the fighters and the people needed at that time.

But we didn't do it until we had a meeting on twentieth of May. The next day in the declarations of the newspaper, it was upside-down. Yes, these fighters, they are right. There are lots of problems, and everything should be given to them – the industries, the plants should be given to the defense, and defense should be self-sufficient, and we should give them some money...

Well, that was not a genuine explanation even, because in '94 again we came back to the same idea, and he was saying, "Why do we need to sell out?" All these things were seen as change of direction, and things like that. So, if you get my point, Berhane, I'm trying to say ...

Berhane: No, I am not giving a justification for the sense of losing direction. I said immediately from '91 to '93 up until May 20th, there was no meeting, as we had had before independence.

Connell: May 20th? That was the first Central Committee meeting?

Berhane: No, May 20th was the fighters' revolt!

Immediately, even two or three months after independence, there were demands from the fighters, as Petros said, for their subsistence and even for their families – for pocket money or for anything, going for tea even. They didn't have anything.

Unless you have well-to-do family who can help you or you are in a position where one way or another you can get some money to work in Asmara and other towns, the fighters didn't have anything. Just immediately after independence. Then they tried to ask for some money to go and see their families. So, we didn't respond to this. We didn't meet and discuss this. All of us. Actually, it is the leadership, starting from the President, who should be responsible to respond to these questions.

Then, slowly problems were accumulating. For three years, we didn't do anything. We didn't have the party meeting. Maybe we had some meeting of Central Committee for some issues. But we were not discussing the real economic – and other – demands of the fighters.

Not only that. In formal meetings or other meetings, the President was trying to justify that these questions, as Petros said, show a sense of losing direction for all of us, he was saying, including himself, because we were in festivities, post-independence, so all of us were going this way and that way.

Not only that. On the 18th of May [1993], prior to the May revolt, May 20th revolt, we had a Central Committee meeting. That Central Committee meeting decided to prolong its term for four years and become members of the National Assembly. And also decided that we would not get salary for the coming four years. It was after that announcement, the next day, that the fighters revolted.

So it was an accumulation of problems. And the explanation was that we were losing direction. People want to get rich quickly. There were excess expectations that every fighter after independence was expecting to be above the people, to get richer.

That was not the real explanation; but that was the explanation the President was trying to give.

Petros: Trying to better your life was considered a loss of direction.

Let me add something to what he's saying.

I accept it in the sense that after independence, we didn't sit down and discuss what we were going to do. Aside from the fact that we discussed about the referendum, which is going to take two years, there was no serious discussion about the future of this country. Problems were drifting, and you react when they hit your head.

So immediately after independence, the first announcement that came as a directive was to send all the fighters who are not fruitful in your ministries or departments to Keren.

Now, when we were in Sahel we had a lot of handicapped people – a lot of people who were not directly useful in any ministry, but were somehow surviving there. Everybody was contributing something, and they were useful somehow. But when we came here, they may not have been directly working at that level. And about 7,000 people were collected in Keren.

Keren had a big problem. They didn't know what to do with these people, and most of them were wounded, handicapped, aged, with family problems and things like that. All of them became frustrated within a short period of time. And then when [Isaias] was frustrated, he said, "Send them all to their units, to the corps."

You are talking about people who cannot see. You are talking about people who are handicapped, old-aged, who cannot even work behind the lines in the departments. They were sent to the corps. And the corps were given the mandate to make housing for them, to make them comfortable, and so forth.

It was hell, literally. It was hell, it was hell, it was hell.

And the corps, you know, were army units. But they became villages, communities, that had to deal with everything – handicapped, children, aged. And it was a problem that was not managed properly.

So, you are talking about something like 15, 20 percent immediately becoming dissatisfied with the way things are run and having grudges and getting confused because they don't know what their future looks like.

Berhane: Another important explanation that he was trying to give – the main reason, the post-independence reason – was, in his words, that the departments, EPLF departments, which were in Sahel, came to Asmara in an unorganized way, so they created problems. That was the main reason for losing the sense of direction and other problems.

. The offices and the other facilities were neglected in Sahel, so they came to Asmara in a disorganized way. But it was not his fault, he wanted to say. It was departments that left Sahel in an unorganized way without being told to come to Asmara.

Petros: Everybody was coming to us.

Berhane: Actually, that was not the reason. But the President said that was the main reason even for losing direction.

Connell: So there was chaos.

Berhane: Yes, chaos.

But he said the problem of losing direction and the other problems were because the departments and other units just flooded to Asmara, though he didn't give them the order. He didn't know who told them to come, and this created problems.

Petros: One thing that developed before independence was that the fighters were not satisfied with the way the organization was run.

The Central Committee of '87 was not as popular as the Central Committee before '87, and the value given to the people who were elected was not that high, because the Second Organizational Congress was so much organized. Everybody was given a paper on whom to select. So many people found themselves not accepting why a certain person was in the Central Committee.

Connell: So the party prepared the slate, and then gave people a paper saying, "This is who to vote for"?

Berhane: For the Central Committee of the EPLF.

Petros: If you have seventy, you get a list of about eighty-five; then you only have a difference of fifteen, but that's all.

After '87, with the performance – even though the military developments were very good and that was the morale carrying the organization forward – I think there was a lot of dissatisfaction on the incapacity, on the lack of management, of many departments in the front and the army. And this was a grudge that was still held by fighters.

Once we came to Asmara, the Central Committee was not famous, was not popular, was exposed, so-to-say. It became very unpopular, and I think one of the reasons that led the President to talk about how the leadership has become "defunct." Not defunct – "rotten."

"This leadership is rotten," he said. "I cannot continue with this rotten leadership. We need to put new blood into this leadership."

And when he was saying that, he was sending a message, which was also true, in a sense, because we were so disorganized.

But we were not sitting down, discussing issues, responding to the needs, looking at the future and things like that in the way that was demanded after independence. And there was a lot of dissatisfaction in the way this country was run. So this was also another complaint.

Connell: So you're saying he was distancing himself from the Central Committee and saying, "It's them, not me."

Petros: Literally, he said that: "Everybody else is rotten, so give me new blood, and I'll show you how to run this country."

Berhane: Prior to independence, in 1986, when actually the *derg* was becoming weaker and weaker, he was conducting seminars. And he called them the "three privileges."

These privileges are that those who are in high position, even in the Polit-Bureau, excepting himself, are drinking and living in good condition while the fighters at the grass-roots are dissatisfied with all the actions of their leaders. This was prior to independence, in 1986

So, the fighters came with a picture, that, except Isaias, all the leaders are drunkards, womanizers, who are living in good condition. He called these famous seminars the "three privileges."

You have to fight these three privileges against the leadership.

Connell: And what are the three?

Berhane: Drinking, living in a good condition, womanizing, something like that.

Connell: This sounds like a classic Chinese formulation.

Berhane: These three privileges were very famous in 1986.

Petros: The "anti-three," he called it.

Berhane: Anti-three.

Petros: And when he made that campaign, he didn't make any kind of meeting of the Polit-Bureau or the Central Committee about what he was doing. He immediately went and made the seminar himself.

So everybody was amazed by the way these seminars happened. Because all the rank-and-file fighters were saying, "Isaias is the only good man." And all the upper cadres, including the Central Committee, were unhappy.

They kept it to themselves, but from that time onwards, their commitment to serving the cause must have been damaged a lot. And this is the first time that we saw, as you said, a purely Chinese style of going to the roots, like a Cultural Revolution.

Berhane: This is one year prior to the second congress of EPLF.

Connell: But the party had a congress the same year. When was the party Congress in relation to this?

Berhane: I think two months prior to the EPLF Congress.

Connell: That's not very long.

Petros: The Great Caesar...

Berhane: So actually it started – the role of the party – started declining in the early '80s – from 1984, 1985 onwards.

Connell: And the role of the great leader?

Berhane: Sure.

Petros: He distanced himself, clearly, and everybody started saying: Look up, only this man is pure, all the others are corrupt, and things like that.

Connell: Can I take you back to the early part of the party, when it formed?

Haile Menkerios argued that the *menqa* incident was important in pushing the party forward. He was not in the party until '75. I didn't quote him for all those things [in the ESA paper], but this is more or less his view, and I wondered about that period.

When did you join the front and the party?

Petros: I joined the party in '76 when I was a battalion [political] commissar.

Connell: That's when I met you.

Petros: Back then I didn't know everything.

Berhane: Myself, too. I became a party member in March 1976, when I was a commissar of a battalion, the same.

Connell: And Sebhat [Ephrem] was also a battalion commissar – is that when he joined the party?

Berhane: Yes.

Petros: I remember Ali Said and Asmorem coming to us – that's when we were in Waukie-Zagr. About the time you were there.

Connell: Yes, I was there in July. Well, in Sabur I met everybody.

Berhane: You should also have become also a party member [laughing].

Connell: A lot of people thought I did…

Petros: But what happened was they called me and they said, we have a party. And we consider you good for it, because you were really suffering after the 1973 crisis, and nobody else went through it like that. What you wanted to do is to make yourself be accepted and known as somebody who is fighting for his country, that's all.

We didn't like the way the problems were handled at that time, because right after 1973 [the *menqa* incident] the people in the Security that were handling the intelligence were really doing it in a very bad way. They were just accusing many people, especially intellectuals coming from certain villages, like Mussie and others. These people were direct victims.

They would take them, ask them questions, intimidate them, and so on. And immediately – these guys know nothing – and suddenly they become – they want to know more about 1973.

And we don't know anything about it, but the way they are treating it is making us become suspicious. And this group distanced itself so far that they became a trend, which was a problem. And it was a really big problem.

Connell: Who were these people?

Petros: There was Haile "Jebha" and Mehare Girmazion, who came from the USSR.

There was Wode-arbate, called "Oosoos," who was a graduate from [unintelligible] University.

Berhane: And Eyob, Dr. Eyob, a Soviet student.

Petros: These people became very unpopular. Nobody liked them.

And they became known as the "rightists." It was just a name given by the grapevine. I don't know if it was an official name. *Menqa* was the left. They were the right, *yamin*.

Connell: I kept hearing about this, but…

Petros: They became so powerful – very, very powerful.

But their influence remained only in Sahel. They didn't come to the highlands. And the units that were in the highlands were more free; they were less influenced by them.

Connell: And this was up to '74?

Berhane: Even up to '76. '75, '76.

Petros: They call this one, they call that one, they put them, they question them, they do this and that, and then they send them back.

Connell: These people were controlling security?

Petros: Sure. Starting from '73, they're the same group.

Berhane: Let me add a few points.
   Menqa, as a trend, had its slogans – that the front doesn't have program, whether it is true or not. That there should be an equalitarian way of handling problems, that there is no justice, something like that. That the leadership of that time was not competent enough to lead the front. These were their slogans.
   Then, the antithesis of this – what Petros was calling this *yamin* or rightists – their slogan was that it was not true. They are mostly a clique from a certain region, from around Segeneiti, and the slogan they were saying that the front had no program was not true. They said they are raising "untimely" issues, something like that.
   And mostly this *yamin* or rightists – some were from other groups, but mostly they were from Hamasien – were organizing people in a regional way. And later they were exposed that they were not fighting the issue in the real sense, something like that. And they were sentenced as rightists who were also destroying the front.

Connell: And when were they sentenced? This was '76?

Berhane: Yeah, '75 to '77.

Connell: And were people killed?

Berhane: Yes.

Connell: I heard seven were killed during the *menqa*.

Petros: I don't know exactly when, because you cannot exactly know what happened. But we know they were gathered to go somewhere at that time...

Connell: The "rightists," as well? There were some from the *menqa* who were killed in '73.

Berhane: They were all imprisoned, but the official explanation given to us, even to the fighters in the meetings, was that they were sentenced.

Connell: But some of them you've never seen again? So some were obviously killed.

Petros: We've never seen them again.

Connell: How many would you guess? Five, six?

Petros: I don't know. At least that.

Berhane: Not more than that.
We are saying the ones who were very active.
You have Mehare Girmazion, Solomon, Haile "Jebha", Eyob, Wode-arbate. Not more than five.
The *menqa* also, the active ones – not more than that.

Connell: Sherifo said there were seven who were killed.

Berhane: Maybe. Something like that.
Actually they are more or less equal number.
The official explanation given was that the other group from the left, raising slogans that were untimely, were sentenced because they could destroy the organization. And the others, the rightists, were also sentenced because they were using this regionalism to fight the *menqa*.

Connell: And were they in someway connected with Sabbe?

Berhane: No, I don't think so.

Connell: How democratic would you say the party was in the early years? You've described how it was not functioning in a democratic way later. Is it a romantic view to say that it was internally democratic, that there really was collective leadership in '76 and '77?

Berhane: I think at that time we were satisfied. We were believing that we had the right way to work, to function.
The party was creating a sense of confidence, not only among the party members, even as leaders they proved to themselves they are

the vanguard, even among non-party members. Because most of them were leaders at different levels, and they were the first ones to sacrifice themselves.

Connell: When did you [Petros] join the front?

Petros: I joined in '72.

Connell: And your name always gets associated with the *menqa* from that time. You and Sebhat.

Berhane: Yes, he was *menqa*.

Connell: But you were "rehabilitated."

Petros: Sebhat was not in the main group…

Connell: Were you [Berhane] in this also?

Berhane: Actually, I was not in the Sahel at that time. I was in Aden.

Petros: At that time, he was in the navy.

Berhane: I was in the navy, the Eritrean navy. Probably I could have joined…

Connell: You were bringing all the arms and supplies across [the Red Sea]?

Berhane: Yes.

Petros: Sebhat and I were in one unit in Algena.
Our unit was one of the troublemakers. Alamin was the commissar of the unit.

Connell: Was he associated with *menqa*?

Berhane: No.

Connell: He is completely with Isaias now.

Berhane: It makes no difference.

Connell: And where was Drue?

92

He was outside the field? He wasn't there?

Petros: Drue was in prison.

Berhane: He was captured. He was in prison.

A Conversation with Ogbe Abraha

August 2, 2001

This conversation took place in the living room of Ogbe's modest one-story house in the Tiro Vollo neighborhood, up the street from the Alla Scala Hotel.

The tape was damaged, so this is reconstructed from notes and is, therefore, a bit choppy, but the discussion was useful insofar as it filled out the picture of how the party functioned in the 1970s and 1980s.

Ogbe was a member of the front and the party in the 1970s and was inducted into the party's core leadership – the Central Committee – in 1976.

The conversation was cut short by conflicting obligations, so I had to pick it up again five days later.

Connell: When did you join the liberation movement?

Ogbe: I joined the EPLF in 1972, coming from Addis Ababa where I had been a member of the clandestine student organization with Isaias, Haile [Wold'ensae] and others. I joined the Ala group, with Isaias, when I came to the field, and I joined the party in late 1974 or early 1975.

Connell: How did you come to join the party?

Ogbe: Members were selected by party leaders. I was recruited by Asmorem Gherezghier.

In 1976, I was elected to the party Central Committee and the Polit-Bureau of the EPLF.

Connell: What is your assessment of the role of the party, looking back on it now, and how did it work? How did it actually operate?

Ogbe: The party played a big role in uniting the EPLF – identifying problems, deepening the ideology, using criticism-self-criticism.

The first party congress was convened at Merera in July [1976].

At that time, it was organized into branches and cells. The Central Committee controlled the branches, and the branches controlled the cells. Each cell had four-to-five members, and there were four-to-five cells in each branch.

The way we recruited and distributed them, each EPLF unit had one or two party members.

After the 1978 strategic retreat, the cells and branches were reorganized to stabilize the base of the movement.

Within the party, we discussed all military, political and social problems. We had a well-organized information system, with regular reports of the meetings of all the branches. All these reports are somewhere now, probably in the President's office.

The party played an important role in consolidating the EPLF after the retreat. During peace-times, we met weekly or monthly. There were internal regulations on the organization of party cells, which met weekly. The higher committee met monthly.

We helped the fighters deal with political issues – the USSR, inside political problems, the ELF, differences among the fighters. And with social issues – marriage issues, cultural projects to increase participation, things like this.

Connell: So happened? Why was the party dissolved?

Ogbe: In the 1980s, more people were becoming aware of the existence of the party but weren't in it. This had a negative impact. There were rumors that some members recruited friends and relatives, not others who had earned it.

And our secrecy was compromised.

There was a big increase in membership, also, which diluted the party – in the thousands.

In 1986 when we had our second congress in Ararab in Sahel, there were big discussions on these issues. There were no votes – we reached consensus on every issue. For example, we decided that Isaias should lead the front at the next EPLF congress.

I was also elected to the Central Committee again.

When the CC met in Afabet in 1989, there were ideas coming up about what to do with the party. Many said that the party and front were merging in outlook, so there was no need for the party.

Now I think there was some brainwashing going on that we agreed to this – that there was no need for the party – but we never took that decision as a group. Only we talked about it. From then on, the party never met, though nothing was formally decided. Instead, our activities were frozen.

Then in 1994, Isaias announced at the [EPLF/PFDJ] congress that there was no party. Mesfun [Hagos] asked in the Central Council – the Polit-Bureau of EPLF – when and why it was dissolved.

Isaias said he took responsibility. It was his decision.

People then were tired of the party. Almost all of us were ready to have an open organization, not these secret programs, so we went with this.

A Conversation with
Ogbe Abraha

August 7, 2001

Like the previous one, this conversation took place at Ogbe's house. It, too, is re-constructed from notes taken during the conversation rather than from a tape.

Connell: Can you fill in a little background on yourself and the roles you've played? What positions have you held since independence?

Ogbe: After independence I was assigned to the Ministry of Defense. This was a continuation of my work with the front.

In the last years in the field, I was the head of the Economic Commission, but my main role was military. After independence, I went back to Defense as a member of the General Staff. I was responsible for logistics in 1991.

Then I was one of the people who went to Europe and the United States in a military officers group that was organized and paid for by the Eritrean government.

In 1993, I was appointed Minister of Trade. Later this was expanded to the Ministry of Trade, Industry and Tourism. Then Tourism was separated to become a ministry by itself. This lasted up to 1996. Then I was changed to the Minister of Labor and Social Affairs.

Connell: Where were you when the war started in 1998?

Ogbe: When the war broke out, I was made the leader of a team that inspected the Ministry of Defense, working under the direction of the President. My task was to assess present military conditions and make recommendations on our preparedness – what we had, what we needed.

Later that year [1998], I was appointed to be an advisor to the President and a coordinator of administration and logistics in Defense – reporting to the President directly, not to the minister.

In the middle of 1999, after the second round [of fighting with Ethiopia], I was given the rank of General and I was appointed Chief of Staff of EDF [the Eritrean Defense Forces]. This lasted only seven months.

Connell: When did you start having trouble with Isaias?

Ogbe: The problem came for me when I began to express my opinions to the President in November of 1999.

There were rumors everywhere, and there were misunderstandings among high officials who were not informed about the situation, but we were not holding any ordinary meetings. I saw this as a real danger to the government, and I told this to the President.

There was no participation in making decisions. Legislative and political bodies were not discussing these things. I told the President that after all this struggle we have passed for the sake of future generations, we should have a collective leadership. I said that institutionalization was inevitable, and we needed to move it forward.

Connell: What concerned you most at that time?

Ogbe: Cabinet ministers were not meeting. The National Assembly was not meeting. The Central Council of the PFDJ was not meeting. There were no institutional meetings. All the information we received was by rumor – *bado seleste*.[1]

I was protesting the lack of participation at the policy level.

Connell: What was his response?

Ogbe: After this, we had a meeting of the CC of the front where very critical opinions of the PFDJ were expressed – on political agitation, economic policy and so on – and we called for corrections.

Several weeks later, I was frozen. The President sent me a letter saying I was "not serious" for a long time. He criticized me for being responsible for the corruption at the Red Sea Trading Company during my time as Minister of Trade and Industry.

Seven or eight months later, we had the ninth meeting of the Central Council of the front. After a discussion of national issues, I appealed these charges to the council in written form. The council set up a committee to assess, but none of the decisions taken at this meeting were followed up.

Connell: What about the war? How did that fit into this?

---

[1] *Bado seleste* or "03" is a common term in Eritrean society for the rumor mill – the grapevine.

Ogbe: To have a war at that time was a very bad thing. If it was only Badme, it could have been solved by other means – the UN, etcetera. But the Tigrayans were expanding into Eritrea elsewhere.

I didn't even hear about the crisis until we were three or four days into it. At first, the only question for us was how to defend the country in a conventional war.

But the reason behind this should be studied. I am not convinced by the explanation of how it started. It is still unclear who made the decision for us to go into Badme.

And this points up the problem in the way all these decisions were taken. There was never any group discussion of strategic questions first. Until now, there is still no national security institution to analyze issues like this with information from all ministries and intelligence sources.

There should be someone responsible for national security. If you leave all this to one person only – the President – you will have dictatorship. There is no other way to explain it.

Connell: How do you think this situation would have turned out differently if there had been discussion within the leadership?

Ogbe: We underestimated Ethiopia. But there was no analysis of this – or of the situation with Sudan.

This was not the right time to open a conflict. The military was not prepared. The economy was weak. The political situation was unsettled, not yet stabilized. If we had to have a conflict with Ethiopia, it would be better to wait ten years and settle the country first.

Connell: The government argues that this is not the time to raise these questions. What do you say to this? What are your objectives in raising such criticisms in the Open Letter and in interviews with the press?

Ogbe: Today, the challenges to the government to democratize, to increase participation should be the legacy we leave to coming generations.

We are trying to discuss national issues in order to open the eyes of the people – on economic and social issues, issues of peace and war. We need to come from our closed eyes and closed ears to hear what is going on and to open the democratic process in Eritrea.

If we hammer on this, the people can follow to see what the needs for change are.

We are saying that the government should move forward on democratization, on multi-party politics, on constitutional government, on human rights issues. First, the Constitution should be implemented.

Conversations

Connell: What do you expect will happen next?

Ogbe: People are coming to understand the need for change. The PFDJ is also aware. But what will happen next is not clear.

Is it going to come to discuss these issues, or to arrest us, or to close the press and the opposition groups?

The highest risk scenario is to arrest the opposition group and close the private press. This is not a solution.

Or he [Isaias] may go to the congress of the front and, using legal means, he can isolate the opposition or arrest us at that time.

For a short time, this could work, but not for a long time in this country. The opposition was not only the fifteen who signed this letter. There is also a very large passive opposition.

A Conversation with
Haile "Drue" Wold'ensae

August 13, 2001

This conversation took place in my apartment in the Sembel Residential Complex in Asmara (known as "Korea" to locals, after the nationality of the contractor), where I was living part-time, while gathering material for a country handbook I was drafting for the Ministry of Information under the supervision of the acting minister, Zemhret Yohannes.

It was with considerable distress that I spoke with Haile in August 2001, as he knew then that he would soon be spirited off to prison for his dissenting views, perhaps never to emerge. And he said he knew, too, that he would do nothing to avert this – or to leave the country – as it was a matter of principle to him to remain in active, visible contention with the repressive apparatus he so strongly opposed right to the end.

I met Haile once more – on September 4 – before he disappeared into the government's secret detention system but without a tape recorder. At that time, he clarified some of the details of early party membership, which I reproduce in the Appendix (the addition of the three generals to the EPLF Polit-Bureau in 1987 and the body's simultaneous reduction from thirteen to nine members that marked Isaias's militarization of the movement at the end of the "three privileges" campaign, for example).

He also said that there had been a number of meetings about the party in the early 1990s, after independence but prior to the 1994 EPLF/PFDJ congress, at which the fate of the party was discussed. At one of these – in a suburb of Asmara near Beleza in 1991 – Isaias presented a paper on the issue, though no copies of the document appear extant today.

Three options were discussed at this and later sessions: Should the party and front be dissolved altogether so new parties could arise from scratch? Should the party be incorporated into the EPLF, which would continue to function throughout the transition? Or should the two disappear and a broad-based movement be formed for the transition to diverse political parties? Though there was never a formal decision on this, what emerged was a combination of options two and three.

The last such unpublicized leadership conference came in January 1994, just before the congress that launched the PFDJ. It was at this meeting, much as had been the case with party/front congresses in the war years, that Isaias unveiled his candidates for leadership, including the core of the PFDJ central office, which was to become the de facto leadership of the political movement. Haile said that war hero Mesfin Hagos, whom Isaias had purged from the EPLF's top leadership in 1987, was absent from the President's list of nominees but was put on by popular acclaim (replacing former ELF leader and Hagaz administrator Tesfai Tekle). Otherwise, Isaias got his way.

But in our conversation on August 13, before I turned on the tape recorder, we chatted about the early political influences on Haile himself. The first such influence was his great grandfather, Bata Hagos, who fought the Italians at the end of the nineteenth century. Haile said he grew up with stories of this warrior and of his maternal grandfather, Ras Tesema, who was active in the independence party "Eritrea for Eritreans" in the 1940s. Later, he said, there was a leader of the underground Eritrean Liberation Movement – Tukuk – who died in the PLF, and, in school, there was Isaias and another activist, Kidane Kiflom, who was killed in 1970 by the ELF.

In our recorded conversation, Haile focused mainly on the charges being leveled at him and the other G-15 dissidents at PFDJ seminars and in the state-run media [see Appendix] and on the likelihood of imminent action against them.

Haile: They want to charge the fifteen-group [the G-15] on three different issues. First, it looks like they want to accuse the group as a group because we are asking for a meeting of the National Assembly and because we have come with an open letter. They call this illegal.

Connell: The request for a meeting is illegal? Or the open letter is illegal?

Haile: Both. That's how they do it. Because they say we have been told by the President that we are doing something illegal and wrong. So one accusation is as a group, accusing the fifteen as a group.

Second, they say they want to accuse individual people on the views we have given through our interviews. They claim it is illegal; it is something that divides the people.

The third accusation is against some of us who have committed something like treason.

Connell: That's what I gathered.

Haile: Yes. And these last are accused on two positions.

One, on the issue of peace and war, is that we have tried to put all blame on Eritrea and to make Woyane free of these war charges.

The second is on the stand some of us have taken during the third offensive. On that, they have put three points: That we were saying we cannot check the advances of the Woyane move towards Eritrea, that we are incapable. Second, that the Woyane have put an ultimatum saying that unless the President of Eritrea, Isaias, is toppled from his post, they will not stop this aggression. So we supposedly said that Isaias has to resign. Third, we are accused of saying that if Woyane occupies the whole country in this advance, there will be a lot of atrocities against our people, so we have to ask the government of the United States or the UN to take over in order to avoid these atrocities. This is defeatist and a collaboration with TPLF.

And they said that although the whole group has committed mistakes, it is only some of us who will be charged for treason. And those are who have taken a position on the letters, too, on the peace and war and on the third round.

Connell: And they said there will be charges of treason?

Haile: They didn't mention "treason," but in Tigrinya it can be interpreted that way.

Connell: It's obvious from the way they're constructing this.

Haile: It is very elastic. The word is elastic. It could go up to treason, I guess.

Connell: And do they say who those are?

Haile: No, no, no. They don't mention names. "Some of them," they say.

Connell: But you and Petros get mentioned by everybody.

Haile: In one of my interviews I said that during the 1967 war when Israel went into Egypt, President Gamal Abdel Nasser wanted the vote of confidence of his people and he said he is ready to resign. So in such kinds of difficulties, the whole government or the President could be asked to resign. So what is the problem, if anybody could put such kind of an idea?

Connell: That was in one of your interviews?

Haile: It was in one of my interviews. And I know what people were saying during the third offensive. So Alamin mentioned, for example, that one of them has said this. He wants to substantiate the accusation that we wanted to topple the President. He put it as a manifestation of the idea of trying to make a *coup* or something like that.

This is one point – that we have made mistakes, some of us. It is criminal, and we will have to be charged. So they classified it as what the group as a whole is responsible for and what individuals will be responsible for. And the message was very clear here saying that it is wrong to say Group-15. It is only a group within this group that has committed criminal offenses. The others are either covering up or are simply stooges.

So they want to separate us into at least three categories. And this is what they have been trying a lot in order to divide this opposition – this group. Now they have failed, they want to classify us separately, so that they can deal with one group and excuse the other group for being only collaborators with us.

The message is very clear here.

Connell: And they also accused you personally of setting up the G-13 [in Berlin in 2000]?[1]

Haile: Yes, not only that – even the student protest for the summer campaign [in 2001].[2] Now, also, they are saying that we are the people who inspired the university students. You will find that if there is any opposition, they will accuse us for that. So, this is one.

The second one is that they said we have started this opposition only for personal interests and sentiments. We don't have any case. We don't have any issue. We don't care about the national interests or people's interest. That was the second thing.

---

[1] In October 2000, thirteen prominent Eritrean academics and professionals, most living abroad, signed a private letter to Isaias that was dubbed the "Berlin manifesto" after it was leaked to the press. In it, they criticized one-man rule and the government's hostility to free expression and called for a debate on the war, implementation of the Constitution, collective leadership, abolition of the special courts, and other reforms. Signers included former EPLF representative to the UN and chair of the Constitution Commission, Bereket Habteselassie; former chair of the Eritrean Relief Association, Paulos Tesfagiorgis; Red Sea Press publisher Kassahun Checole; and former EPLF health department head Dr. Assefaw Tekeste, as well as Khaled Beshir (U.S.A.), Miriam M. Omar (U.K.); Mohammed Kheir Omar (Norway); Mussie Misghina (Sweden); Reesom Haile (Belgium) and Lula Ghebreyesus (South Africa.) Several signers met with Isaias in November to discuss the letter, but the exchange was hostile and unproductive, according to participants. Lula later withdrew her association.

[2] In July 2001, University of Asmara Student Union president Semere Kesete was arrested after criticizing the government's summer work program for university students. Hundreds of protesting students were subsequently rounded up and forcibly dispatched to summer work camp at Wi'a (Dankalia), where two died of heat stroke. In the aftermath of these protests, the University of Asmara Student Union was disbanded and replaced by a PFDJ-controlled youth union chapter. Semere, who was never charged with a crime, later escaped. He is now abroad and active in opposition politics.

The third thing they said is, people have been asking the government and the leadership to take action against this group, the G-15. Because of the tradition of PFDJ to be very quiet and because there were other pressing national challenges, they did not want to take action so far. But they will be accounted. Not all of us, but those who have committed criminal offenses will be charged.

Our reply to the first charge is that the G-15 has not committed any offense, nor has done anything illegal or unconstitutional, because it was the PFDJ headquarters in January 2001 that started a conspiratorial campaign against some leaders, and that campaign, that seminar, was not endorsed by the Central Council nor by the Executive Office of the EPLF [PFDJ], nor was it endorsed or discussed by the National Assembly or the Cabinet of Ministers.

Connell: No institutional body?

Haile: And the worst thing is that it was very conspiratorial. Because in every ministry the minister is the top PFDJ official. And if there is any meeting, seminar or anything – even if the headquarters of the PFDJ has to send discussion papers or seminar papers – it was the ministers who have to organize those meetings.

In the January seminars, they did not inform us. For example, our Minister of Trade and Industry. They simply invited the heads of the departments, heads of divisions, and branch heads of the PFDJ in the ministry, as well as in other ministries. And they started to campaign.

In those meetings – which we were not informed of, which we did not know their objectives, their content – we only knew after the people dispersed and some of them came and told us that there is a conspiracy and even people were afraid that we would not see the light tomorrow.

And in these meetings, they were telling them that we are higher officials who had a defeatist position and who were praying for the TPLF to advance and conquer the whole country.

The people in the seminars – it was a very shocking thing for them!

And there were people in these meetings who were prepared to come and say, "Well, the government has delayed. It has to take action against those people. They should be imprisoned and taken action against."

This stirred the people up.

Connell: I have to say this sounds exactly like what happened in the U.S. back in 1978.[3]

Haile: And the worst thing they did was that...

People, for example, Ali Abdu, who is the head of the television department in the Ministry of Information – him and another, Tadessay or something like that – they were the ones who raised their hands and said: "The government should take action. It should imprison them."

It was orchestrated.

But they didn't know that people would be talking about who said what.

So the same people, Ali Abdu and the other guy, Aron Tadessay, went to another meeting, and they were the ones that raised their hands there and said the government should take action and imprison us.

They went to several different meetings, but they didn't know that people would tell me about it – that Ali and Aron Tadessay have said the same thing in another meeting.

So it was something orchestrated.

Connell: Who's Aron Tadessay? From some ministry?

Haile: They have now made him in charge of a PFDJ branch or something like that. He was the head of the shop of Auget [Ed note: a PFDJ bookstore in Asmara].

Previously he was a member of the National Guidance, and he was in the place on the way to Port Sudan, the place we had the garage – in Suakin. He was a storekeeper.

Connell: So he's a rising star?

Haile: Yes.

And the others were shocked by this accusation. So they asked, who are these people, and what are the crimes they have committed?

The leaders told them: No, you will know later.

So people raised [the question], if there is such kind of treason, you don't bring it to seminars. You take action, and then you tell us. So everybody knew there was something cooked.

---

[3] After the Soviet Union intervened in the liberation war on behalf of Ethiopia, ultra-"left" cadres within the U.S.-based Associations of Eritreans Students and Women, working with pro-Albanian communists in U.S. and Canadian micro-parties, used false accusations and rumors to engineer a break with the EPLF. Once the deceit was exposed the effort collapsed. See Dan Connell, *Against All Odds*, Chapter 10, "Retreat."

Haile "Drue" Wold'ensae – August 13, 2001

When we heard this, well, we don't want to be irresponsible like what they are doing because it has created a lot of confusion within the cadres, within the people. And people were saying, there are some who are working on sub-national issues, creating regional and religious divisions.

So we said, well, you don't correct mistakes with wrong ways. We said, this is very dangerous. If there is anybody who has committed any crime, it should be legally addressed. And, therefore, we should ask for a meeting of the National Assembly and the Central Council. The regular meeting time was already passed.

Connell: February was the next scheduled meeting, wasn't it? It didn't happen.

Haile: It didn't happen. It was in August, the last meeting of the Central Council. So in December there should have been the next one.

But for the National Assembly it is every six months. It was supposed to be convened in August immediately after the Central Council, but the President has to go to the Millennium Summit at the UN, so we had to postpone it. That's why it convened in September.

Even by that schedule, at least by January there should have been the National Assembly meeting as well.

So we started to say, this is a very dangerous move. And many of the members of the Central Council, who are members of the National Assembly, thought that this is a very dangerous move, that these people in the [PFDJ] headquarters are committing a grave mistake and that it has to be corrected in the regular meeting. The majority of the Central Council members were opposed to the seminar and were in favor of handling it in the meetings of the Central Council.

We said: Well, the President is not going to convene this meeting, so we have to ask him. We have to write our names, make a petition. Already the regular meeting time has passed, and there are important issues to be discussed. Therefore, we have to go ask the President.

When we raised that question, many of them said: Well, if we ask the President, he will react, and he might even take excessive measures. But we have to wait until *he* convenes the meeting.

The majority had supported this idea of having the meeting, but some were afraid to ask the President for it.

So we said: No problem, we have to ask. This is legal. And in fact, in January of 2000, when there was the meeting of the Central Council and the National Assembly, at that time it was really the first challenge the President got.

The first question he got was: Why don't we have the regular meetings of all the legislative bodies of the front and the government and the executive bodies of the front and the government?

109

The President at that time said: Well, it was not convenient.

And he was challenged: Why?

He said: Because of the war situation.

People told him: No, the war has stopped since seven months at least. Because it was January 2000.

So he said: I am the chairman. I am telling you it's not convenient.

And he even went as far as saying: And in the future, if I don't feel it's convenient, I am not going to convene these meetings.

So people became furious.

People told him: The country is in a very difficult situation. Let alone the regular meetings, there should be *extra* meetings because the issue of peace and war should be decided by the legislative bodies.

This was the issue raised in the January 2000 meeting.

And when he insisted that it is only when he feels it is convenient to meet, then people told him: If it is not convenient to you as a person, then Sherifo as Vice-President can convene the National Assembly, and Alamin as Secretary of the Front can convene the Central Council meeting.

Connell: Now was this the Central Council or the National Assembly?

Haile: The Central Council.

Connell: And who was saying this?

Haile: Many of the now G-15.

And not only that, it was raised also then that the Front is not doing its business. It has created a lot of problems interfering with the government's institutions.

Connell: This ended up being part of the Open Letter. You're talking about economic business? Or are you talking about all its business – what it's supposed to be doing?

Haile: No, in all the governmental institutions.

The problem is that the President wanted parallel structures, and he wanted to control one structure by using the other structure. There was a lot of interference in government institutions by PFDJ people. This was also raised in the January [2000] meeting.

From that one, everybody knew that the President has openly told us that if he does not feel it is convenient, he will not convene the meeting of the legislative bodies.

But after the third offensive and all the setbacks, even then, people started to say because he has insisted that he will only convene a meeting when he thinks it is convenient – in June [2000], particularly, when

I had to sign the Cessation of Hostilities agreement in Algeria – people started to say, we have to write a petition asking the President to convene the meeting of the legislative bodies because he has told us in January that he will not abide by the Constitution.

But we told them – Sherifo as Vice-President and myself as heading the peace process and as the signer of the Cessation of Hostilities told them – give us the chance to ask him to convene these meetings. If he refuses, then we can take the other steps.

Because of the outcome of the third offensive, he was in a very demoralized position, and he knew that when we asked him, if he does not abide by that, then we'll write this petition. At last, with some hesitation, he accepted to convene the meeting in August.

And in August...

Connell: And this was you and Sherifo who approached him?

Haile: Separately. Separately.

And we said that we have to look forward. These people will try to personalize things and try to create all sorts of defensive mechanisms to abort this. We have to forget everything. We will leave this assessment and evaluation of our experience, too.

But in this August meeting, we said, we should look forward and make sure we guarantee an orderly, peaceful and democratic transition to a constitutional governmental system. So we have to ask for the convening of the Congress, as far as the Front is concerned, and to set a timeframe for the national elections.

We had discussed it among ourselves, and we said we have to be very rational. We cannot ask for national elections. At least we will need six months for drafting and discussing the election law and party law, and then we should give at least one year for elections. So we said at that time we can ask for a year-and-a-half, so that we could have a timeframe of one-and-a-half years to the end of 2001.

We said we should dwell on these things because these people – and because of the failure in the third offensive – will be on the defensive and try to create all sorts of problems. So we should forget all the other things, look forward and set the timeframe, and the basic things we need to go forward.

So that was how we were able to decide on all these issues. It was not accepted by the headquarters of the PFDJ, nor by the President. But at the [September National Assembly] meeting, and because the morale at that time was affected, they had to accept all these things.

Even the issue of the party law – they strongly opposed it, but they were defeated.

Connell: They being?

Haile: Yemane [Gebreab], Zemhret [Yohannes], for example, from the PFDJ.

And Isaias. He kept quiet and when he saw–

Connell: And Hagos and Abdallah Jabr?

Haile: Hagos and Abdallah were not in the meeting because they had some assignment, either to buy things, or I don't know. They were not around.

Isaias himself prior to the meeting, in order to set the mood, made an interview and said we don't have an incubator to hatch political parties at this time. So he was trying to set the mood.

But in the discussion, it was only Yemane and Zemhret who strongly opposed the formation of parties. And when he saw that the majority was for it – President Isaias – said, there's no problem. We can have a committee to draft it.

He had in mind, rather than opposing such a position, he thought he would strangle it during implementation. Because outside the Parliament and the Council he knew there would be rumors, people would be talking – Isaias opposed these things – so rather than oppose it, make it unimplementable.

And I know the people in the headquarters would tell you that the August and September meetings were unproductive. The August one was Central Council; the September was the National Assembly. They were dissatisfied of the resolutions, and therefore they will tell you it was not productive.

I mention all these things to tell you that in February 2001, when the PFDJ people came with this conspiratorial theory, and when members of the Central Council were discussing having a meeting, some of them were not ready to sign because the President could take measures. But we knew the President would not convene any meeting. That is why we said we have to write a letter, or otherwise we have to confront him. We did not choose that.

That is why although there were many people who supported to have a meeting, many of them failed to support the signing. And even some of those who signed – there were eighteen of them who signed it earlier – some of them had to retreat because they were intimidated.

One of them is the Head of the Police, Brigadier General Musa Raba. He signed with us but later they told him you are a military man, and doing such kind of a move, you will be court-marshaled. So he sent a letter, "Because of my position it is not – because I am a military man, I cannot join such kind of…"

And the other one was Worku, the ex-head of ERREC [the Eritrean Relief and Refugee Commission].

Connell: Where is she now?

Haile: In the September 2000 meeting of the National Assembly, there was a hot discussion on our treatment of our friends – the NGOs and other partners – and people were saying – myself and the others – that we have made a lot of mistakes with them.

She supported my view, and immediately after the meeting, the President told her she is out of office. And he told her she is assigned to Keren.

She refused to accept it and she was one of those who signed it, but later Yemane "Charlie" from the Office of the President, who is not a member of the Central Council, nor of the National Assembly, told her that she had made a mistake – she will have to face severe consequences.

In fact, she said, and I quote, "You are heavyweights. They might not take any action against you. But I will be a victim. They will imprison me, so I cannot do this. Please remove my name from the list." It is a mockery.

So in February, we told the others, the President had already told us in January he will not convene if it is not convenient for him. He will not convene. So we have to ask him. And that's what we have done.

So asking the President to convene the meeting of both the Central Council and the National Assembly according to the Constitution is not illegal. It is constitutional.

Connell: Though there is no Constitution...

Haile: Well, the transitional Constitution at least.

In the transitional Constitution it is very clearly stated that the National Assembly should convene every six months, and the Central Council should convene every four months. The Cabinet of Ministers should convene every month, and the Executive Office or the Front Office, should convene every month. So this is a constitutional right for these bodies to convene then.

So the first request, he responds saying: You are mistaken.

The second one, we said we don't only have to ask him to convene, we have to tell him why we think it is important to have the meeting.

So we said: There is this dangerous campaign of the PFDJ. If there are people who have committed anything, let us come to the assembly, come with our concrete things and let the law take its own course.

And the other thing is that because he has disbanded the Committee on Drafting, and he was taking all actions, and all the decisions we have taken in August or September were violated, so we told him all the resolutions are being violated and we want to implement them. So that's why we need the convening of the committees.

He refused. And there also we have told him, if we don't get any positive response, we have a responsibility to inform our people the dangerous things that are going on and our views on how to handle this crisis.

Our response was that this is legal, constitutional, and there is nothing that we can be accused of.

For the second – individuals making interviews – our response was that it was the PFDJ headquarters that started those conspiratorial things. We wanted to address it in its proper way. We have asked and were refused, so we have to come open. So it is the headquarters of the PFDJ that should be responsible for this crisis and improper handling of the problem. And the President is responsible for not convening the assemblies, so he is the one who should be accused.

For the individual interviews, we said it was President Isaias and Alamin Mohamed Said who started the interviews. They were making interviews with the government mass media and abroad with private mass media, and they were discussing issues that did not have consensus in the Central Council and the National Assembly. More than that, they have been propagating ideas contrary to the decisions of the Central Council and the National Assembly.

So, any member of the Central Council has a right to voice his own opinion, and the people have the right to hear from different corners about the particular issue. It is the people's right, and it is the obligation of officials to bring it to the attention of the people to look at it from different corners and different angles.

Nobody should be accused of it. It was President Isaias and Alamin who started the campaign. They have been campaigning on issues where there was no consensus – even, they were propagating opinions contrary to the decisions of the Council.

So this is another issue.

Connell: Number three is the charge of treason.

Haile: On treason, there were the two issues.

First, on the position of peace and war, our response is: This peace and war issue related with *woyane* has a long history. Even before war broke out, it is a very complex issue. Therefore, we feel – and it is very sensitive – therefore we prefer to handle it in the way it is sensitive.

For national security interests, we cannot discuss this exhaustively publicly. But on the conduct of the war and the conduct of the peace process, we've assessed them in the August and September meetings. And as in every case when assessing the military performance or the conduct of the peace process, one has to talk about the strong and weak points of your side and strong and weak points of the other side. And people could differ on their assessment of this.

So, if you differ on the assessment of your weak point and the strong points of the enemy, one cannot accuse you of being a collaborator of the other side. We can differ. Somebody might like to say, "No, we do not have any weakness."

And if we differ on what was the strong point on the other side, it does not mean because you talk about your weaknesses and talk about the strong points of the enemy or the other side, it does not mean you are selling out to the enemy.

You have to be objective. You have to accept weaknesses. And you have to recognize strong points of the enemy.

This has been discussed in the Central Council and National Assembly, and nobody from the fifteen tried to accuse Eritrea in order to make the Woyane innocent of the war.

But in order to talk concretely, we said we propose that the Central Council and National Assembly meetings concerning the assessment on the war and peace process be public.

Connell: This is what you're saying now?

Haile: In our reply, yes.

Let us make the proceedings of both assemblies public, and let everybody see if there is somebody who has tried to blame Eritrea for all the war and make Woyane innocent.

And, if because of the tradition that we are not allowing people to know the discussions of the Parliament, we said, let us allow responsible elders – a committee of elders, who would be responsible to keep things separate – to go and look on the records of the two assembly meetings.

And we said, in order to cover weaknesses if you want to blame somebody as collaborating with the enemy, this is not acceptable.

In our experience with others, when there is a victory in a battle, everybody wants to be the owner of that victory. But when there is a setback, then you try to find somebody who would be blamed for it. And an innocent one who cannot defend himself could be a victim.

So we said this is the case. Otherwise, come and open these things. This is how we replied to this one.

On the second one…

Connell: Asking Isaias to resign?

Haile: Yes.

Prior to the second round, the public in general was made to believe that if there was another battle or war, we will have miracles. This was all the propaganda.

So everybody was expecting that the day the bullet is shot, we will advance inside Ethiopia, and the majority thought that we might reach

Conversations

up to Makele. These were the psychological preparations that were made.

And prior to the third round, there were people who were pushing for trying to avoid another war. And these people were accused by President Isaias and the others as cowards prior to the battle.

So, when the third offensive came – day one – it was on day one that they broke our front lines – and in areas where the whole population and many of the administrators were saying that they had been sending, the *woyanes* [the TPLF leadership in Ethiopia] had been sending, reconnaissance teams – intelligence people – to that area, and they are going to come through this area.

Everybody was saying that. But our defense did not take care about it, and it was in this area that they broke through. And it was Day One.

So in the first three or four days, people were not only surprised but felt that we had been betrayed by the government. And when the retreat of Barentu came, everybody panicked.

Everybody thought that whatever had been said was a lie, and everybody started to think about the different scenarios. And everybody was saying – particularly in Asmara – everybody was saying, this man is responsible for all these things.

Even outside, when people were saying that the *woyanes* are buying a lot of modern arms, and they were asking are we prepared really, he was saying they are only buying things looking at catalogues, and they are buying things like the Chechnyans and ridiculing that and being very confident. So people were afraid. People were saying that the President has failed us. That was a very clear sentiment in all of Eritrea.

I tell you, ministers did not have any information on what things were going on. So they were going to anybody that could tell them what is happening, how are things going on.

And people, cadres, were saying, why shouldn't we be deployed? It is not only the military, but the people are at risk. People, cadres, could go and at least stabilize things, give morale to the people.

But the cadres, they don't know how things are going. The information was blocked, while the Ethiopians were saying they are advancing, they have occupied this area and that. And there was nothing from the government mass media. So it was a disaster.

Almost everybody was saying: Oh, this president should resign. That was a public statement. And even many cadres would say that.

The day we were retreating from Barentu, Isaias went to the command post where General Sebhat was. And all the others were voluntarily going there to help our defense capability – Petros Solomon, Berhane Gebreghzabhier, Ogbe Abraha. They took individual initiative to go there and to help because immediately after January 2000 – after the meeting – President Isaias told Ogbe Abraha that he was fired.

116

On May 12, when the third round started, Ogbe called the Office of the President and told them, I cannot wait here at home while there is a war, so let me go to *any place*. He was not asking to be the Chief of Staff.

Connell: This is in May?

Haile: On May 12th, when the third round started.

But they simply dismissed him. They did not want to allow him even to participate. So he has to individually take initiative and go to the command post of Sebhat Ephrem as the others were doing. Even Mesfun Hagos, who was the governor of Debub, he had to stay there with the people and see how things are developing. When all these people had led all the wars for the final victory in '91!

So Isaias went to the command post and told them we are retreating from Barentu. To be very precise, they were: Sebhat Ephrem, Petros Solomon, Ogbe Abraha, Berhane Gebrezghier.

Abraha Kassa most probably was around, but I don't think he was in that particular meeting. He is the Chief of the National Security.

So when Isaias told them we are retreating from Barentu, they told him: "Okay, now we have to sit down and discuss and look at all the different options we have because now it has become very dangerous."

When they told him that, Isaias said, "I don't want to bother my head with brainstorming." So he left them and went to his office.

When he went to his office, he told his secretary he wanted to see me and Yemane Gebreab.

I didn't have the information on what was going on in Barentu at that particular moment. It was the secretary that told me that he was asking for me and for Yemane to come. And when we went there, he told us it is impossible to defend Barentu, and we are withdrawing, so what can we do?

"What can the UN do?" he asked me.

"Well," I told him. "There is nothing that can be done." I told him the *woyanes* have an excuse for continuing the war, and the international community will not condemn them.

The international community is saying that in '98 they did not condemn Eritrea because [the Ethiopians] were saying that we had occupied areas that they were administering. Whether it is an Eritrean or an Ethiopian territory – that is not the question now. But they were administering it, and that's why they were asking us to withdraw from this area. They did not condemn us. They will not condemn them now.

And the *woyanes* have openly declared that they have advanced in western Eritrea, not because they claim it is an Ethiopian territory, but they are saying that Eritrea has occupied other territories and they have the right to go wherever for military purposes.

So we should not give them the excuse for continuing the war, and we should make sure that the international community will support us to stop the war.

I told him the only way out diplomatically is to declare that we will unilaterally implement the OAU peace plan.

Because we have accepted it already.

Therefore we withdraw from those areas that we have accepted – from Zal Ambassa and the nearby places.

Let us say we have been committed to the peace process. The Woyane is creating a problem. We will unilaterally implement, and therefore we have withdrawn our troops from Zal Ambassa and what not and what not. This is the only way, diplomatically, we can play.

Connell: And then call on the international community to press Ethiopia to cease?

Haile: Yes. Let us call for a unilateral implementation of the peace plan.

He does not like that.

The point is that always, in all the peace process also, he only accepted the peace plan after Woyane occupied Badme because always there is an internal insecurity for him about the issue of Badme.

This is my reading and my understanding.

He accepted the peace plan because Woyane has occupied the territory and therefore Badme will not be an issue. Who started what will not be an issue. This is childish.

Because immediately after Badme, the Ethiopians said Eritrea has to leave the other places, because the principle applies – what applied to Badme applies to the other. Because after May 6th, even if Eritrea claims it is an Eritrean territory, but it was administered by Woyane.

Now, on the Woyane, the accusation is targeted against me. Because I was saying the Woyane have been consistent as of May 13th when they went to the Parliament and said Eritrea has occupied areas which we have been administering – Badme at that time – and unless the Eritrean forces withdraw peacefully, we have the right to liberate our territory by the use of force. This has been the consistent policy of the Woyane.

But in our case, on May 14th, immediately the second day after the Ethiopian Parliament declaration, there was a Cabinet of Ministers meeting. At that time, we came with a very constructive proposal. We said this is a border problem. It can only be solved peacefully and legally. We reject the use of force, even the intimidation of the use of force. And it can only be legally resolved on the basis of the colonial treaties.

And even we went farther to say, in order to diffuse the tension and allow a third party to help us to demarcate the border, we are ready to withdraw our troops from our own territory – let alone from contested areas – but from our own territory. And let the other side also withdraw its troops, so that there will be a demilitarized zone.

That was a very constructive proposal. But we did not keep it consistent.

We did not accept the American-Rwandan recommendation. That recommendation went to the OAU, and the OAU endorsed it. We did not accept that also, and in February '99, there was the second offensive. They took over Badme, and immediately we declared: We accept the OAU framework agreement.

And later they were asking us to withdraw from Zal Ambassa because the principle applies to them. And we were trying to say the OAU says only Badme.

Well, it was Badme, but when there was the war after May 12th, we had taken over Zal Ambassa and the others, so it applies. But he does not want to accept it.

Later, prior to the third offensive, when a "non-paper" proposal came to us, we as the Ministry of Foreign Affairs said for bargaining purposes we can insist on the technical arrangements. But if things do not go the way we want it in the legal sessions, then the "non-paper" does not jeopardize our strategic interest of demarcating the border on the basis of the colonial treaties. Therefore we have to accept it. Let us take it as our bottom line.

Connell: I don't think I know the "non-paper."

Haile: The "non-paper" is the one that was proposed to reform the technical elements.

It was an American proposal. But it is the same thing that we have accepted after the third offensive.

Connell: So basically to withdraw from any contested areas, from any areas the Ethiopians claim?

Haile: No. In fact, it was in June or July '99, when there was the OAU meeting in Athens at which there was a proposal – the modalities for implementation. In that, it was very clearly stated: Both forces to withdraw to May 6th positions.

And I know how hard we fought against our President to accept this proposal. And later after the third offensive, we have to accept not only this proposal, even to accept a temporary security zone within our own territory.

So, in assessing the peace process, one has to be very clear with his conscience.

Connell: Gayle Smith told me there was a point when the U.S.-Rwanda proposal was accepted, and then the next day it was withdrawn.[4] And that's when the U.S. negotiating team went public.

Haile: Yes. During the American-Rwanda mediation, they came with a proposal saying that there should be a return of civil administration in Badme.

Connell: And it turned on this question of police and militia.

Haile: No, no. Wait a minute.

First, there was a proposal to have a civilian administration in Badme.

Although we were supposed to be a team, always it was the President. They were coming to us – myself, the President – and Yemane Gebreab was always there.

All of the sudden, the President said, Yes, we accept the return of Ethiopian civilian administration in Badme.

For me it was a shock. Because we did not discuss about it. We did not exchange ideas among ourselves.

What was a concern for me was that – immediately after that – was that when he promised that Eritrea will accept Ethiopian civilian administration in Badme, I think that was the time when the negotiating team decided to have the American-Rwanda proposal.

I feel – I don't know for sure – that that is the time the team told the [U.S.] State Department that there is a breakthrough.

Connell: The U.S. team?

Haile: The U.S. team.

And therefore, they can now table a final proposal. Because they thought that Isaias has accepted it, and this will be a breakthrough.

So I think that is the time the team got a blessing from the State Department – my guess.

Immediately when we went out of the meeting, I told the President, why should you hurry to accept this? Because, I told him, these are mediators. And mediators have their technique of mediation. They always want a win-win solution from their own point of view. And in order to have a win-win solution, they would ask or request compromises from both parties. So even if we have to accept this Ethiopian administration, it must be after we have exhausted the negotiation and accepted it as if making a compromise on our side. It is our bottom line.

---

[4] Gayle Smith (my former wife) was at that time a high-level U.S. AID official for the Horn of Africa and one of four American members of the negotiating team.

Connell: He doesn't have the patience for that though.

Haile: Yes.

So I told him this is the technique.

You know what he told me? "We don't care about the techniques of these people. We always work on principles. For us it is a question of principle and what-not, and what-not..."

Mr. President, I told him, you should know the rules of the game. And I said, if you have accepted this, how about if they want to push us to accept more compromises? This is too early to accept this.

But, he told me, he accepted it for two reasons. One, as I said, he is not interested in these mediating techniques; he always looks at principles. Second, he told me, this will create a confusion within the TPLF leadership – meaning that if we accepted this there will be one group that will accept and another who will not accept and then it will create a problem among themselves.

I didn't have any information about the internal situation in the TPLF; he had the information. But for me, to accept this is too early, and it might harm us in negotiations.

So Gayle Smith is correct when she told you that he has accepted. But later, when they have finalized the proposal, and it came, he brought up the issue of the militia in order to not accept this thing. Because it was not a genuine acceptance of the proposal itself the first time.

And at that time, there was the OAU meeting in Ouagadougou, so I had to leave. I had to go via Europe.

I was in Asmara when he accepted it. While I left, the team came back and said this is the proposal that we are tabling. And he said, if there are going to be militias we cannot accept the civilian administration.

They [the U.S. negotiators] wanted to create a *de facto* situation. They gave it to the Ethiopians. Meles accepted it, so they declared that they have given a proposal to both sides.

Connell: They made a big mistake with that.

Haile: But I think that was a calculated move. They wanted to pressure us.

Connell: I know they did, but Isaias doesn't react well to this.

Haile: So that's why they said they have put a proposal to both parties. Ethiopia has accepted it; Eritrea has not yet accepted it.

By that time, you know why they wanted to rush it? Because there was the OAU meeting. They had to go there.

If he had accepted it, then it would be finalized, and it would only be reported to the OAU. If he does not accept it, then they want to pressure him through the OAU.

Connell: It doesn't sound like there was any way to solve this.

Haile: But these are the facts. It was only a question of the militias, which was raised in order not to accept it.

So, on the assessment of the peace process: One – this is not only my view but the others – we were not consistent.

What we were raising was that in the negotiations, it is not a question of making the other side believe you, it is a question of making the international community believe that you are committed to peaceful and legal resolution of the problem.

We will never satisfy the TPLF. We should not think to convince the TPLF to agree with us. And, of course, when you are in negotiations, we are mainly negotiating with the international community in order for them to believe that we are committed to a peaceful and legal resolution.

And we were saying, even if the international community accepts our position, we do not have any illusion of thinking that the international community will come and prevent Ethiopia from going to war. But at least if the international community is convinced, then while we are defending ourselves, the Ethiopians will have a hard time to continue pushing on war.

But Isaias was saying, whenever you bring such kind of an issue, there are people who think the international community will come and fight for them.

Connell: In his view, it's all or nothing. There's no in-between understanding that though the decisive factor remains inside, you can influence external factors in your favor.

Haile: So, now anybody who would comment on how we conducted the peace process – when there was a need for some flexibility without jeopardizing the strategic objective – is accused of incriminating Eritrea. And the issue is not Eritrea – it is him, himself. That is the point.

He preferred to accuse people who would assess the peace process by bringing whatever he could maneuver. Rather than meet, he wants to accuse us of collaborating. So, the stand on peace and war is this issue.

In our reply, I just want you to be aware of the internal dynamics. But on that we said, in assessment one could have a difference of opinions on the weaknesses and strengths of yourself and your enemy, and any difference of opinion on that should not be taken for collaborating with the enemy or making the enemy innocent of all these things.

So it is only his personal attitude.

And on the third round and what people have said, most probably he wants to accuse those three people: Petros Solomon, Ogbe Abraha, and Berhane Gebrezghier. Because they have told him we have to sit and discuss and look at all possible options.

And then immediately after what I told you, he refused to discuss things. He said that he doesn't want to bother himself with "brainstorming." He went to his office; he wanted to see me and Yemane Gebreab and whatever he thought – I told you those things.

But immediately when he went to his office, Petros, Ogbe and Berhane thought this was very dangerous. He doesn't want to talk with them.

So Petros called Sherifo and told him of the withdrawal and the need to discuss what to do next. He asked Sherifo to intervene and get him to discuss what should be done. And while I and Yemane were in his office, Sherifo came there and joined us. So it was four of us there.

I was calling for unilateral withdrawal from the contested areas and acceptance of the OAU plan, but Isaias and Yemane were not agreeing.

After this, I made a call to all the ministers to come for a meeting to inform them of the withdrawal and of the need to stabilize the situation. It was not a "meeting." It was called a "briefing." The last CC meeting was in January 2000. There was none since then.

After the meeting – the briefing – many were frustrated. Some went to the command post trying to help.

At last the advances were checked. Many individuals have stepped up and done their best. My guess, though, is that it was from this time that the accusation against us was fabricated.

There was nobody who said we should have to satisfy the TPLF demand to topple the President. Anyone might have said individually that the President has failed and should resign, but there was no organized effort to push it, nothing anyone could say was a *coup*.

Connell: So how do you know they will charge you with this?

Haile: Last week, on 6 August, they called a meeting of ministers, union heads, PFDJ branch heads. And Yemane and Alamin told them to prepare the population for war. And they told them they have prepared charges, so start the campaign against the G-15.

First, people argued that they cannot take this to the people, who are just now resettling from the last round of fighting. They said that this would create panic, and they cannot campaign on this.

Second, they said the G-15 has raised a lot of issues. Our reply should address all these issues. If our reply doesn't address all issues, we can't campaign on this either. They are asking to convene a National

Assembly meeting or a Central Council meeting. Why can't we convene them and solve it that way?

Then Abraha Kassa tried to intimidate him, but many people argued against this, and at last Alamin acknowledged their mistake and moved on.

At the end, they declined to wage a war campaign and asked to wait and see on number two [the G-15 issue]. It was an indecisive ending. Action was postponed.

Immediately after this, one went to Sherifo and begged him to go to Isaias to try to resolve this thing. But I think it is too late. They already have their plan to divide the G-15 into three and get the core for treason – Ogbe, Petros and Berhane for defeatism in the third round, and me for my position on the peace process.

A Conversation with Petros Solomon

August 23, 2001

This conversation took place in Petros Solomon's family home on Martyrs Boulevard in Asmara.

Before I turned on the recorder, Petros remarked that he had started to become disillusioned as early as 1992 but couldn't then quit – could not detach himself from the massive challenge of reconstructing the country. Nor, he said, was there anyone to talk with about his concern that Isaias was on the road to becoming a dictator – no one but Ogbe Abraha, the only one to whom he voiced his early reservations.

He said that twice in the mid-1990s he asked Isaias to relieve him of the post of Minister of Foreign Affairs in favor of a non-political position but that the President refused. Then, when he continued to raise concerns to Isaias over the direction the country was taking, he was suddenly transferred to the Ministry of Fisheries – to many observers a demotion but to him a relief.

We started the recorded part of the conversation with a discussion of who was in the leadership at the time the party and the front were founded, as well as at later congresses. See the Appendix for a complete list.

Connell: I talked with Drue, and when he started looking back, he mentioned...

Petros: Drue is somebody who writes. And a writer is more perfect than a soldier.

Connell: I'm not sure...

Petros: I don't think. I just act.

Connell: Well, he talked about seeing Romedan pushed out of the leadership in 1994, and as that being a point where he should have acted but didn't.

Petros: Romedan was talked to, but not there.

Connell: That's what Drue said. And that that was –

Petros: Romedan the man and Romedan the character are two different things.

Connell: He clearly put the nation first instead of making a fuss.

Petros: He just needed a little bit of guts to become the next president of this country. He can be that. He is so popular. But you don't know his character. He is very timid, timid, timid – very timid.

Only yesterday I saw him.

Now they are accusing me of being a coward and giving this country up to the UN and America, and I'm telling him, "Okay, you are the witness – what are you going to say?"

But I am quite sure [Isaias] is not going to say anything in public, and I am quite sure he has nobody who is going to accuse me in court. It's just a mockery, a slander game.

Connell: They tried to discredit you with corruption charges and that didn't work.

Petros: Corruption! They are still two months working in the Ministry of Fisheries with six security guys. Not even one of them an accountant! They cannot even find if I stole some money.

They are just questioning people, putting them in prison, asking them, what do you know? Okay, you don't tell us, you stay there. That's human rights...

Yesterday Yasin was out. He was there [in prison] one month and twelve days. He told me, "I was in a dark room. I would hear the voices around me. They are telling me you are here for nine years, and you have been tortured. And don't lose hope."

I told his wife to go to court. And maybe that's why he's out.

Nobody dares to ask in this country. Nobody dares to ask for *habeus corpus*.

Connell: He worked with you, didn't he?

Petros: Yes.

I was shocked. You know, Yasin is from Tiyo. He's an Afar. He doesn't know anything of this politics.

He's a hero. He was a super commander, a marine diver. He was the best this country ever had.

He was from Tiyo in Dankalia – a nomad, a fisherman. He came, he joined, became a commander, finished twelfth grade. And now he was the head of the Eritrean Diving Center.

He's a marvelous diver. He knows a lot about diving. He's a navigator. He has a license, he can drive boats.

He can be the best manager you can think of in any tourism company, because he knows every part of the sea.

And they put him in jail, just to find something about me.

For forty-two days.

And it makes me wonder, why did I fight?

Connell: You fought for your country, not for this.

Petros: I mean, you just become hopeless when you see these things.

He said, "I don't have any relative to ask about this, because I'm an Afar, and I have no one here."

Oooh, you feel very sorry about it.

Connell: [Pause. Points at a photo on the desk.]

Petros: That's my wife. She's in the States now.

Connell: And your daughter?

Petros: My daughter is here. I have two daughters in the States.

So, what do you have? Come on, bring your questions.

Connell: I want to ask you, what was the point where you decided that things had turned bad – but you're getting into it earlier than I expected.

And my second question is, why did you wait so long to talk?

Whenever I raise these issues with other people, that's what they come back with: Why did you wait until now?

Petros: Isaias was the main waiter, I think.

He had very good ways of treating you and making sure that people didn't converge.

He was enjoying when people fight, and he was utilizing it. And he has outsmarted everybody for a long time. He was out of this comradeship way back, and he was using it before we realized it.

By the time we realized it, it was too late.

Connell: You said you held back in '92.

Petros: I'll look into my diaries now.

Connell: When were you the Foreign Minister?

Petros: 1994. I became a minister of the Ministry of Defense in October '92.

Connell: And that lasted until…

Petros: '94, February or March.

Connell: And then, when did you end up in Fisheries? Was that '98?

Petros: '97.

Connell: What did you do to deserve that?

Petros: Too much opinions…
Opinions.

Connell: Ogbe [Abraha] told me about writing a critical letter to Isaias. He said that's what got him canned.

Petros: Well, what I said that got me in trouble when I was Foreign Minister was that we need not fight, we need not go to war, with Sudan, something like that.[1]
And when I was on a tour abroad, diplomatic relations with Sudan were cut without even me knowing.

Connell: That was at the start of 1995?

Petros: I was abroad. So that pissed me off really.
Then there was the Yemen issue, and there were too many opinions, and I don't know what happened…
But I did ask him that I didn't want to be Minister of Foreign Affairs. I asked him two times. I said, "I don't want to be a Minister of Foreign Affairs."
And he said, "Why?"
I told him I don't have the capacity to be a Foreign Minister.
"Well," he said, "you know things are not as they were in the field, but we have a lot of time to change it."

---

[1] Eritrea broke diplomatic relations with Sudan in December 1994 after a cross-border raid by Islamist guerrillas based in northeastern Sudan.

But I told him that I don't believe I can continue in this position. I said it's better if I move somewhere where I am not in a political position.

And when I became the Minister of Fisheries, I was really happy.

Connell: You completely turned it around, too, in terms of its economic potential.

Petros: I really had a dream. I really wanted to do something. I'm a dreamer.

Connell: What about Yemen? Were you critical on that one? Were you consulted on that?

Petros: Let me tell you.

The first time I was the Minister of Foreign Affairs, we had a workshop, and we discussed issues.

We talked about the worst scenarios, and we said, we cannot have problems with three countries: Djibouti, Ethiopia and Yemen. And we said, okay, let's study the nature of these problems. Let's see what we can do. Let's see how we can avoid them.

Then all the problems one-by-one came – you know.

That was the worst scenario. And the worst scenario happened.

You know, it's very foolish people that cannot discuss this. You can see how inflexible we were, regardless of how much we knew about what kind of problems we can have.

Connell: Who was making the decisions to send military force? Was it Isaias in each case? In Yemen, for example?

Petros: Yemen.

You don't even know the story. They tell you the Yemenis were there, and the argument was there, and it happened.

I didn't even know until I heard about it afterward.

It just happened.

You know, they called our ministry the "fire brigade."

We always said, "The President throws a bomb past us, and then we have to move in and put out the fire."

[Interruption for a phone call. The conversation resumed with a discussion of the situation Isaias faced in the summer of 2000 after the third round of fighting with Ethiopia.]

Connell: And he was getting strongly criticized?

Petros: He was strongly criticized, and he was very arrogant.

"Why do you want to make meetings? I don't want to make meetings," he said. "What is the necessity of meetings? I don't make meetings. I don't see any necessity of making meetings. Have the people of Eritrea asked me about that? Who are you guys?"

Connell: I had a small taste of this myself in 1988 when I went to see him. You know, I was not in the field every year in the 1980s because I had problems with my family, my kids. And so I built Grassroots International as a way of doing solidarity work.

And we had an interview, and at the very end of it, he turned to me and said, "You know this Grassroots will never amount to anything. It's been a waste of your time. If you had done the book that you said, you could have done us some good work." And then he turned around and just walked out, didn't even talk about it. Girma Asmorem was there, too. But he was no help.

Petros: Girma is an opportunist.

He was with me at the Foreign Affairs, and I was telling him everything. He was a friend of Yemane, and he wanted to become an ambassador to the U.S. And the President, I tell you, has never, ever believed that Girma is a useful person. He used to say it in front of him.

You know, a revolutionary is a stage that you have to pass through in some part of your life.

Connell: This is probably the wrong time to ask you this, but where does that leave you today in terms of what you believe?

Petros: Well, really, I'm a very optimistic man.

Connell: Still?

Petros: I believe that we can work for a society that responds to what the people want. That might be difficult, but materially speaking, people want prosperity, people want equality, people want security. People want a good life in all its forms. These are good goals, and you can still have them.

And the best way to have them is to have competing ideas from the best that you have – that will give you the guarantee that nobody is dominating the scene and trying to do it his own way.

I believe more than ever that freedom of expression is one of the most important pillars within a society.

A long time ago, we used to say we were for the dictatorship of the working class. Hey, you are black, you are red, or white. It's either here or there, no in-between.

The problem of having only one color is that you lose all creativity.

Connell: When I met Isaias in '94 – the last time I really had a serious interview with him – he talked about the old politics as if it had been a religion, which in many ways it was. And he warned about the dangers of being "obsessed." Yet he seems obsessed with the issue of personal corruption. And there's a quality of obsession about many of the things that he says.

Petros: Actually, in 1994, I don't think there was big corruption in this country. But he wanted to differentiate himself from the others by saying that everybody else is corrupt except me. Just like in the '80s – his campaign of the three privileges.

That is exactly what he was doing. He was talking to the young people, saying the leadership is corrupt. That's exactly what he was saying.

Finally, he did it with his friends – Desu, and "Papayo," and others.[2]

If Papayo wasn't a coward, he would have talked about how much money he paid for this man to enjoy himself in a geisha in Japan or Taiwan or Hong Kong. It's more than the money that all these people have stolen.

The $50-60-70,000 he was spending on geishas – taking them to geishas in Japan, in Hong Kong.

They were telling us how they enjoyed it – Papayo was. He might have translated that into nakfa and told the Eritrean people that they paid so much for a woman.

This man was accusing these people, and he was enjoying it himself. He should have said: No, let's not waste our money on these kinds of things.

Alamin was accused in 1982, 1983, in Paris, of buying a BMW from the money that was contributed by the members. He bought a BMW.

Connell: What was he doing out there in '82?

Petros: He was at one time the head of Foreign Relations.

---

[2] At the end of 1996, Ermias "Papayo" Debessai, a member of the EPLF since its inception who held a seat on its Central Committee in the 1970s and 1980s, was one of ninety high-ranking party members and businessmen arrested in a corruption scandal in the PFDJ's largest commercial enterprise, the Red Sea Trading Company. He remained in detention in 2004.

This is the man who bought a BMW at that time. And now he's talking about corruption....

Connell: Nobody is completely pure. But, as you said, there isn't big corruption here. It shouldn't be the main issue.

Petros: I don't see this corruption as the biggest problem in this country.

Yes, there is corruption. There is no society that is corruption-free. But compared to other countries, Eritrea is not big corrupt.

There are corrupt leaders, and you have to be very tough when you find them. But now he is talking about it every day, and everybody is seeing in the papers, "Oh, the leaders are corrupt!"

It is hypocrisy, hypocrisy.

Connell: Where do you see this going?

Petros: I don't know. He's going to face a very big problem in the summer.

Connell: The elections are most likely going to be postponed until sometime next year.

Petros: I don't know, most probably he won't even do it.

He will try to freeze us as members of the Central Committee, make a majority decision on the party laws according to his own ways, make a deadline for the elections, and then court-marshal us according to the traditions and ways of doing things of the party.

Connell: Before the election? Before there's a congress?

Petros: Before the elections – before the Congress. Because if you are talking about a PFDJ Congress, it will be a problem.

All these issues might come up. So he has to do it before that.

Connell: These meetings that have been held to level charges against you – the Embatkala seminars and the others – these are non-formal, unofficial meetings, so you have no right to representation.

Petros: They are illegal meetings.

Connell: They're just invited-only guests.

And there are going to be more, I assume?

Petros: No. I don't think.

Connell: Is this a preparation for the Congress?

Petros: No. They have to act fast!

[Interruption.]

Connell: The events of the war are now being talked about and not-talked about, especially the third offensive and the withdrawal from Barentu.

I gather that when Isaias made the decision to withdraw, he did it by himself. And that there were other options discussed that ranged from withdrawing from Assab to going back to Sahel. But this is the period – that's the part they're trying to get after you for – you, and Ogbe and Berhane.

Petros: It was a crisis, a crisis.

Going to Sahel was not an option. The PFDJ was trying to prepare the people that we are going to Sahel and fighting back again in the mountains. But this was not an option.

Our opinions were very clear: After Barentu, withdraw from Zal Ambassa, withdraw closer to Assab, accept the peace plan, and make sure that you are not against the United States government. Full-stop.

And it is what happened.

But he did not accept it.

Connell: Withdraw from Barentu? Withdraw from Zal Ambassa? Withdraw from…?

Petros: Withdraw from the controversial areas.

And then it means – if you withdraw from the controversial areas – that the peace plan is accepted because the Ethiopians were saying that we should withdraw from the areas we occupied by force. That was the logic of it.

Withdraw from the areas, accept the peace plan, let the UN peace force come in and don't be against the U.S.

And that's what happened.

Connell: What does it mean not to be against the U.S.?

Petros: He was saying that the U.S. is against us, U.S. is blah-blah-blah…

You know, if you want to succeed in diplomacy at least make sure that you are working within, not against.

Connell: How long was the position put forward to withdraw from the controversial areas?

Petros: The whole thing happened in about a week or so.

Connell: Right around the defeat – or the "setback," what everyone calls it – at Barentu?

Petros: Yes. So that was the issue.

He was nervous. He didn't want to withdraw from Zal Ambassa, so he didn't withdraw. And then he was forced to withdraw, but he declared that we withdrew according to our plans.

Which is not true, because by that time they couldn't defend Senafe even.

Connell: And there was some talk of withdrawing from Assab?

Petros: And Assab was a good thing because the commander there was smart – he withdrew in time.

Connell: Assab?

Petros: He withdrew from the 71-kilometer marker to 57. He defended his position and stayed there.

Connell: Did he do that on his own?

Petros: Yes, he was told to withdraw.

Connell: Altogether? Back, how far?

Petros: To withdraw to where he thinks he can hold his position.

Connell: I had heard there was talk of withdrawing from Adi Qayeh, too.

Petros: I don't know about that, but nobody would have.

The point was that, it was not an orderly withdrawal, as they claim to say.

They cannot talk about these things, but they were pushed, and that's why they left Senafe. And where they landed, God made it, okay?

But if they had done it beforehand without being pushed, they would have been in a better position, in a better place – at least defending Senafe, or something close to that.

So to cover up all these things, he says a lot of things.

Our dear president.

Now, he says that Eritrea is less than the President. The president is more than Eritrea.

APPENDICES

INSIDE THE EPLF

The Origins of the 'People's Party'
and
its Role in the Liberation of Eritrea[1]

Dan Connell

Abstract

At the third congress of the Eritrean People's Liberation Front in February 1994, delegates voted to transform the 95,000-person organization
into a mass political movement, the People's Front for Democracy and
Justice. The congress gave the PFDJ a transitional mandate to draw the
general population into the political process and to prepare the country
for constitutional democracy over the next four years. Near the close
of the three-day conference, Isaias Afwerki, the country's acting president, surprised many of those present with an announcement that a
clandestine Marxist political party had guided the Front for almost 20
years and that it had been disbanded in 1989, shortly before the end of
the independence war. Since then, however, there has been little public
discussion of the historical role of the party or its legacy. Drawing on
interviews with key participants, this paper explores the origins of what
was known as the Eritrean People's Revolutionary Party and its impact
on the liberation struggle during the nearly two decades of its clandestine existence. Questions I address include: How, why and by whom
was the party formed? How did it function in relation to the Front as a
whole? How did this change from the 1970s to the 1980s? And why was
the decision taken to disband the party in 1989? Still to be examined is
the party's legacy in the post-liberation era and how its political culture
and mode of operation shapes the contemporary political landscape.

---

[1] This article is based on a paper presented at the Eritrean Studies Association
in July 2001 in Asmara, Eritrea. It was revised based largely upon comments,
corrections and suggestions made at or shortly after the ESA conference and
then published in the *Review of African Political Economy*, Sheffield, UK, No.
89, September 2001.

Appendices

Introduction

During the first decade of its existence, in the 1970s, the Eritrean People's Liberation Front (EPLF) developed a reputation at home and abroad as a highly disciplined political movement whose members consistently – sometimes eerily so – articulated its outlook, promoted its programs and modeled its values. One of the key features that differentiated the EPLF as a national liberation movement was its commitment to simultaneous social and political struggle and the incorporation of this approach into its political culture as well as its practice. It was this aspect that made it a *revolutionary* nationalist movement, as it worked to transform the society it fought to liberate.

The EPLF accomplished extraordinary things with meager resources. Despite the continuing absence of sustained external support, the Front steadily improved its military capacity, while simultaneously building basic infrastructure (construction, transportation, communications), promoting economic development (agriculture, animal husbandry, commerce and trade), delivering social services (education, health, emergency relief), and campaigning to alter fundamental power relations within rural society (land reform, marriage reform, restructuring of village administration). A dynamism was evident that was easy to appreciate but difficult to explain. Visiting journalists often described the EPLF as a "well-oiled machine," marveling at its accomplishments while at the same time signaling their unease over the refusal of the Front's members to acknowledge weaknesses or faults.

The quality of organization and the high level of consciousness among its members were among the Front's most distinguishing features. But so, too, was its opacity. How could a steadily expanding guerrilla army with so little outside support function so well and have such a high degree of consensus within it? The answer was not immediately apparent, but it was obvious that leadership was central. As is now clear, it was not only *who* led the Front but *how* they did so that explained their effectiveness in action and their unusual degree of political and organizational unity – how the leadership was able to make use of collective strengths, to identify and correct deficiencies, and to steadily replenish and expand its ranks. It was the existence of a highly disciplined, secret party within the Front that accounted for much of this.

For nearly all of its existence, the EPLF was guided by a clandestine Marxist party – the Eritrean People's Revolutionary Party (EPRP, usually known simply as the 'People's Party') – that gave it vision, program and direction while molding its members to reflect its goals and objectives

---

[2] This paper draws heavily on interviews with several long-time party members conducted in Asmara in 2000 and 2001. A fuller exposition of party history and program awaits a study of the extensive documents now in the archives of the People's Front for Democracy and Justice, and further interviews with former party leaders, members, supporters and critics.

and to spread its message. Despite the secrecy surrounding the party, its impact was readily apparent in all that the Front did. A grasp of its origins is central to appreciating the role it played in building the EPLF and in liberating Eritrea, as well as in shaping the political culture that continues to define the country's post-independence political landscape.[2]

The Origins of the Party

The seeds for the People's Party were planted in the perilous political environment of the 1960s, when the only armed nationalist force in Eritrea was the Eritrean Liberation Front (ELF), whose politically conservative leaders, based outside the country, were anxious to end Ethiopian rule but not to see Eritrean society changed. On the contrary, they had powerful vested interests in preventing initiatives in that direction, and they acted ruthlessly to suppress them. Yet they were also divided amongst themselves and deeply distrustful of one another. This created spaces for various opposition currents to arise and grow in the field.

At that time, to voice support for a secular nationalist perspective within the front, let alone a left political agenda, could put one at risk of isolation, imprisonment or even death, so much of this evolved quietly, in one-on-one encounters among the liberation fighters. Radical ideas were swirling around the liberation movement at that time, and activists from a wide array of political trends were joining it. However, most did so with little grasp of the movement they were entering or the dangers they would soon face because of their outlook, or simply because of their ethnic or religious origin.

Some of the ELF's first foot-soldiers came out of the Sudan Communist Party. Others joined after studying in the Middle East where they were exposed to left parties and Arab nationalist movements and ideas. Among them was Romedan Mohammed Nur, a student from the coastal lowlands who joined the ELF in 1963 while studying in Cairo and was immediately sent to Syria for military and political training. Romedan was one of the early ELF recruits who would go on to play a key role in the formation of the People's Party and the EPLF. By the middle of the decade, other recruits began to come from the mostly Christian, Tigrinya-speaking highlands as well. This in itself posed a problem for the highly factionalized ELF, then dominated by warlords from the mostly Muslim western lowlands and eastern coastal areas, whose personal ambitions overshadowed any semblance of nationalism.

Many of the newcomers brought an eclectic agenda for social and political change drawn from Marxist "classics" and popular accounts of other liberation struggles then circulating on the campuses – an agenda at odds with the disheartening reality they found in the field. Fighters sent outside for training – to Syria, to Cuba, eventually to China – also brought back ideas and experiences that clashed with the situation in rebel-held Eritrea and the backward thinking of the ELF's leadership. One of the student radicals from the highlands to join the ELF in 1966 was Isaias Afwerki, the country's current president and another People's Party founder. He told me later that he was stunned at what he found when he arrived at the ELF's offices in Kassala, Sudan that September:

> In those days it was something like an obligation to join the movement for national liberation. Emotionally and sentimentally, everyone was with the ELF.

> But when I joined the armed struggle in 1966 with many of my friends, we began to know the real ELF. The first day I arrived in Kassala [Sudan], I was frustrated, people telling me about the ugly nature of the ELF. It was a nightmare. For some reason that no one explained, we were ostracized. There was an atmosphere of terror where you had to go out in groups, especially at dusk. There were no instructions, there was no organization, but if you asked questions, you were labeled as an agent of the Ethiopians. Not only highlanders – everyone who joined the ELF found himself in this situation.

> The shocking thing was that during high school, you never knew who was from what tribe, from what region, because there was not a hint of that kind of thing. But in the ELF everything was based on your clan or tribe. This created the ground for a new outlook, a reformist trend. Anyone who got there with high nationalistic feeling would be in the camp against the ELF leadership. It was not a battle of ideas or ideals – it was a question of whether there was nationalism or not. You would never talk about 'Eritrea' inside the ELF – always it was tribes or clans or religious affiliations that mattered. Revolutionary ideals had to be injected into the ELF to make it a real nationalist movement.[3]

Isaias had been a member of a secret nationalist organization in secondary school in Asmara. He and others of this group went on to university in Addis Ababa where they expanded the organization and developed contacts with Ethiopian revolutionaries. Once in Kassala, Isaias wrote to his comrades to alert them to what he found there, but the letter didn't reach the others. That December Haile Wold'ensae, another leader of the Addis Ababa student organization, joined Isaias in Kassala, where he heard the bad news firsthand:

> When I opened the gate, he told me to shut my mouth, make no comments, no proposals. He would tell me everything when we could talk separately. I couldn't imagine what was going on.

> He took me to a restaurant to talk. The first thing he told me was that the situation was a complete mess. There was no national leadership, no national program. To raise questions about this was to risk everything.

> The idea of having a clandestine organization within the ELF was the order of the day from the very beginning. It was a very dark moment for us, but we knew there was no other way, that we had to commit ourselves

---

[3] Interview with the author, Asmara, April 8, 1992.

> *to be dedicated no matter what the cost, that we even had to differentiate between those nationalists who could be committed to a long-term strategy and those who were only emotional.*
>
> *This was a very dangerous endeavor. In the beginning there were three – Isaias, myself and Mussie [Tesfamikael]. We took an oath to rebuild a genuine national movement, and we signed it with our blood.[4]*

Each man carved an "E" into his upper arm to signify his commitment. The scars are still visible today.

At the time they made this pledge, the ELF was organized into autonomous geographical (and also ethnic or clan-based) divisions, drawing on the experience of the Algerian liberation movement. However, by structuring the front this way, ELF leaders were able to carve up Eritrea into personal domains allied to one another but not functioning as a coordinated national army (or political movement). "None of these people ever talked about Eritrea," said Haile. Everyone wanted to have his own fiefdom. We called them the 'generalissimos.'"

At first, there were four such divisions, ringing the center of the territory. Each one had its dissidents, though it was difficult and dangerous for them to maintain contact with one another. In 1965, as more and more highlanders sought to join the ELF, a fifth division was formed in the Hamasien highlands. The ELF took this step both to mobilize manpower and resources there and to balance a power struggle taking place within the front's Revolutionary Council (RC).

From the outset, the form, structure and leadership of the 5th Division was contested. A highly respected Christian serving in the Sudan army, Tsegai Gebremedhin, was selected to head it, but he soon fled after one of the ELF-RC leaders, Idris Ghalaudios, circulated rumors that Tsegai was a target for assassination. "At that time, no Christian had any guarantee of safety," said Haile. "We were not even taking any malaria pills for fear we would be poisoned. In battles, we were mainly guarding ourselves against bullets that came from behind."

Meanwhile, a growing Chinese interest in the Eritrean struggle introduced a new element to the volatile political mix. ELF leaders had approached China for support, but the Chinese had reservations over the front's weak leadership. When they agreed in 1966 to provide the ELF arms, they conditioned it on a promise to send the political commissars from the front's five divisions to China for special training. Among them were Isaias, chosen to represent the new 5th Division in the highlands, and Romedan, representing the 4th Division from the coastal lowlands. As Haile recollects it:

> *The Chinese said there would be no arms, no money, before they trained these people. Isaias was chosen partly to get him out before [the ELF lead-*

---

[4] Interview with the author, Asmara, March 13, 2000.

ership] eliminated him. I went to the new 5th Division to be a link with our clandestine organizations in Eritrea and Ethiopia. The third one of us [Mussie] was to stay in Kassala, where he had started a magazine, 'The Renaissance of the Youth,' and be a link there.

Throughout the next year, tensions built within Eritrea over control of the 5th Division, its mission, even its size and operational objectives. ELF leaders also acted to isolate and punish dissidents in all five divisions. According to Haile, this harrowed the ground for the political lessons Isaias and Romedan were learning in China:

This was why there came a need for a clandestine organization that had to go beyond a national program. We needed an ideology that could match or challenge all these problems – not just the corruption of the ELF leadership but the narrow nationalisms that dominated the movement. We needed an ideology to use as a tool to fight all these things, and we needed a revolutionary party to wage this struggle. This reality created an incentive for an outlook to deliver a solution to all these problems.

The Chinese idea from the beginning was to give us this ideology through their training, but only two of the ones who went – Isaias and Romedan, who met each other there – looked at the Chinese experience to see how Eritrea could benefit from it. For them, it was enlightening to see that the Chinese revolution had gone through a lot of problems, some of them similar to ours.

At a minimum, this was a stimulant. At best, the Chinese experience offered us some possible solutions. This is when they decided on their own to have this 'inside' organization. But the other three [ELF commissars in China] were totally alienated. They only saw the trip as a vehicle to get arms.

Along with their military training, Romedan and Isaias got lessons in party-formation, as their Chinese teachers insisted that no revolution could succeed without a party to lead it.[5] The two began to discuss the problems in the ELF with their lecturers, according to Haile, who said that this polarized the delegation as the other three accused them of working against the ELF: "When they took their meals together, these three would take their knives and make threatening gestures, saying, 'This is what will happen to you when you get back.'"

ELF leaders knew some of the trainees would come back ideologically charged – this was the height of the Cultural Revolution in China – so they were wary of the group to begin with. One of them, Idris Ghalaudios, was also worried that RC rival Osman Sabbe, who had set up the trip, was conspiring to reap the benefits of the arms that would flow from the arrangement, so he traveled to Beijing to meet the students

---

[5] According to Isaias, the most useful lessons were those regarding military strategy and tactics.

144

and establish his own links with the Chinese. When he arrived, the three conservative trainees told him of Isaias's and Romedan's growing radicalism. His response was to assure the Chinese that the five students would be their disciples and radicalize the whole of the Horn of Africa with their teachings. "He told them that they would be the ones to form a party and spread the Red Book, and the Chinese believed this," said Haile.

Idris left China at this point, but there was little doubt that a confrontation was in the offing. When the five students finished their training and flew to Damascus, Idris was waiting. On their arrival, he told them the whole thing had been a trick – there would be no Red Books in Eritrea, no party, no new ideals, only a chance to get arms and money. He also insisted they turn over their political texts and study materials to him for safe keeping, as they were to fly through Saudi Arabia on their way to Sudan, and carrying such documents could be dangerous. They never saw their materials again.

When the group returned home, the ELF was imploding. The 5th Division had disintegrated into political infighting. Many people suspected of disloyalty to the ELF leadership had already been killed. At the same time, Ethiopia had begun a series of devastating military offensives that threw the entire front into disarray. The result, said Haile (who was in Sudan most of this time), was chaos:

> Many villages were burned, and many people became refugees, but when one division was attacked, the others relaxed. There was no coordination. ELF units were going from village to village to get food, but then they fled, leaving the people to pay the price. Women were giving food to the fighters even when their children were hungry. At last, some of them started to protest, saying the fighters escaped when the enemy came without even helping them to escape, too. People began to withhold food. Many also went to Sudan where they saw what the leadership was doing while they suffered. This discredited the ELF and the model of the five divisions, and it helped the nationalists in each division to organize opposition to it and to the division between the field and the outside leadership.

This opposition coalesced around three issues: unifying the fighters, bringing the leadership inside, and guaranteeing the human rights of the civilian population, whose only role to that point was collecting money and supplying food to the fighters. "These three slogans were the mobilizing tools for a rectification movement," said Haile, who fled to Kassala as the Front descended into an orgy of political repression and violence. And this was when Romedan and Isaias returned. The turmoil in the field helped them to survive despite plans by the leadership to eliminate them. But it also disrupted efforts to consolidate the clandestine nationalist opposition into an organized party. "The idea of forming a party was short-circuited," said Haile. "There was no breathing space for it then, so from 1968 to 1971 we worked on a mass basis."

Appendices

Two left trends – guided by distinct political lines – began to emerge within the nationalist opposition then. One, fiercely nationalist but with Maoist overlays, would form the basis for the Eritrean People's Revolutionary Party in the early 1970s and, through it, the EPLF. The other, a more conventionally pro-Soviet grouping, would crystallize as the Eritrean Labor Party and take nominal control of the ELF after the RC disintegrated. But before this happened, there was a fierce battle for control of the liberation movement and the resources it commanded, followed by a lengthy process of political struggle within and among the breakaway factions.

In 1968, representatives of the 3rd, 4th and 5th ELF Divisions met in the field to select a twelve-man provisional leadership for what they called the United Force. The group included radical nationalists and individuals who went along simply because they had problems with the old leadership. This uneven political mix carried within it the seeds of future discord. "It was a mistake to include reactionaries in this group," said Haile. "They became a Trojan Horse to make more intrigues later. Still, when the enemy tried an offensive to take advantage of the situation, the United Force succeeded in defending territory for the first time. This sent a big signal to the people and to the other divisions, and it threatened the old leaders."

With fighters fleeing the other two divisions in droves and the United Force organizing and politicizing both their members and civilians in the regions where they operated, the beleaguered ELF-RC, led by Idris Ghalaudios, made a final bid to control of the movement. At a hastily convened conference at Adobha in 1969, Idris called for "unity" while mobilizing his supporters and allies to purge the radical nationalists.

As Haile tells it:

> They dominated the conference and immediately began to imprison and kill the democratic forces. Before we could organize ourselves to resist, we had to escape. Isaias went to the Ala Valley. Others went to Sudan, so there was no way to coordinate the establishment of an alternative. The situation was even worse than before, and it was very difficult to have confidence in anyone.

Three groups broke off from the ELF at this point. Romedan went to Aden with a group led by Mohammed Ali Omaro (now Eritrea's ambassador to Kenya). In the months they remained there, the fighters were exposed to numerous left and Arab nationalist political movements and governments, as South Yemen was then a haven for radical ideas and organizations. During this time, members of this group began to discuss the need to form a party to reform the liberation movement. Among those in these exchanges – which did not lead to conclusive action – were Omaro, Romedan, and Mahmoud Sherifo (the Minister of Local Government in post-liberation Eritrea, often characterized as the second-most important position in the new state). This group sailed to the Dahlak Islands in small wooden dhows from where they made their way to the Eritrean mainland.

A second group, under Isaias, took refuge in the highlands in the Ala valley, south of Asmara. A third remained in Sudan. The Aden group took the name People's Liberation Forces (PLF). The second one, in Ala, became known as the PLF 2. The third, nicknamed the Obel group, was called the Eritrean Liberation Forces. Together, they would evolve into a coalition they were to name the Eritrean People's Liberation Forces. Once consolidated at an organizational congress in 1977, this was adjusted to the Eritrean People's Liberation Front. But it took them a while – and a lot of struggle – to get there.

The Launch of the Party

The initial step in launching the party was taken at a clandestine gathering in the scorched desert of Eritrea's Dankalia region in 1971, when revolutionary activists from the PLF1 and the PLF2 met for the first time since the fracturing of the ELF.

On April 4, 1971, like-minded revolutionaries from the two PLF groups established a secret political formation to rebuild the national movement on a more unified and a more radical social and political basis. Among those at this meeting were Isaias, Abu Bakr Mohammed Hassan, Omaro, Ibrahim Afa, Mesfin Hagos, Ali Sayid Abdella, Mahmoud Sherifo, Hassan Mohammed Amir, Ahmed Tahir Baduri, Ahmed al-Qeisi and a handful of others.[6]

"We met there and discussed the need to form a core among us before uniting the new forces, to campaign on the basis of nationalism and progressive ideas, and to rid the others of the prejudices and grudges of the past," Sherifo said later. "We decided to work in a very secretive manner. Marxism would be our leading ideology, and we would call ourselves the Eritrean People's Revolutionary Party."[7]

---

[6] Ibrahim Afa, Abu Bakr Mohammed Hassan and Hasan Mohamed Amir died in the liberation war. Romedan, not present at the meeting but part of the core group, retired from politics in 1994. Ahmed al-Qeisi was "frozen" in place after independence and dropped from party leadership. Mesfin Hagos, Mahmoud Sherifo and several charter party members who were not at this meeting, including Haile Wold'ensae, were censured in 2001 after circulating a public letter criticizing President Isaias and the PFDJ Central Office and were later arrested on charges of breaching national security. Omaro and Ahmed Tahir Baduri were assigned to Eritrea's diplomatic corps. Al-Amin Mohammed Said, not present at the first meeting but part of this circle, heads the PFDJ Central Office today. Two from the clandestine student movement who joined the Front later – Petros Solomon and Sebhat Ephrem – rounded out this group. Petros was sacked from his ministerial post in 2001 for signing the public letter critical of the PFDJ. Sebhat served as Minister of Defense. Of the original party founders, only Ali Said Abdella and Al-Amin Mohammed Said remained in the movement's inner circle ten years after independence.

[7] Interview with the author, Asmara, August 1, 2001.

Haile Wold'ensae (then in an Ethiopian prison) and several others who were not present at this first meeting – Romedan and Alamin Mohammed Said, among the most prominent – were also among the party's charter members. Most of them would figure in the EPLF's top leadership throughout the liberation struggle and in the post-independence state, with the exceptions of Ibrahim Afa, Abu Bakr Mohammed Hassan and Hassan Mohammed Amir, all killed in the war with Ethiopia.

Much of the early work of the People's Party was aimed at molding the EPLF into a coherent political and social force – one that could model revolutionary behavior as well as promote new values and that could develop a national identity capable of subsuming the sectarian divisions that had undercut the liberation movement until then. "The main achievement of the party was national unity," said Haile.

> It brought youngsters from the different Eritrean ethnic groups to work together in the most difficult conditions of survival, and it gave them an ideology that provided some light at the end of a very dark tunnel.

> Even now we can say that the party made miracles. It made people commit themselves. It made each and every individual think of himself as part of the whole organization and even in the most difficult situation not to lose his bearing. Each individual fighter was facing challenges without looking backwards – and addressing the basic issues of the society in order to transform them. One of its main strengths from the beginning was to address the woman issue.

Nevertheless, the party barely functioned as a distinct political force during the first years of its existence, as the emerging front fought to survive against attacks from both the ELF and Ethiopia while consolidating its own organizational and political structure. One of the factors that pushed party-formation to the top of the political agenda was an eruption of political infighting in 1973, initially identified with a 'leftist' group known as *menqa* (Tigrinya for "bats," referring to those who fly about at night) just as the front was preparing to move into the densely populated highlands.[8]

The stage was set when the two PLFs, which were in the process of integrating their respective forces, shifted their bases to the Sahel in 1972.

---

[8] See Ruth Iyob. 1995. *The Eritrean Struggle for Independence: Domination, Resistance, Nationalism, 1941-1993.* London: Cambridge University Press. See also Poole, D. 1998. "The Eritrean People's Liberation Front," in C. Clapham (ed), *African Guerrillas.* Bloomington: Indiana University Press.

[9] They were also joined there by a small contingent from the nascent Ethiopian People's Revolutionary Party, which left Yemen in 1972 to get training from their comrades in Eritrea. Whether or not there was a conscious decision to adopt nearly identical names for the two parties, there was clearly a shared political tradition upon which each drew. The two parties maintained links into the mid-1970s, when the Eritreans lost confidence in their Ethiopian counterparts and distanced themselves from them.

They did this in order to give themselves the security to work out their political differences while maintaining their logistical links with South Yemen, from where all their arms and supplies came. Once the first two groups relocated, the Obel group, whose politics were more eclectic and whose links with the other two less organic, joined them.[9] The plan was to politicize the rank-and-file of the three former ELF forces to develop a basis for unity-from-below through a congress to be convened once the main differences were worked through. But pressures from both the left and the right threatened to abort the project.

Haile Menkerios worked in the information and propaganda department of the joint forces at the time these events took place, though he was not yet a member of the secret party-building group. He recalls this period as one of increasing political tensions from both ends of the political spectrum. A leftist faction within the Ala group associated with Mussie Tesfamichael became frustrated with the slow pace of political development and pushed for a rapid transformation of these groups into a revolutionary political formation, challenging Isaias's leadership in the process. As word of these developments reached Osman Saleh Sabbe – the rightist former ELF RC member who was then representing himself in Yemen as the head of the new liberation forces (which he called the ELF-PLF) and securing arms and supplies for them – he began to mobilize his loyalists to oppose what he correctly perceived as a threat to his increasingly tenuous position by the direction the movement in the field was taking. This placed the revolutionaries grouped in the new People's Party in a squeeze from both political flanks.

Their response was to preempt their attackers in the summer of 1973 by hurriedly combining the leaderships of the PLF1 and the PLF2 under Isaias's command.[10] The Obel group, where Sabbe's influence was strongest, pulled out of Sahel and shifted its base of operations to Adobha and Barka to avoid participating in this process. Once there, however, it was hammered by the ELF, whose main strength was in this region, and most of the group's fighters fled into Sudan.[11]

Meanwhile, weeks after the merger of the two PLFs, the *menqa* faction, whose leaders were marginalized in the command of the newly combined forces, stepped up its opposition to the unified PLF leadership. This apparently galvanized Sabbe loyalists and others on the right flank into action. In the ensuing political struggle, which paralyzed the movement, a number of fighters were arrested. Some, including Mussie and five or six others, were executed. Others in the 'leftist' faction were brought back into the fold through an extended process of criticism/self-

[10] Isaias was chosen to head the ten-member combined leadership of the PLF1 and the PLF2. He continued in this role after three more people were added to this body from the Obel group, when it merged with the others in 1974.

[11] Telephone interview with the author, Gloucester, MA, to Arverne, NY, July 11, 2001.

criticism. Several others, identified with the rightist faction, were executed later. Whatever the details, the experience reinforced the leadership's
conviction that greater political cohesion and more centralized organizational control were needed if the Front was to advance its liberation
agenda. Building the party was to be the vehicle for this.

Haile Menkerios, who joined the party in 1975 but was never a
member of its leadership, points to these events as the seminal experience that gave the People's Party its prominent role in the formation
and development of the larger liberation movement. "This party did not
form to deal with external issues," he told me. "The need for the party
arose from this internal disunity. We were all saying that there was no
guarantee of the continuation of our revolutionary outlook unless we
formed a revolutionary organization." Haile was invited to. Others,
like Sherifo, downplay the incident, insisting that it retains significance
largely because of the executions that took place afterward. However,
few dispute that this period was a turning point for the EPLF and for the
party that was to lead it.

The Politics of the People's Party

During the organization's early years, Isaias was the leader of both the
party and the liberation front. Romedan was the second in command
of both. Another half-dozen or so individuals made up the collective
party/front leadership – mainly those I have already named. (Throughout most of the EPLF's existence, its Politburo was composed of the
party's smaller central committee.) When the armed struggle entered a
new, expanded phase in 1975, and the PLF began to grow rapidly, they
met in Bahri and decided there should be a distinct party leadership
outside the front leadership. At that point, Haile Wold'ensae (recently
released from an Ethiopian prison) and Alamin were charged with organizational and political party development – preparing manuals for
political education, drafting a party program, drafting a party constitution, developing a group of highly conscious cadres and so on.

In 1976, with some 150 active members, the party held its first clandestine congress in the slopes north of Asmara, near the small village of
Merara. There, they committed the organization to a socialist political
program for the long-term future and a national democratic agenda
for the liberation of the country now. Delegates elected a central committee with Isaias and Romedan as the Secretary General and Assistant
Secretary General, respectively. Haile Wold'ensae and Alamin were confirmed in their political roles, and Haile was tasked with setting up an
ideological department and a cadre school.

Nearly a year later, in January 1977, the EPLF held its first organizational congress, adopting a National Democratic Program drafted
by party members and circulated among fighters and civilian members
before its acceptance. The party also drew up a leadership slate that was
accepted more or less as presented. Henceforth, the Front would be led

by a 13-member political bureau selected from within a 37-member central committee that was chosen at the congress. Romedan was to be the EPLF's general secretary, Isaias the vice general secretary. Haile Wold'ensae would head the front's political department and Alamin would run its foreign relations department.

By this point, the EPLF functioned as a disciplined political organization whose members shared a common outlook and acted as political emissaries in their interaction with civilians and rival factions. It was separated into military and non-military wings. The Eritrean People's Liberation Army (EPLA) was organized, U.S.-style, in tiers of three units each, starting at the squad level and up to 500-person battalions. For example, three squads comprised one platoon, three platoons one company, and so on. However, the command structure drew on socialist models, with a three-person leadership composed of a military commander, a political commissar and a vice commander, and no other forms of rank within frontline units. Decisions were made collectively by the three leaders, but once in battle the military commander had undisputed authority.

The notion that each fighter had to model the EPLF's politics was embedded in the structure of the organization, which set out to re-mold its members in order to transform the society at large. This started in training camp, which lasted six full months for most new recruits, and it continued within the front as members met three times weekly for political education led by cadres within their units. The content of these sessions varied according to issues of the day, but in the mid-1970s, as the EPLF went through a major growth spurt, the main thread followed a curriculum produced in the field that started with a reprise of Eritrean history and proceeded to a highly sophisticated analysis of the revolution's goals and objectives. Marxism was the methodology.

The political education for fighters and civilians alike followed a formal curriculum contained in a book produced under party direction in 1975 titled *General Political Education for Fighters*. Each chapter provided a focus for discussions. The topics ranged from the origins of Eritrea and an analysis of its cultural and class composition to reflections on the revolution and its goals, the identification of Eritrea's friends (workers and oppressed peoples of the world, all progressive forces, the socialist countries) and enemies (Ethiopian colonialism, imperialism, zionism, internal reaction), the tactics of the revolution, the handling of contradictions and the political economy of ancient and modern societies.

The last chapter concluded: "If you fight against imperialism as a united people, organized and led by the workers, you step toward socialism." On the back cover was inscribed the slogan: "An army without

---

[12] The contents of the manual were summarized for me by members of the EPLF Office of Public Administration in October 1977.

a revolutionary ideology is like a man without a brain. An army without a brain can never defeat the enemy."[12]

The EPLF cadre school, through which many party members were recruited, took up more advanced study of Marxist methodology and politics. Topics included dialectical and historical materialism, common political deviations and the nature of "revisionism." The People's Party also ran its own intensive cadre school.

Despite its clandestine nature, Estifanos 'Bruno' Afeworki, a veteran of the party from the early 1970s but not in its leadership, says that it functioned for most of its existence as an effective vehicle for collective, action-oriented leadership:

> The People's Party was a very democratic and egalitarian party [he said] – a platform where EPLF cadres could openly discuss any issue – military, political, social – any issue that surfaced in that period. We drew up short- and long-term programs – the NDP for the EPLF, socialist transformation for the EPRP. The party tried to transform the EPLF society itself, while the front was liberating Eritrea and its people, step by step. That was the key that enabled the EPLF to succeed. The party was very strict about the role of the army and its relations with the population, for example. You were demoted immediately if you did anything wrong to the people.

> The party also had its own structures – a cadre school, a politburo, a central committee, even regional administrations – just they were smaller than those of EPLF. We had members in Asmara – in the factories and among the intellectuals – among the peasants in the villages outside Asmara, in the refugee camps in Sudan, in Europe and the USA. No one had a special office for the party, everyone was immersed in the EPLF structure, not like today when we have professional politicians – people who are only doing politics. In fact, a politburo member might also be a brigade leader.[13]

The EPLF's most decisive interventions came in the areas of land reform, village democratization and gender equality. Organizers surveyed land tenure in rural Eritrea – which varied widely from one region to another – and set about reorganizing it on a more egalitarian basis through newly elected village administrations. The EPLF mid-wifed these committees into existence through a system of sectoral representation based on new mass organizations of peasants, women, workers and youth, themselves segmented by class position. Each sub-set selected its own representative, producing a People's Assembly of mostly poor women and men of all ages. Though this formulaic approach was modified as the years wore on, it signaled a commitment to empower the disenfranchised majority through entirely new social and political mechanisms.

---

[13] Interview with the author, Asmara, December 12, 1999.

Party cadres were instrumental in carrying this out, while the process itself served as a recruiting ground for new party members.

Village elections were held as often as every three-to-four months as people learned to evaluate the performance of their new officials and to oust those who didn't measure up. Quotas were set for women's representation in the new assemblies, and marriage laws were reformed to free women from arrangements that in many cases kept them in life-long bondage. These and other such measures antagonized some conservatives, but they were accompanied by the provision of social and economic services – health care, early childhood education, adult literacy, agricultural extension, veterinary assistance and so on – that were often channeled through the new associations and committees rather than directly administered by the front. This helped to stop the grumbling by those whose prerogatives were curtailed. By arguing that women's full participation in the independence struggle was essential for the country's liberation, the front also tried to make it unpatriotic to contest women's increased prominence in social and political affairs.

Most of this was party-driven.

The Convergence of Party and Front

In 1977, the Ethiopian army was collapsing and the liberation of the country appeared in sight. However, the national movement remained deeply divided. Political unity was a heated topic in the EPLF and the ELF and throughout the society, but the two fronts made little progress toward it. Negotiations were carried out on a party-to-party basis with no lasting results. Several attempts to cooperate on the frontlines, including joint assaults on government positions, failed badly and led to sharp recriminations, mostly aimed at the ELF, whose command structures were weak and whose fighters lacked the discipline under fire of their EPLF counterparts.

Unity talks, carried out sporadically through the late 1970s, never got beyond the formal stage as both fronts – and the parties operating within them – held out for approaches that played to their respective strengths. The EPLF favored a gradual process of coordination and dialogue at all levels in order to build a united front from below. The ELF called instead for an agreement to combine the two forces through a one-time, movement-wide congress in which each front would be represented according to the size of its membership. These positions reflected obvious organizational self-interest, as the EPLF, with its highly politicized membership, would have an advantage over the ELF in an extended political encounter, while the ELF, with its larger numbers, might have an edge in an abbreviated contest where size alone determined power. This divergence was consistent with each organization's way of dealing with political matters. It was never resolved.

Meanwhile, the 1978 strategic retreat triggered a gradual rethinking of the party's and the EPLF's general strategy and tactics and a modification of their approaches to social transformation. There were no sudden ruptures, but there was an acceleration of the trend toward the "Eritreanization" of the movement on the organizational, political and ideological levels. Not only the direct involvement of the Soviet Union but also the behavior of the rest of the world, socialist or otherwise, encouraged the movement to believe that when the chips were down, there was no one to trust but the Eritreans themselves.

Political education remained a constant feature of life in EPLF areas, though it gradually altered in form, substance and frequency. It took place in small meetings, through intensive courses of study, and in large public seminars. It could involve military units, sectoral groups or whole villages. Its aims were to discredit the enemy, to build commitment to the EPLF, to transmit specific lessons on the meaning and method of political struggle, or simply to increase morale and self-confidence. After the retreat, this process opened up to include more dialogue and more exploration of topical issues. Organizers were advised that meetings should be short and "untiring" and that they should be scheduled in consultation with the participants to ensure active involvement. Sessions ranged from the difference between Ethiopian-sponsored *kebeles* and EPLF-supported peoples' assemblies to interpretations of Middle East politics, discussions of the meaning of democracy and disquisitions on women's right to sexual satisfaction in marriage.

To support the intensified political work, the EPLF reopened its cadre school – run by the party – and trained over 400 new organizers from 1979-82 (compared to 266 in 1975). Meanwhile, basic education continued in civilian society and within the military. Adult literacy was a major focus of the mass organizations, and frontline combat units routinely met behind their trenches to study language, mathematics, geography and other primary subjects, as I witnessed in 1979 during a two-week trek on foot from Nakfa to the highlands outside Asmara. Each unit also had its own cultural troupe, which regularly performed the songs and dances of all Eritrea's ethnic groups for the fighters and for villages where they were stationed.

But disunity in the field continued to plague the movement. EPLF attempts to revive the unity talks with ELF near the close of the decade were unsuccessful. By 1980, tensions were at a peak, and the number of armed clashes between the two fronts steadily increased, even as the EPLF prepared for another round of fighting with Ethiopia. (ELF forces were no longer on the frontlines.) In the spring of 1981, renewed civil war broke out, and the EPLF drove the ELF out of the country altogether. Remnants of the defeated front took refuge in Sudan, some to eventually reconcile with EPLF and rejoin the war with Ethiopia, others to remain in opposition and to attack the postwar EPLF government in the 1990s. Many ELF members simply scattered into the diaspora, as had happened in 1970 during the front's first big split.

Though the ELF's collapse allowed the EPLF to turn its full might against Ethiopia for the first time, it also put enormous pressure on the Front's (and the party's) political resources, as it tripled the size of its operations. In 1982 alone, during one of Ethiopia's most brutal and protracted military campaigns (Red Star), the EPLF organized over 550 new village committees.

At about this time, the Front stopped sub-dividing its mass organizations on the basis of class. It took this step in part due to the demands of its expanded area of operation, in part to the leveling effects of a drought that was ravaging Eritrea, and also because party leaders began to see it as too mechanical an application of Chinese-derived political formulas. However, there was a renewed emphasis on socio-economic development in the liberated and semi-liberated areas.

Land reform remained at the core of the Front's work in the densely populated highlands where it was seen as a springboard to social revolution. From 1981 onward, mutual aid teams were organized among poor peasants to increase the scale and cost-effectiveness of their farming activities. Despite problems with resources and logistics and in the midst of yet another, even longer Ethiopian military campaign in 1983, the EPLF also renewed its efforts to improve rural productivity through agricultural extension work, assistance with animal husbandry, and projects such as poultry-raising and vegetable gardening run by the mass organizations. Consumer cooperatives were established, and loan cooperatives were set up to finance village infrastructure projects. Perhaps the most effective project in the first half of the 1980s, though, was the public health program under which scores of traditional village health workers and mid-wives were given special training and linked into a national network of preventive and curative medicine. Throughout, the watchword was self-reliance: doing more with less.

In retrospect, the signature of the People's Party is readily apparent in this fairly rapid adaptation to otherwise disastrous conditions. But a much more detailed reconstruction of these events and the party's role in them needs to be carried out. Questions to be asked include: How, when, where and how often did party leaders meet? How did they communicate with mid-level cadres and with the party rank-and-file? Who were the key players in the party at this time? What lessons did they take from their new experience in the field and internationally, and how did the party's political line evolve through this tumultuous period? What criteria were used to select new members or to advance to higher levels of party leadership? How did the rapid growth in numbers affect the party's internal discipline, political coherence, and outlook? And much more.

Whatever was exchanged in the clandestine party meetings – most of which were rigorously documented at the time – conditions in the field in the 1980s played a central role in the party's changing outlook. As difficult as things seemed in the late 1970s, they soon worsened. The two longest and most destructive Ethiopian military campaigns of the war were conducted in 1982 and 1983. Then, in the mid-1980s, war and famine combined to create a human crisis of almost unimaginable proportions.

Persistent drought sered the brittle land until the population of northern Ethiopia and much of Eritrea teetered on the brink of starvation. By this time, some 360,000 Eritrean refugees had already fled to Sudan, most due to the war, some as early as 1967. Several hundred thousand more were internally displaced, either subsisting with help from relatives or under the care of the EPLF, whose humanitarian arm, the Eritrean Relief Association (ERA), mounted a cross-border relief operation from logistical bases in northeastern Sudan. However, though millions of dollars in aid poured into Sudan once news of the famine broke, relatively little of it made its way into Eritrea, since most international donors – with the exception of the European Protestant churches and a handful of solidarity groups – declined to support work in guerrilla zones. In December 1984, when I toured the area, ERA was feeding more than 100,000 people in thirty camps inside Eritrea, and the numbers were growing by the day. Much of the money for this came from the Eritrean diaspora, though by early 1985 Western NGOs finally became significant contributors.

Not surprisingly, this situation had a further dampening effect on the party's political mobilization. Organizers found it increasingly difficult to produce convincing results from social experiments in an economy where there was no surplus, and where people were almost entirely preoccupied with basic survival. As one frustrated cadre put it to me at the time, "The people can't eat ideology."

Other factors also fostered a moderation of the radical socialist politics of the 1960s and 1970s. The end of the civil war with the ELF encouraged the EPLF to be more inclusive, as the Front reached out to Eritreans of all political stripes on the basis of their nationalism. The need to assign scarce cadres around vast new areas of the country to reach people in former ELF areas limited the ability of the EPLF to carry out its social reforms and its political mobilizing at the level of complexity it had brought to its early experiments. Seeing nearly every socialist-oriented movement and government in the world troupe in and out of Addis Ababa helped undermine faith in the litanies of the Left that had informed the Front's early ideological development, even as protracted internal debates over the nature of the Soviet Union continued without resolution within the party. The experience of administering the liberated zones also fostered a growing sense of the limitations of state-centered development models.

Taken together, these factors did not provoke a political about-face, as one might have expected, but they did foster a more pragmatic approach to economic policy and more openness to experimentation. Precisely how they did so deserves further elaboration, as the ability to steadfastly maintain focus on the commitment to national liberation, whatever the ideological or political tools appropriated to advance it, is a definitive feature of this movement. But it became harder and harder to operate in the way they had.

Former party members say that the clandestinity of the party made it increasingly difficult to convene formal meetings, the more so as the Front expanded in membership and geographical reach. (One party activist said his marriage nearly ended in divorce because his wife became convinced that the excuses he was giving for attending secret meetings were covering up a liaison with another woman.) It became less and less practical to gather party members or party leaders together to discuss the issues of the day in the manner they had in the early years. As a result, much decision-making in the later years was done informally, with little accountability even to other party members.

Nevertheless, the Party was engaged in a continuing process of reflection throughout this time whose outcomes found expression at its 2nd secret congress, in late 1986, where it changed its name to the Eritrean Socialist Party and adopted a more social democratic program.[14]

This shift in outlook was carried into the planning for the Front's second congress in March 1987. A party-led preparatory committee circulated a draft of a revised National Democratic Program to every member of the EPLF, including fighters and those in the mass organizations, soliciting comments that were incorporated into the document during a year of intense debate. The party also drew up its own slate for the EPLF elections, which it quietly but effectively promoted in the lead-up to the congress.

Among the changes from the 1977 program adopted at the congress were the deletion of references to "imperialists" and "Zionists" in favor of allusions to "foreigners hostile to Eritrean independence." The "masses of workers, peasants and other democratic forces" became "the people." "Anti-feudal and anti-imperialist" popular organizations became "nationalist" associations. More significantly, the rights of all "nationalist political parties" were explicitly guaranteed; pledges to confiscate all land in the hands of the Ethiopian government and all foreigners and Eritrean collaborators were scaled back to include only lands held by the former regime; plans to establish large-scale, state-run

---

[14] Party documents from this period, including the 1986 party program, are on file in the archives of the PFDJ in Asmara.

[15] There were 1,359 delegates at the congress, with civilians outnumbering military personnel three-to-one. A quarter of the participants were women. Every nationality in Eritrea was represented. A new 71-member Central Committee was elected by secret ballot, after 120 nominations were taken from the floor. The former members of the EPLF Political Bureau were the top vote-getters, with Isaias and Romedan coming within one vote of each other. The newly elected Central Committee chose Isaias to be General Secretary.

farming cooperatives were dropped; Eritrean capitalists were encouraged to set up factories and enterprises without reference to size; trade was to be "regulated" by the state rather than "handled" by it; and more emphasis was given to public education, treatment of prisoners of war and attention to the rights of Eritreans living abroad. While the rhetorical level dropped a notch, the most important pattern in these changes was a diminished view of the role of the state in Eritrean development and an explicit commitment to multiparty politics.[15]

After this congress, the structure and substance of the front's political education for the mass organizations – and for the fighters – lightened up further. Study groups that used to meet three times weekly for political education began to meet once each week or less. The content of the political education curriculum came from a new manual, published in 1989 to replace the text of the 1970s. The main focus was on Eritrea – the place and the nation – with less theory and more emphasis on practical issues facing the country and the liberation movement. There were also short sections on Ethiopia, Africa and the Horn of Africa; the Middle East; and the international situation. The syllabus was prepared for discussions at three successive levels, starting with a basic introduction to the concepts, then going into more descriptive and explanatory detail, and finally, in advanced sessions, approaching the material from a more analytic perspective.[16]

The shift in content and in intensity had been a long time coming, according to Alemseged Tesfai, an EPLF veteran but not a party member who worked on the development of the new curriculum.

> Political education within the EPLF had already been on a decline in the last years of the struggle [he said]. This was because Marxism had lost its attractiveness to many of the new breed of fighters who were joining the front in order to run away from the derg's similar rhetoric. More serious than that, even veterans were getting disenchanted with the old ideology – Soviet intervention, Cuban and South Yemeni direct military engagement on the other side and Chinese abandonment of Eritrea's cause were some of the reasons. But then, the EPLF itself was, by the mid-eighties, distancing itself from hard-line Marxism. In 1989, it assigned quite a few of its university-level cadres to re-draft a new program of political education, one that was to be in tune with the 'realities of the day'. Ahmed al-Qeisi and Haile Menkerios led that effort and several cadres were part of it. It was decided in one of the meetings there (in Himbol) that the new political education, to be given to the EPLF rank and file and to members of the mass organizations simultaneously, should be free from Marxist content and dogma.[17]

---

[16] Interview with the author, Orota, Eritrea, November 1990.
[17] Email to the author, October 16, 2000.

The Decision to Dissolve the Party

Throughout the last decade of the liberation struggle, the party steadily converged with the front – in its political line, its program, its methodology, and its leadership – even as membership in both bodies expanded geometrically. This made the management of a secret party more and more difficult, and it led to anomalies in the quality of the cadres – so much so, that party leaders began to question the rationale for sustaining two parallel organizations. Haile Wold'ensae was among them:

> We had expanded so much we had a lot of problems. Party cells were distant from the center. Unhealthy ways of recruitment began to crop up – people recruiting their friends, for example. We began to see a lack of competence in the primary organizations of the party. Rather than leading the front, they started being problems for it. In some cases, they were more a problem than a resource. Finally, the CC [central committee] realized this and decided to intervene in the process of selection.

> By the 1986 congress, the party was diluted from what it had been, and the CC began to question the validity of the primary organizations, the primary cells. They carried a lot of ideological weight but they were sometimes not very practical – always debating the question of the Soviet Union, the socialist camp, etcetera.

> There was a tension between realistic and unrealistic objectives, but this movement always had an inclination to be more pragmatic than ideological, to define a realistic, achievable program rather than to become idealist in our approach.

> During these years, we began to shed some of our naiveté. We were committed not to sacrifice our national interests to idealist philosophical interests, and we began to see that this clandestinity had its own problems. Also, some of our [party] members were less competent than non-members, some less disciplined. The party became a hiding place for unhealthy elements.

> In the beginning, the party had to be clandestine. We existed in a hostile surrounding environment. We could not survive unless we were secret. But now the party had served its purpose and it was no longer a club of the best ones. So the issue we faced was: do we make it open and evaluate every individual and every cell in front of all the front and all the people, which was the only way to rectify the party? Also, with all this streamlining, the setting up of achievable objectives, was there a gap between the objectives of the party and the objectives of the front? If not, there was no reason to have two organizations.

> We saw that the two were coming closer and closer, that there was little difference between them, so we asked, why shouldn't the party become the party of the mass? By 1986, the issues were there, but they were not resolved. By 1987, we became convinced of the need for change. The majority of the front was now sharing the objectives of the party but were not members of it.

In 1989, we said, now we are entering a new phase. Therefore, the broad-based movement should replace the party in order to allow not only the front members but the population as a whole to work for the objectives of the party, which had now become the objectives of the front.

This was not an easy decision. Some thought it would be diluting it, that it was a wrong decision, that the party would be gone if it turned out that we needed it, that this would be irreversible. Others thought the party would be a privilege that they would lose. Myself, I thought it was not possible to continue that way, but was there the possibility of a transition that every member of the party could feel part of that decision? Why not the whole front being the party? But the front was still narrow. There were remnants of the ELF still around, for example. So we determined that there was a need for a broad-based movement, not a party.[18]

This thinking led to the functional dissolution of the party in 1989 and to the decision to transform the EPLF into a mass political movement, the People's Front for Democracy and Justice (PFDJ), at its third congress in 1994. "There was no major shift in our orientation," said 'Bruno' Afeworki. "We were always a socialist-oriented movement, but slowly we started to be more nationalistic, more concerned about our national interests. And we lost a large number of our leading cadres during the war. This had a big effect. Finally, it matured into a nationalist party, and we dissolved it because there was no longer a need for it.[19]

However, this left the nation with a yawning gap in collective political leadership during the country's first postwar years, when the locus of power shifted to the new government. Even the mass organizations ceased to function but for that of the women, which maintained its network of services and self-help programs, as the leadership's attention was riveted on state-building and on meeting the urgent but long-delayed needs of a war-weary population. Then, at the EPLF's 3rd congress in February 1994, most of the party's veteran leadership was sidelined, as a younger generation assumed responsibility for the administrative center of the reconstituted front, its secretariat, where authority for day-to-day operations would reside.

"A debate came up after the war over the need for the continuity of the Front and its work – should it be the old leadership, or should there be new elements? We decided new ones were needed, so we chose a leadership from the generation that was mobilized in the '70s, not the '60s," said Bruno. But six years after the shift, he was less sanguine about its prospects. "The PFDJ is not a party in the way we were then," he said. "It is more amorphous, more diffuse. But it is a transitional organization, a nationalist umbrella, out of which parties could develop when

---

[18] Interview with the author, Asmara, March 13, 2000.
[19] Interview with the author, Asmara, December 12, 1999; Interview with the author, Asmara, August 2, 2001.

the time is ripe. The basic belief of the People's Party was that that there should be a multiparty system in Eritrea. I hope this is still alive."

Summing Up

The People's Party had its origins in the brutal internecine fighting of the 1960s, when the ELF imploded, devouring its children. The commitment to build it clandestinely was reinforced in the early 1970s as three breakaway but disunited ELF fragments struggled to reach common ground while battling for their survival against both the new ELF and the Ethiopians and as further infighting (the *menqa*) threatened to derail the consolidation of the new front. Out of these experiences came the conviction that a tightly organized, highly conscious political core was needed to build and direct the movement as it sought to transform the society in a revolutionary democratic direction while liberating it from Ethiopian rule.

The party functioned as an extremely effective instrument of political leadership throughout its first decade. During this period, the EPLF fought off the threat to its existence from the ELF, broke its dependence on the rightist Osman Saleh Sabbe for external relations and established its own distinctive presence on the regional and global political scene, vastly expanded and deepened its social base within Eritrea and among the Eritrean diaspora, and survived the onslaught of the new Soviet-backed Ethiopian military machine (with the political disorientation that accompanied the geopolitical realignment of the two superpowers). The EPLF, with the People's Party at its head, went on in the mid-1980s to carry the population through the worst human disaster – the 1983-85 drought and famine – the region had ever experienced, even as Ethiopia sought to use the crisis to further its military and political agenda.

However, the rapid, extensive expansion of the front and the party in the 1980s, then the only nationalist forces engaged in combat, had a moderating impact on their politics. Coupled with an extended process of reflection triggered both by the changing regional and international alliances and by accumulated experience on the ground, this tempered the party's revolutionary outlook to the point where it and the Front began to converge. By the end of the 1980s, there was little substantive difference between the program and line of the two organizations (or their leadership).

At this point, the need for a clandestine "vanguard" leadership began to come into question. With the difficulty party members had convening meetings without giving themselves away and the growing perception that party membership itself no longer reflected the best and most dedicated fighters and civilian activists – some suggested it had become a club of old-time party members and their friends – this sentiment spread. The impending end of the liberation war and the shift in focus to postwar nation-building accelerated it. However, exactly how, by whom and under what circumstances the decision was taken to dissolve the party, and how this was communicated to party members is not clear. Several former party central committee members say it was never actually dismantled. Instead, it was simply "frozen" in place and then permitted to disappear with no formal closure. Among other things, the peculiar character of this ending makes it more difficult today to examine the party's experience and its lasting legacy. It also feeds the tendency, inherited from the years in the field, to exercise political leadership through non-formal channels, rather than institutional ones.

The People's Party came into existence as an instrument of leadership. It succeeded on the planes of ideology, politics, organizational coherence, personal behavior and the construction of a genuinely national culture. But it also functioned as an instrument of command and control. It did so at first to maintain the Front's line, to ensure that elements did not develop that would disrupt the organization or weaken it from within, and to mediate the relations between its members and the outside world (including other Eritreans) so that the movement could present a solid front to its friends and its enemies. In time, however, it inevitably became more an instrument of control than one of leadership. How much of this has carried over into the post-liberation political environment needs to be better understood.

Eritrea's contemporary political culture reflects a paradoxical mix of self-imposed secrecy and social consensus, of authoritarianism and collective action. The ability to maintain a balance between these contrasting impulses served the people well during the struggle for liberation. But in the post-liberation transition, it has played a more contradictory role – on the one hand helping to promote the development of a unified national culture, while avoiding the ethnic, religious and geographical fragmentation that has torn apart other African nation-states, but at the same time impeding the evolution of this embryonic popular democracy to its next level.

A rigorous examination of the party's history – its strengths and its weaknesses, its successes and its failures, its pluses and minuses, and above all its lasting impact – is an important piece of the democracy-building process underway now. The chronic difficulties that armed political movements have exhibited in the transition from resistance to democratic governance are well-documented. Can this political movement transcend the proclivity toward self-perpetuating authoritarianism that so clearly comes with this territory? I would argue that it has a far better chance to do so if its own heritage is available to those struggling for such goals.

Selected Bibliography

Cliffe, L. and B. Davidson (eds). 1989. *The Long Struggle of Eritrea for Independence and Constructive Peace*. Lawrenceville, NJ: Red Sea Press.

Connell, D. 1997. *Against All Odds: A Chronicle of the Eritrean Revolution*. Lawrenceville, NJ: Red Sea Press.

Eritrean People's Liberation Front. 1982. "Creating a popular, economic, political and military base," an unpublished paper prepared for a conference in EPLF-held Eritrea.

———. 1975. *General Political Education for Fighters*. Fah, Eritrea: EPLF.

———. *Memorandum*. 1978. New York, NY: EPLF.

Firebrace, J. and S. Holland. 1985. *Never Kneel Down: Drought, Development and Liberation in Eritrea*. Lawrenceville, NJ: Red Sea Press.

Pateman, R. 1990. *Eritrea: Even the Stones are Burning*. Lawrenceville, NJ: Red Sea Press.

Poole, D., 1998. "The Eritrean People's Liberation Front," in C. Clapham (ed). *African Guerrillas*. Bloomington, IN: Indiana University Press.

Ruth Iyob. 1995. *The Eritrean Struggle for Independence: Domination, Resistance, Nationalism, 1941-1993*. London: Cambridge University Press.

The Eritrean People's Revolutionary Party Leadership

Founding Members (1971)
1. Isaias Afwerki
2. Abu Bakr Mohammed Hassan [martyred]
3. Ibrahim Afa
4. Mahmoud Sherifo
5. Ali Said Abdella
6. Hassan Mohammed Amir [martyred]
7. Ahmed al-Qeisi
8. Mohammed Ali Omaro
9. Ahmed Tahir Baduri

The following were part of the core that created the People's Party but were not at the party's launch in April 1971:
10. Haile Wold'ensae
11. Romedan Mohammed Nur
12. Alamin Mohammed Said

EPRP Central Committee (1976)
1. Isaias Afwerki
2. Romedan Mohammed Nur
3. Haile Wold'ensae
4. Ibrahim Afa [martyred]
5. Mahmoud Sherifo
6. Alamin Mohammed Said
7. Ali Said Abdella
8. Ahmed al-Qeisi

Several of the founders were not on the first official party CC. The following were added to the leadership at this meeting:
9. Mesfin Hagos
10. Petros Solomon
11. Sebhat Ephrem

12.	Ogbe Abraha

EPLF Political Bureau (1976)
1.	Isaias Afwerki
2.	Romedan Mohammed Nur
3.	Haile Wold'ensae
4.	Ibrahim Afa [martyred]
5.	Mahmoud Sherifo
6.	Alamin Mohammed Said
7.	Ali Said Abdella
8.	Mesfin Hagos
9.	Petros Solomon
10.	Sebhat Ephrem
11.	Ogbe Abraha

The following were in the front's top leadership but not the party CC at this time:
12.	Berhane Gherezgihier
13.	Mohammed Said Barre

EPRP Central Committee (1986)
1.	Isaias Afwerki
2.	Mahmoud Sherifo
3.	Ali Said Abdella
4.	Ahmed al-Qeisi
5.	Haile Wold'ensae
6.	Romedan Mohammed Nur
7.	Alamin Mohammed Said
8.	Ogbe Abraha
9.	Petros Solomon
10.	Sebhat Ephrem

The following were elected to the party CC for the first time:
11.	Berhane Gebreghzabhier
12.	Teklai Habteselassie
13.	Haile Samuel
14.	Saleh Hirui
15.	Abraha Kassa

EPLF Political Bureau (1987)
1.	Isaias Afwerki
2.	Mahmoud Sherifo
3.	Ali Said Abdella
4.	Haile Wold'ensae

5.   Romedan Mohammed Nur
6.   Alamin Mohammed Said
7.   Petros Solomon
8.   Sebhat Ephrem
9.   Mohammed Said Barre

The PFDJ Executive Council (1994)

1.   Isaias Afwerki, Chairman
2.   Mesfin Hagos
3.   Ali Said Abdella
4.   Alamin Mohammed Said
5.   Abraha Kassa
6.   Tesfai Gebreselassie
7.   Abdella Jabr
8.   Yemane Gebreab
9.   Zemhret Yohannes
10. Hagos Gebrehiwet
11. Askalu Menkerios
12. Muhyadin Shengeb
13. Osman Saleh Mohammed
14. Fawzia Hashim
15. Germano Nati
16. Amna Nur-Hussein
17. Yusuf Sayiqh
18. Hamid Himid
19. Alamin Sheik Saleh

COMMENTARY

EPRP Founders – Where are they now?

EPRP founders Abu Bakr Mohammed Hassan and Hassan Mohammed Amir were killed in battle before the EPRP's first congress in 1976.

EPRP founder Ibrahim Afa was killed in battle between the 1976 and the 1986 EPRP congresses.

EPRP founder Ahmed al-Qeisi has been "frozen" by President Isaias since independence.

EPRP founder Romedan Mohammed Nur was forced into retirement in 1994 and has remained out of the PFDJ leadership since then, though he has taken on limited political assignments at the President's request.

EPRP founders Haile Wold'ensae and Mahmoud Sherifo (both of whom signed the Open Letter to the PFDJ in May 2001) were jailed in September 2001. Haile served as the new government's Minister of Finance and Economic Affairs, Minister of Foreign Affairs and Minister of Trade and Industry.

EPRP founders Mohammed Ali Omaro and Ahmed Tahir Baduri are abroad on diplomatic assignments (respectively, the Ambassador to Kenya since 2000 and Ambassador to the United Nations since 2001) and have played no significant role in the post-independence national leadership.

Of the original EPRP founders, only Ali Said Abdella (PFDJ Executive Council, Minister of Foreign Affairs) and Alamin Mohammed Said (head of the PFDJ Secretariat) remain in the leadership with Isaias today.

EPRP Central Committee (1976)

Of the four elected to the EPRP Central Committee who were not among the founders, Petros Solomon and Ogbe Abraha (both of whom signed the Open Letter to the PFDJ in May 2001) were jailed in September 2001. Petros had served as Minister of Foreign Affairs, Minister of Defense, and Minister of Fisheries since 1991. Ogbe served as the head of the EPLF's Economic Commission at independence and went on to serve as the Minister of Trade and Industry, the Minister of Labor and Social Affairs and the Chief of Staff of the Eritrean Defense Forces.

Mesfin Hagos (an Open Letter signer) was abroad when the crackdown on dissent occurred and has remained outside Eritrea since. The popular former war hero and, briefly, Minister of Defense in the post-liberation government was elected to the PFDJ executive Committee at the front's organizational congress in 1994 over Isaias's objections. He resigned as Defense Minister that year in protest over what he termed "Presidential interference" and was appointed Governor of the Debub *zoba* [region], a position he retained until going into exile in 2001.

The fourth new CC member, Sebhat Ephrem, is the current Minister of Defense and a member of the PFDJ Executive Committee but has little actual power, as the four generals who command the operational theaters in Eritrea report directly to the President.

EPRP Central Committee (1986)

Four of the five new members elected to the EPRP Central Committee in 1986 were military commanders. The fifth, Abraha Kassa, came out of the EPLF's security apparatus and went on to head the office of National Security after liberation. The militarization of the party leadership, just as it was losing its distinctive political role, was hardly a coincidence.

Three – Gen. Teklai Habteselassie, Gen. Haile Samuel and National Security chief Abraha Kassa – remain close to the President today.

Gen. Berhane Gebreghzabhier, a signer of the May 2001 Open Letter to the PFDJ, was jailed in September 2001.

Saleh Hirui was imprisoned around the time of independence on allegations of homosexuality and kept in jail for ten years. He is now in exile in Saudi Arabia.

PFDJ Executive Committee

Few of the old guard from the EPRP or the EPLF leadership carried over into the PFDJ Executive Committee, whose ranks included the leadership of the front's new secretariat, most of the heads of the mass organizations, several military people, and others, both in and out of government.

However, the PFDJ Executive Committee had little of the leadership responsibility held by the party's Central Committee or the front's Political Bureau during the liberation struggle.

Real power in post-independence Eritrea resided in several distinct centers – mainly the PFDJ secretariat, the top ranks of the armed forces, and the President's Office (a constellation of policy-making groups that paralleled but did not link to the main cabinet ministries). All of them reported directly to Isaias.

This created conditions of one-man rule at the top and a sharply divided second tier of power whose competing centers could be balanced (or played off) against one another at will.

An Open Letter to All Members of the PFDJ

May 5, 2001

Introduction

This letter is a call for correction, a call for peaceful and democratic dialogue, a call for strengthening and consolidation, a call for unity, a call for the rule of law and for justice, through peaceful and legal ways and means.

For some time now, regular meetings [of the Central Council and the National Council] have not been held. Believing that the best way to resolve problems is through meetings and democratic dialogue, we requested twice through signed letters that President Isaias Afwerki, as chairman of the Central Council [of PFDJ] and the National Council [of the state], convene meetings of both bodies, but he twice failed to respond positively to our requests. Those of us who made these requests have, as responsible members of both bodies, now chosen to write this open letter to all members of the PFDJ.

Most of us have spent more than a quarter century in the struggle for independence, and many of us have at different times served our country at high levels of responsibility. We have witnessed and taken part in the bitter struggle of our people for liberation, and are now serving the Front, the State and the people as members of the Central Council (the legislative body of PFDJ) and the National Council (the legislative body of the State).

It is obvious that our country is in a crisis. This crisis is the result of the weaknesses of the PFDJ and the Government, and the invasion of our country by the enemy.

Our aim is to find remedies for the weaknesses of the PFDJ and the government so that people participate in discussions and decisions of important national issues to enable Eritrea to come out of this crisis, to pave the road for peaceful, legal and democratic transition to a truly constitutional government, and to establish guarantees for Eritrea to become a peaceful and stable nation where democracy, justice and prosperity shall prevail.

In the Eritrean reality, guaranteeing and consolidating internal democracy within the PFDJ is essential to ensure a democratic process of transition and the establishment of a democratic constitutional government; and our aim and message is this, and only this.

I. Experience of Eritrean People's Liberation Front Before Liberation (1970-1991)

1. Background

The Eritrean Liberation Front (ELF), in its experiences from 1961 until 1969, was unable or unwilling to:

– Establish a clear national program,

– Form an effective strategy for liberation,

– Ensure and protect the human and democratic rights, unity and cohesiveness of the people and its army,

– Tolerate differences of views, and

– Adopt a participatory approach in the execution of its programs.

This created an internal crisis within the ELF.

As democratic resolution of the problem was denied, the EPLF was formed as a democratic alternative in order to confront the challenge effectively and to establish a free and democratic Eritrea through the consummation of a national democratic revolution.

2. Preliminary stage (1970-1976)

For those forces who later formed the EPLF, this was a stage of rejecting the negative experiences of the ELF, identifying weaknesses in their internal unity and in their capacity to effectively defend themselves in the civil war, and the promotion of the principles of democratic dialogue and peaceful resolution for secondary contradictions.

The doctrine that "the Eritrean field could not tolerate more one liberation front" was defeated. The bitterness of the civil war and the losses and setbacks it caused created a suitable environment for nationalist and democratic principles and practice, and led to the weakening of sub-national ideas and groupings, as well as undemocratic and corrupt practices.

Although the road to such an outcome was not always smooth and flawless, it led to the creation of the EPLF which in its congress in early 1977, came out with a clear political program, established strict laws to guide its practice, declared a strategy of people's war, i.e. liberating the land and the people step by step, introduced transparency and accountability appropriate to the stage of the liberation struggle.

3. EPLF until liberation (1977-1991)

- From 1977 until the liberation of Eritrea (1991), although it can not be said that the EPLF was perfect in its leadership and its organization of the people, or that its internal democracy equally satisfied all its members, not only its legislative and executive organs, but also its institutions which were governed by the conditions of the war were, in accordance with the constitution, transparent and accountable, and relatively satisfied the expectations of most members and the people.

- Even if there were some problems and certain people were occasionally mistreated mainly due to lack of proper management, the majority of the members of the front:

  – Believed that they played a part and contributed in all aspects of the struggle;

– Had unity of purpose and action that astonished friend and foe alike;

– Accepted organizational decisions and regulations not as edicts and decrees from higher authority, but as their own decisions, which they executed with dedication;

– Had strong ties and unshakable faith in each other and the various levels of their leadership;

– Held meetings (admittedly not regular always and at all levels) to identify deficiencies and take corrective action, built on strengths, and used criticism and self-criticism as well as objective periodic evaluations;

– Strengthened the struggle by keeping secrets from the enemy while obtaining secrets from the enemy;

– Respected and cared for not only each other but also the people, listened to people's problems and tirelessly worked to solve them; and

– Above all else, were confident and ready for the highest sacrifice.

- Although not completely successful, the EPLF made an effort to work together with other liberation forces to achieve unity. At its Second and Unity Congress in 1987, it formed a broad national democratic front and decided that it will form a multi-party democracy in independent Eritrea.

- In order to defeat the colonizer, the EPLF made optimum use of its human, financial and material resources. It made accurate and objective assessments of itself and the enemy. It reinforced its strengths and corrected its weaknesses, while exploiting the enemy's weaknesses and trying to weaken enemy strengths. It did this without boasting and shouting, preserving its resources, and taking considered decisions of when to attack, when to defend, and if necessary, when to retreat.

- While no one denies that there were problems in organizing and mobilizing people inside and outside, there is no doubt that the EPLF:

– Raised resoundingly the voice of Eritrean revolution around the world;

– Reflected the Eritrean people's desire and longing for independence;

– Raised expectations for a democratic Eritrea.

Until independence, the people had absolute confidence in the EPLF, EPLF members trusted their leaders, and the leaders equally put excessive trust in the General Secretary. All activities were based on trust and more or less family type style of work. Beginning the late 80's, however, absolute trust and the uncontrolled family type of work started to cause problems.

4. EPLF later PFDJ: After Liberation

A. Before Referendum (1991-1993)

- From the time of liberation until Eritrea was declared a sovereign nation through the referendum, the EPLF had recognized itself as the Provisional (Interim) Government without making any changes, and ruled Eritrea as such. If it had any difference with the pre independence phase, it is only that during this time, the concentration was on setting up government departments, implementing emergency rehabilitation and resettlement programs and preparing for the referendum.

- Although it was understandable that problems associated with transition would arise during the two-year interim period, no attention was given to handling veterans and the disabled, mass organizations and the people in general. Although problems and complaints were there, they were simply ignored and brushed aside as "results of loss of direction" instead of being handled seriously.

B. After Referendum (1994-2001)

1. Regarding the PFDJ

1.1. Its goals and plans

In its third congress held from 10-16 February 1994, the EPLF changed its name to Peoples Front For Democracy and Justice (PFDJ), and to reflect the new era, revised its programs and constitution and established a new national charter and a transitional constitution with the following tenets:

Vision: The establishment of a peaceful, just, democratic and prosperous Eritrea.

Vision goals: To ensure national harmony, political democracy, economic and social progress, social justice, cultural revival, regional and international cooperation and stability.

Principles: To be governed by national unity, active popular participation, the decisive role of man, social justice, self reliance, strong link between the leadership and the people

Core political program: To establish a democratic, constitutional political order that allowed pluralism.

Important issues discussed or decisions taken at different meetings of the Central Council of the PFDJ included the following:

The Eritrean Liberation Front (ELF), in its experiences from 1961 until 1969, was unable or unwilling to:

Appendices

- At the second session of the Central Council (28-02-94), a proposal was presented for the Council to work through committees and to establish internal rules and regulations.
- At the third (26-08-94) and fourth (14-08-95) sessions, it was decided:
  ° To identify and separate government assets and PFDJ assets;
  ° That PFDJ businesses work strictly obeying the trade law and the laws of the market, and aim at helping the disadvantaged in our society;
  ° To establish a trust (Hidri) to administer PFDJ businesses.
- At the fifth (25-03-96) and sixth (22-04-97) sessions, it was decided to postpone the holding of the fourth party congress until the first half of 1998, and a preparatory committee was formed.
- At the eighth (29-01-00) and ninth (02-09-00) sessions, the following decisions were made after thorough discussion of the issues:
  ° To form a body to study the structure and method of work of the government and the PFDJ;
  ° Meetings of legislative and executive bodies to be held at regular intervals;
  ° To immediately commence preparation necessary for the implementation of the constitution and to work in accordance with legal procedures;
  ° To accelerate resolution of issues of land allocation;
  ° To regulate and improve the salaries of military personnel;
  ° That people's complaints should be heard and resolved;
  ° Government media should be effective and invite wide participation;
  ° PFDJ organization must allow wide participation as before;
  ° Internal democracy in the PFDJ must be ensured;
  ° To form a committee that would review in detail the conduct of the war with the Woyane as well as the peace process, and to advise the President on the same in the future;
  ° To form a committee to study policies, decision making processes, method of work, distribution of authority, and accountability and control in the PFDJ and the government;
  ° To form a committee to investigate allegations of violation of the rights of a Central committee member.

In addition, it was decided that the fourth congress be held within six months (i.e., by 02.03.2001), and preliminary preparations were discussed.

1.2 What happened after all these decisions?

- Until now, the Central Council has neither internal rules and regulations nor committees to facilitate its work.

- Regular meetings of the Executive Committee (scheduled to be held monthly) and Central Council (scheduled to be held every four months) of the PFDJ have not been held. Since 1994, the Executive Committee should have met 84 times; instead, it met only 11 times. 73 meetings (i.e. 86.9%), which should have been held, were never convened! In the three years of the war with the Woyane, the Central Council met only twice, both in 2000, instead of the scheduled nine times! As the Chairman decides on all matters between meetings of the Executive Committee and Central Council, he became the sole decision-maker as a result of these circumstances. The negative consequence of this became evident during the Woyane invasion. Transparency, accountability, democratic processes and participatory decision-making were abandoned.

- Traits that were instrumental to the success of our struggle for liberation like transparency, accountability and wide participation were slowly forgotten. Mismanagement in the affairs of the PFDJ and the government became worse and worse. Even at critical moments, people were sidelined. The confidence of the people in the front, front members in the front's leadership, and the front's leadership in its chairman was shaken and diminished.

- On the basis of the constitution of the PFDJ, the Central Office of the PFDJ should administer the affairs of the Front, ensure the independent existence and continuity of activities of the Front, execute the policies, programs and decisions of the Central Council, and, through its Secretary, be accountable to the Executive Committee and the Central Council. The Central Office has, however, exceeded its mandate and interfered in the affairs of the government, and taken measures that weaken front and government institutions and institutional work in general. The Central Office has gone so far as to endanger the unity of the PFDJ and the people, as well as the security of the nation, by conducting a dangerous and malicious campaign, without the approval or knowledge of the legislative and executive organs of the front, against some members of the Central Council.

- Smear campaigns and name-calling have replaced constructive criticism and self-criticism. No periodic, objective and productive evaluations based on concrete realities and criteria are made; thus, it has not been possible to correct errors and consolidate strengths. The lack of concern for the common good, nurtured complacency and a "why should I care" attitude in others.

- The establishment of PFDJ business entities had an honorable purpose. However:

- ° They lack transparency and accountability;
- ° They don't follow legal procedures;
- ° They are neither guided by a clear policy nor have professional administration;
- ° They mix front and government businesses;
- ° They have become vengeful enemies of and negative examples for private businesses instead of encouraging them through fair competition and partnership;
- ° They are not run by a trust as decided by the Central Council, and they have never presented reports of their accounts to the Central Council as they should;
- ° They have never been audited, and thus have never paid taxes to the government on the basis òf audited statements;
- ° Even if it cannot be said that they have done nothing good, they have lost credibility and goodwill among the people and front members.

- It was decided that the 4th congress of the PFDJ shall be held at the beginning of 1996, and if conditions did not permit, it would be postponed for a maximum of only six months. The fact that it has not been held up to now (2001) is inexcusable. Cognizant of this fact, the Central Council, in its 9th session, decided that the congress be held in March 2001, but none of the tasks (appraisals) that have to be done as preparation to the congress have been done, and the obstacles to its holding have become obvious.

2. Regarding the Government

2.1 The Goals and Programs that were adopted:

After the referendum, as it was not possible to establish a constitutional government before there was a constitution, it was decided that a transitional government be formed for a period of four years within which a constitution and all the institutions necessary for a constitutional government would be put in place. Conscious of the fact that the EPLF, even if it bore the responsibility of leading the struggle to liberation and sovereignty, should not form a government alone as before the referendum, it was decided to issue Proclamation number 37/1993, later amended as proclamation 52/1994 on 19-05-1993, delineating the structure, powers and duties of the government of transition.

- The Eritrean Government of transition would have legislative, executive and judicial branches, which provide checks and balances on each other. It would establish the rule of law, consolidate national harmony, uphold political pluralism and ensure transparency, tolerance and accountability. It would be free from corruption, and would develop a common national outlook. It would further develop, as guarantees for a democratic political order, a free and powerful judicial branch, a conscious civil society, a free, reliable, critical and responsible mass media, and other democratic institutions.

- As it was not proper for the PFDJ to form a government alone, half the seats of the National Council were set aside to be filled by representatives of the people elected to Regional Assemblies, while the other half were reserved for members of the Central Council of the PFDJ.

- The National Council was to have a life of no more than four years and meet at regular intervals of six months. It would elect the President, and approve or ratify the cabinet, government ministries, commissions, authorities and offices proposed by the President. It would review and approve the budget, development plans, proclamations and treaties proposed by the cabinet. It would establish and employ committees to oversee the drafting of the constitution, laws governing political parties, press law, and other laws necessary for constitutional governance. It was to be a legislative body with the highest authority of the government of Eritrea.

- The Cabinet of Ministers was to be accountable to the National Council, and work as the highest executive authority between meetings of the National Council. Its authority and duty was to run the government with collective responsibility, decide on the policy and size of the defense and security forces, direct and follow-up the implementation of political, economic and social policies. It would decide on issues related to foreign aid and foreign credit. It would hold regular monthly meetings.

- The President is accountable to the National Council, and is the Head of State and Commander in Chief of the Armed Forces. Besides representing the government in matters domestic and foreign, the President appoints diplomats, delegates and emissaries, and he supervises, controls and coordinates the implementation of government policies and programs. In the absence of the President, the Minister of Regional Administration acts as President.

- The judicial branch is independent and free from the legislative and executive branches, and guards the rights, interests and freedoms of the government, organizations and individuals guaranteed under the law.

- The authority and responsibilities of each ministry, commission, authority and office of the state of Eritrea must be published in the legal gazette.

- The National Council, in its second session of 7.6.93, discussed the need for the establishment of Council committees and its own rules of procedure.

- During the third session of the National Council (2-4 March 1994), the proposed Constitution Commission, the Land Proclamation and the Cabinet of Ministers were approved. Even though the budget for 1994 was not presented, it was decided that starting from 1995, the budget would be presented to the National Council for approval.

- In the seventh session of the National Council (1-2 November 1995), restructuring of the Government;

- In its eighth session of 22-24 January 1996, the Press law;

- In its ninth session of 2 July 1996, the draft constitution were discussed and finalized.

- In the twelfth session of the National Council (1-2 February 2000), which followed the eighth meeting of the Central Council of the PFDJ (25-29 January 2000), the issues raised in the CC pertaining to the state were raised here too and discussed. The issues included, continued neglect of regular meetings, mismanagement in government, non-separation of authority between PFDJ and the Government, the need to address complaints from the public, the need to speed up the work of the Election Law Committee, steps necessary for the implementation of the constitution, and problems concerning the implementation of the Land Proclamation.

- In its 13th session held 29 September to 2 October 2000, which followed the ninth meeting of the Central Council of the PFDJ, the National Council decided to form committees to make overall review of the 10 year performance of the government, as well as specifically of the third Ethiopian offensive. It also decided to form a military committee to review the organization and performance of the Eritrean Defense Forces and the peace process with Ethiopia, and to advise the president in these areas in the future. It further decided to hold national elections on the basis of the constitution no later than the end of 2001, and to declare the laws governing the formation of political parties. To that effect, a committee charged with drafting laws governing political parties was formed. This committee was instructed to organize public discussions of the party law it drafted, review the views provided by the public, and bring its final draft to the National Council for approval.

2.2 What was done on the basis of the decisions above?

Even though a lot has been accomplished [during the interim period], much that was illegal and unconstitutional (we did have transitional constitutions for the PFDJ and the government!) was also done. Had this negative experience been avoided, it would have been possible to redouble our achievements and completely eliminate or reduce the problems we faced.

180

Our pre-independence successes were made possible because there was a very high level of motivation created by our collective responsibility and a very high level of participation. After independence, disillusion set in; and even if there was an attempt to dismiss it as "loss of direction", it was the result of abandonment of the above values and practices. "The president has no one to help him!" became a daily propaganda to blur collective work and individual responsibility. The democratic, participatory and institutionalized method of work we were used to was abandoned. Trust, cooperation and good will were eroded. Holding each other accountable and correcting errors disappeared. Let alone building on the strengths of the EPLF, it even became impossible to maintain what we had. The people's respect for and confidence in the PFDJ and the government slowly changed to doubt and fear. There are many valid reasons for this:

- The interim government, which was not to continue more than four years, has now been in power for eight years.

- Preparations for constitutional government have not been done, and continue to be deliberately delayed. These include:
  ○ Proclamation of the law governing political parties;
  ○ Proclamation of election law;
  ○ Formation of an Electoral Commission;
  ○ Revision of existing laws to ensure consistency with the constitution;
  ○ The ratification of regional and international treaties;
  ○ The establishment of committees of the legislative branch;
  ○ The establishment of internal rules and regulations of the legislative branch and their practical introduction;
  ○ The evaluation of the judicial branch;
  ○ The establishment of the Supreme Court;
  ○ Dismantling of the Special Courts;
  ○ Infrastructure for the offices of the National Council.

- The checks and balances between the legislative, executive and judicial branches are non-existent.

- The National Council has no committees or internal rules and guidelines. It does not convene every six months as scheduled. With the exception of the first Cabinet of Ministers it confirmed in its fourth meeting on 2-4 March 1994, it has never confirmed nor has it ever been consulted about all the ministerial changes made since then. It has never been presented with regional or international treaties for its consideration. One of its main oversight functions over the executive branch is to review and approve the national budget, but it has never been presented with any national budget.

In fact, since there is no budgetary law, the government has so far operated without any budgetary restraint, and continues to do so.

- The Cabinet of Ministers does not meet every month. From the scheduled 84 meetings, no more than twenty have been held. The cabinet has no system of checking and reviewing implementation of policies, decisions, laws and programs of the government and its agencies. The cabinet has not decided on issues relating to external aid and credit. The cabinet has not decided on the policy and size of the military and security forces. The cabinet has no coordinated plan or control of national security.

- The President has not convened the regular meetings of the National Council or the Cabinet of Ministers. He has interfered especially in the sensitive Ministries of Defense and Foreign Affairs, as well as other government agencies, preventing the creation of stable government institutions in the country. When overall restructuring was proposed and implemented in all ministries, he did not implement the reorganization plan in his own Office of the President. For no explained reasons and without the approval of the National Council, the President has changed, "frozen" and demoted Ministers. [In the past ten years after independence, 4 Defense Ministers, 5 Foreign Affairs Ministers, and 6 Finance Ministers have been change]. As Commander in Chief of the Armed Forces, he clearly has authority to direct the Ministry of Defense, but the President has directed subordinates of the Minister to report directly to him and has continued to bypass the minister to attend to minute administrative details in this manner. He has encouraged the direct interference of the Central Office of the PFDJ in government ministries thereby compromising their institutional integrity, and creating unnecessary confrontational tension and mistrust between the Central Office and the concerned institutions. Because of his method of work and his demeanor, he has lost the confidence of many front members and people.

- By taking illegal and unconstitutional measures, he has usurped the mandate of the committee entrusted to draft the law governing political parties, and has arbitrarily broadcast the draft election law and the draft party law, causing unnecessary delay. He has also trampled over other Central Council and National Council decisions.

- Because of the weaknesses of the legislative and executive bodies, the President has been acting without restraint, even illegally. Having been used to taking his unrestricted power for granted, he finds it unacceptable now when attempts are being made to have those bodies work properly as well as correct the weaknesses of the system. The President has become so accustomed to acting freely and as he pleased, he is rejecting democratic dialogue, refusing to convene legally required meetings.

- While the judiciary lacks adequate human and institutional capacity, instead of providing resources to build up its capacity, the President has created a competing Special Court reporting directly to him. People are being jailed for years without the knowledge and agreement of the judiciary, and independence of the judiciary and rule of law are being violated.

- As no institution or plan for national security exists, the people have become victims of unexpected threats to its security. In the war with Ethiopia, even if the enemy did not achieve its maximum goal, the Woyane has occupied our land and inflicted incalculable harm on our people, economy and society. What happened has revealed fundamental weaknesses in the way we function which is in need of correction.

II. What Type of Crisis are we in?

A. *What is the Crisis?*

The problem is that the President is conducting himself in an illegal and unconstitutional manner, is refusing to consult, and the legislative and executive bodies have not performed their oversight functions properly.

The confidence of the general membership of the front as well as the general public in the leadership and the party has been reduced. This phenomenon has come as a result of alienation that accumulated over time, and it was highlighted as a result of the war with the Woyane and its disastrous consequences. People want a transparent, accountable, institutionalized and legal administration. The people are asking for past experiences to be objectively assessed, corrective measures to be taken, and on the basis of lessons learned, illegal practices to be discarded and correct and institutionalized practices developed to create an atmosphere in which confidence can be restored.

One side is saying:

- Human and democratic rights of citizens should be guaranteed.

- As there was in the defense of the sovereignty of our nation, let there be now too broad participation by PFDJ members and the general public in the appraisal and evaluation of past experiences.

- Let the PFDJ and the government take concrete measures to implement and guarantee their professed aims of establishing a constitutional government.

- Let a constitutional government be established through free and fair elections.

- Let differences inside the front and the government be resolved peacefully, democratically and legally.

The other side:

- Argues saying our professed goals cannot be implemented now because suitable conditions have not yet been created, and there is the danger of "sub-national sectarianism";

- Argues further that the we should not have an open discussion, assessment and evaluation because this could lead to a rift between the government and the people, and our enemies may exploit the situation;

- Characterizes any criticism as anti-front and anti-unity, and is quick to portray it as and equalize it with serving the enemy's agenda.

- Closes all legal avenues and forums for dialogue and shelves decisions that should be implemented;

- Is delaying the front's congress and national elections to perpetuate the existing order;

- Attempts to muzzle any serious views and opposition by instilling fear, and threatening to take illegal and undemocratic action.

After liberation, the people expected peace and improvement in their lives. However, when the unexpected war with the Woyane came, the people, on top of all the sacrifices they made during the struggle for liberation, had to make heavy sacrifices again to defend their sovereignty, and now find themselves victims of heavier hardships and agonizing displacement. As long as the danger from the enemy was present, the people restrained themselves and chose not to speak loudly against government weaknesses and mismanagement. But instead of taking action to correct its mistakes, the government has tried to cover them up and to silence criticism by threats creating an atmosphere of fear and intimidation. The people have thus now started to express their concerns and speak out.

B. How can the crisis be resolved?

- When the President is ready to be governed by the constitution and the law, and when the legislative and executive branches perform their legal functions properly;

- When confidence is placed on the members of the front and the general public, and they are allowed to exercise their right to participate in open discussions of important national issues, and when the legislative and executive organs of the PFDJ and the government hold their regular and emergency meetings and exercise their powers;

- When the PFDJ's and the government's experiences of the past seven years are discussed and reviewed in open forums with wide public participation, and lessons learned are utilized for the future;

- When the law of party formation is proclaimed, and parties are allowed to form and are encouraged to compete peacefully and freely;

- When elections to the Fourth Party Congress are conducted freely and fairly, and the future of the PFDJ as a political party/ organization, which must be governed by the same party laws to be proclaimed, is democratically decided at the fourth congress;

- When assurances are in place for free and fair national elections, and when preparatory steps (proclamation of election law, party law, and formation of electoral commission) for the elections are quickly taken;

- When the impartiality of the mass media is assured to encourage the protection of human rights, freedom of expression and political discourse; when the formation and freedom of action of civic organization are allowed and encouraged; when the Special Courts are dismantled; when those who have been imprisoned for a long time without a court order are brought before a regular court of law; when the independence of the judiciary is guaranteed;

- When participatory procedures are established to formulate clear and declared policies to address the gap in the standard of living, the lack of job and educational opportunity in different localities and communities.

III. Why this letter and at this time?

BECAUSE all legal means to resolve this crisis in the legislative bodies have been blocked, frustrated. The President has refused to convene meetings of the legislative bodies, but continues to express his views and taking illegal action. Front members have the legal right to know the current situation and to state their views and criticisms.

As the conduct of the PFDJ and the government deteriorated and became more erratic, particularly concerning the Woyane war and its consequences, an attempt to revive wider participation in decision-making, eliminate existing weaknesses and reinforce our defense was made at the eighth session of the Central Council (28-29 January 2000). At this meeting, the president was asked why regular meetings of the legislative organs were not held, and an impassioned demand was made to hold regular meeting on time in the future. The president, however, not only tried to present the unacceptable excuse that conditions were not conducive to hold meetings, but arrogantly added that he was not going to call meetings in the future either if he did not feel it was conducive to do so.

Appendices

Since the Woyane was getting ready for its offensive, the issue was not raised at the twelfth session of the National Council to avoid giving moral ammunition to the enemy. The president however continued to take wrong, illegal and vengeful measures that could serve the enemy's purpose.

At the ninth meeting of the Central Council which was convened from 31 August to 2 September 2000 (after the third invasion), and to some extent at 13th session of the National Council, which was held from 29 September to 2 October 2000, the following were raised, among others. Genuine reviews to be conducted, to look forward and establish deadlines for holding the front congress and national elections, measures which are necessary preparation for such to be taken, and important issues requiring preparatory study to be studied. Since military and diplomatic efforts had to be strengthened, the Council also decided to form a military committee to do an appraisal of our record in these areas and to advise the president in the future. However, obstacles are being placed to block the implementation of any of these decisions.

In January 2001, the president, by way of the Central Office of the PFDJ, conducted a disturbing open smear campaign accusing high officials of regionalism and treason. Seminars were conducted that suggested there was a fifth column inside the country, that equated honest criticism with aiding the woyanes' agenda, and that threatened action would be taken against the targeted high officials. This was done to silence free expression and muzzle criticism, and to avoid proper evaluation. This disturbed and created serious concern among the people and members of the front.

Although the illegal and negative handling of the issue by the President and the Central Office of the PFDJ was provocative, we decided to avoid confrontation as there was as yet no guarantee for a peaceful end to the war with Ethiopia, and took the initiative to resolve the problem through legal means and dialogue. We started to consult with other members of the Central Council to ask for meetings of the Central and National Councils whose regular time was past due.

Upon hearing of our initiative, the central office of the PFDJ had circulated a letter (Annex 1), on August 7th 2001, threatening members of the National Council not to sign on a petition calling for a meeting of the National Council. We thought this action improper and were forced to counter with our own letter to all members of the National Council the following day explaining the situation (Annex 2). On 12-03-2001, the President rejected our request (Annex 3).

Copies of our letter of 20 February 2001, asking the President to convene meetings of the Central Council of the PFDJ and the National Council, which reached him on 13 March 2001 (Annex 4), his negative reply (Annex 5), our second letter again asking for meetings explaining the reasons for our call (Annexes 6 A & B), and the President's second negative response (Annex 7) are all enclosed with this letter. Legal requests received illegal responses, and our attempts to resolve problems through meetings and democratic dialogue, not only fell on deaf ears, but attempts were also made to mis-present it in an illegal and undemocratic way.

Thus, our efforts to amend and correct the mistaken path of the PFDJ and the government, our attempt to ensure a democratic transition to a constitutional order, our resolve to obtain these results through democratic and legal means at the leadership level has failed to bear fruit. Having no other means at our disposal, and rejecting resort to illegal means, we bring this open letter to you. We believe every member has the right to know about the crisis and our views on how to solve it. We believe every member has the right and the duty to know about the democratic solutions available, and we perform our duty in bringing this crisis to your attention in this open letter.

Just as we bear ultimate collective responsibility for our performance as leaders, we are obliged to bear equal responsibility for correcting our failures. Since our failure to lead properly has injured the people, we are prepared and determined to make amends and compensate our people by working tirelessly to build, in concert with other PFDJ members and the general Eritrean public, an accountable and responsible government in Eritrea.

If there is any accusation against any member of the Central and National Councils, from the President on down, then we support and believe, that instead of blackmailing, the accusation should be openly leveled at the subject member during a meeting of the appropriate Council, and if it merits legal action, for the appropriate court to handle it through due process of law. Every member of the Central Council of the PFDJ and the National Council must be accountable in the performance of his duties or his handling of financial records, and, as a public official, in his morality. We call for the creation of an independent body that includes members of the general public, to investigate every member.

If we do not take corrective action immediately but instead continue as we have been, then it is not hard to imagine from the experiences of the past ten years the devastating consequences that await us. We need act in concert to resolve our differences, to avoid our security being compromised and our internal unity is weakened, thereby exposing us to becoming victims of external forces. This is a serious national affair. Determined, courageous, capable and nationalist Eritreans must play their role. Let them utilize their capacity to contribute their share to their country. Let us take practical lessons from the Woyane invasion. We should never risk compromising our hard won independence and making our fertile land barren. Time is passing, and our external enemies have not folded their hands waiting for us.

Appendices

We shall continue our struggle to establish the rule of law. We shall continue to struggle to implement the sacred ideals and principles of the front and our national constitution. We shall continue to struggle using every legal and democratic means available. We have no ambition other than making these sacred ideals a reality. We take this opportunity to call on all PFDJ members and the Eritrean people in general to express their opinion through legal and democratic means and to give their support to the goals and principles they consider just.

Signatories:

1. Mahmoud Ahmed Sherifo
– Member of the Central Council of PFDJ
– Member of the National Council

2. Haile Wold'ensae
– Member of the Central Council of PFDJ
– Member of the National Council
– Ministerial cabinet member

3. Mesfin Hagos
– Member of the Central Council and the Executive Committee of PFDJ
– Member of the National Council

4. Ogbe Abraha (General)
– Member of the Central Council of PFDJ
– Member of the National Council

5. Hamid Himid
– Member of the Central Council of PFDJ
– Member of the National Council

6. Saleh Kekya
– Member of the Central Council of PFDJ
– Member of the National Council

7. Estifanos Seyoum (Brigadier General)
– Member of the Central Council of PFDJ
– Member of the National Council

8. Berhane GhebreEghzabiher (Major General)
– Member of the Central Council of PFDJ
– Member of the National Council

9. Astier Feshatsion
– Member of the Central Council of PFDJ
– Member of the National Council

10. Mohammed Berhan Blata
– Member of the Central Council of PFDJ
– Member of the National Council

11. Petros Solomon
– Member of the Central Council of PFDJ
– Member of the National Council
– Ministerial cabinet member

12. Germano Nati
– Member of the Central Council of PFDJ
– Member of the National Council

13. Beraki Ghebreslassie
– Member of the Central Council of PFDJ
– Member of the National Council

14. Adhanom Ghebremariam
– Member of the Central Council of PFDJ
– Member of the National Council

15. Haile Menkerios
– Member of the Central Council of PFDJ
– Member of the National Council

Annex 1

Peoples Front For Democracy and Justice (PFDJ)
Central Office

7 March 2001

Honorable Members of Central Committee
Peoples Front For Democracy & Justice

Based on information provided by some members of the Central Council, a petition calling for a meeting of the Central Council is going round to collect signatures from members.

Our transitional Constitution provides for an emergency meeting to be held where 2/3 of the members call for one. Even though this right exists, it has never been exercised in the past. Before such a step is taken, it is appropriate to ask the Chairman, directly or through the Central Office, to convene such a meeting. Prior to the distribution of the petition paper, an application for a meeting was not rejected. Even if there is no reason to collect signatures to call a meeting, it would have been proper for the members who have chosen to take this action to present it openly to all members of the Central Council. For this reason the current circulation of a petition calling for a meeting is out of order.

The Central Office of the PFDJ, with this letter, transmits this notice to members of the Central Council.

Signed (illegible)
Stamped

Annex 2

8-3-2001

Honorable Members of the
Central Council of the PFDJ

We refer to a letter dated yesterday, 7 March 2001, written under the letterhead of the Central Office of the PFDJ with an unknown signatory, and distributed to members of the Central Council. It states that, "certain members of the Central Council are circulating a petition collecting signatures to call for a meeting of the Central Council," and that this is "out of order."

This letter states:

- Our transitional Constitution requires the Central Council to hold an emergency meeting upon the application of 2/3 of its members;
- This right admittedly exists, but has never been used;
- Before such a step is taken, it is appropriate to ask the Chairman, either directly or through the Central Office, to hold a meeting;
- Prior to the distribution of the petition letter, a request for a meeting was not rejected;
- There is no reason to collect signatures and to call for a meeting;
- It would have been appropriate for the members who have opted to take this action, to present their request openly to members of the Central Council.

The letter declares that the Central Office of the PFDJ is issuing this notice because the current circulation of a petition calling for a meeting is out of order.

We, the undersigned members of the Central Committee are some of those who have been meeting and talking quite openly with any member of the Committee calling for a meeting of the Central Committee. Because based on the constitution of the PFDJ the meeting is overdue, because there are urgent situations regarding our unity and security as a people and a nation, because it is our public and national duty and responsibility, and because all responsible members of the Central Council, cadres and members are eagerly awaiting that the unity of our people and the security of our nation are safeguarded.

1.　　　　Based on our constitution [PFDJ transitional Constitution], between the regularly scheduled meetings to be held every 4 months, it is mandatory to hold an emergency meeting if 2/3 of the members call for it. This is a right guaranteed by our struggle, not a right to be begged for or handed out. The letter, while it admits the existence of this right, claims that we have never exercised it in our history. It is true that because of innocent trust in our leadership and its central organs, and because to a certain degree collective participation and understanding existed on many issues, meetings were not held as scheduled, and obviously it cannot be said that problems were not created as a result. This was not only wrong, but as genuine trust was betrayed, collective action was abandoned, and collective understanding was eroded, no one can deny that the negative consequences have continued to grow.

To say that we should not use a right because we have not exercised it in the past, however, is failing to learn from past experience, only looking backward, not to know your realities, and to fail to look forward and to building a responsible and accountable government in the future. Innocent trust cannot be exploited forever.

At the January 2000 meeting of the Central Council, the argument that meetings should be held as scheduled and the consequent holding of the follow up meeting of the Central Council on time was a step forward, and it is a fact that this permitted the discussion of some issues on a timely basis. At that meeting, a call to hold all future meetings on time was made. What is being requested now is convening a meeting that is overdue, and that does not require a call by 2/3 of the membership. This is a right of the Central Council and not a gift from someone or other. This is not something that should be cancelled because it is problematic or inconvenient for the Chairman of the Central Council. If the time for the regular meeting is up or past, a call for the chairman to convene the meeting can be oral or written, made individually or collectively. Because it is a legal right. There is no reason or obligation that the request be made through the Central Office.

2.   The letter states that there is no reason to collect signatures to call for a meeting. This is an extremely regrettable and irresponsible statement. In spite of the fact that the campaign by the Central Office in January 2001 among PFDJ members (and the general public) caused major upheaval and concern on the one hand, and provided the enemy with moral ammunition on the other, the Central Office fails to recognize the importance of calling an emergency meeting of the Central Council to safeguard the unity and the security of the nation, although the due date for the regular meeting is long past. Maybe the Central Office did not want to.

This illegal and irresponsible smear campaign by the Central Office of the PFDJ, which contradicts the discussions and decisions passed at previous meetings of the Central Council, which is unknown to and certainly not a decision of the Executive Committee of the PFDJ, which has been kept secret from members of the Central Council, which can divide the nation and create chaos, which can destroy the people's hope of restoring their lives after the damage they have sustained, which appears aimed at controlling the preparation for elections at any cost, which has seized the authority of the Central Council and the Executive Committee of the PFDJ, and prevented them from performing their constitutional duties, which is being conducted in a manner devoid of national responsibility by the Central Office of the PFDJ, has created an undeniable political crisis, for which responsibility must be borne.

Not only for those responsible members of the Central Council who care about the unity and security of the nation above all else, including above holding office, but also for any Eritrean nationalist, the need, reason and urgency to convene the meetings is obvious and they are anxiously awaiting them. To state that there is no reason for convening meetings is to choose chaos, regardless of its consequences, instead of solving problems legally in constitutionally mandated meetings.

3.   The letter states, "It would have been appropriate for the members who have chosen to take this action, to openly present it to members of the Central Council."

- Was it not clearly stated at the January 2000 meeting of the Central Council that henceforth all regular meetings would convene on time?

- Has four months not elapsed since the August 2000 meeting of the Central Committee?

- Had the date for the regular meeting not arrived or passed when the Central Office commenced its irresponsible smear campaign?

- After the irresponsible smear campaign, didn't members of the Central Council as well as cadres and other members of the front express their concern and openly declare their support for a resolution of this issue at a meeting of the Central Council?

- Aren't those members of the Central Council calling for a meeting, conducting their contacts with other members openly?

- If there is an issue a member wants to communicate with other members of the Central Council, other than meetings of the Central Council, or the Central Office wills it, is there any way or means (Magazine, Radio or other communication device etc...) to do so?

- Is it illegal to call for a meeting of the Central Council when the due date has elapsed or when there are problems? Is trying to hide reality openness, or is openness calling for a meeting whose due date has elapsed and which is desperately needed to solve problems?

Finally, the set date for the meeting of the Central Committee has come and gone (two months have passed). There are important situations requiring a meeting, and the right to call for a meeting is in order. It is a right that cannot be revoked by any hapless posturing of the Central Office of the PFDJ. The responsibility entrusted to us by the PFDJ and the people demand it, and we would like all members of the Central Council to know that, along that of others, our call for an urgent meeting of the Central Council also remains in place.

If we do not get a positive reply, after a limited period, since we have no open access to the mass media which is in the hands of the Central Office of the PFDJ, in order to fulfill the responsibility and trust placed in us by the front and the people, we shall be forced to express our views openly to the PFDJ membership and the general public. We shall not be responsible for the consequences.

Signatories:

1. Mahmoud Sherifo
2. Haile Wold'ensae
3. Petros Solomon
4. Mesfin Hagos
5. Ogbe Abraha
6. Berhane Gebreghzabhier
7. Saleh Kekia
8. Hamid Himid

Annex 3

The State of Eritrea
Office of President

Date 12.03.2001

Sherifo (Mahmoud)

This morning you sent me a letter with signatures. If it is for my information, I have seen it. In general, I only want to say that you all are making a mistake.

Annex 4

Date 20-2-2001

To the Honorable Isaias Afwerki
Chairman of Central and National Councils

The date for the regular meetings of the Central and National Councils have passed, and in addition, there are issues (situations) that call for an emergency meeting. We, the undersigned members of the Central and National Councils thus request that you convene the meetings shortly.

Victory to the Masses

Signatories:

1. Mahmoud Ahmed Sherifo
2. Haile Wold'ensae
3. Petros Solomon
4. Mesfin Hagos
5. Ogbe Abraha
6. Illegible
7. Saleh Kekya
8. Hamid Hmd
9. Alamin Sheik Saleh
10. Estifanos Seyoum
11. Berhane GebreEghzabhier
12. Astier Feshatsion
13. Mohammed Berhan Blata
14. Germano Nati
15. Musa Rabaa
16. Nati Ibrahim
17. Beraki GhebreSelassie
18. Adhanom GhebreMariam
19. Haile Menkerios

Annex 5

The State of Eritrea
Office of President

Date 13.03.2001

Mahmoud Sherifo

Again today you have sent me another letter. I have seen it. I repeat, you are making a mistake.

Annex 6a

20.03.2001

To: Honorable Isaias Afwerki
President of the State Of Eritrea

Subject: Request for meetings of the Central Council and National Council

Those members of the Central Council and National Council who previously sent a request for meetings of the Central Council and the National Council accompanied with their signatures, are not satisfied with your response of: "You are making a mistake". We say there are problems that should be solved in meetings, and steps that need to be taken urgently to guarantee a democratic transition to a constitutional order. Now again, we ask you to convene the meetings, whose mandatory regular dates have already passed, within the month of March.

We are sending, as an attachment, a document describing the problems we see and the solutions we expect.

Victory to the Masses!
Those members of the Central Council who previously sent a signed request.

Annex 6b

Problems that have been created and their solutions

Eritreans living inside and outside, initially to make independence a reality, and when the war with the Woyane erupted to defend national sovereignty, enlisted their beloved children with their blessing, gave their money, property and labour with complete dedication to their country. Their goal was, not only seeing an independent Eritrea, but also to see the unity of the people assured, with all around equality and social justice, with public accountability and with peace and harmony. However, the general public and front members are not satisfied with the leadership and management of the front and the Government. The illegal and irresponsible seminars of the PFDJ Central Office and the inexcusable steps being taken by the President are creating not only concern, but may also create harmful consequences.

196

There are attempts, in some quarters, to explain these problems as results of frustration caused by the war with Woyane. However, these problems started largely after independence, especially after 1994, and accumulated thereafter becoming worse, until at the time of the war with Woyane, these problems put the nation's existence at risk. The problems are that legal and institutional methods of working, collective decision making in important issues, accountability and democratic management became slowly weakened and diminished. Mutual concern, respect and trust disappeared; the powers of legislative and executive bodies were usurped.

In order to solve these problems and to guarantee transition to a constitutional order, the meetings held in January and August-September 2000 addressed these issues and made important decisions. However, later on, the decisions were twisted, misinterpreted and shelved. Observing the danger in this crisis, concerned embers of the Central Council, without being tempted into a tit for tat, presented their request for already late, legally mandatory meetings of the Central & National Councils. But this was rejected. While a legal and responsible request was rejected, the misguided seminars of the Central Office of the PFDJ, which had no blessing of the Executive Committee and Central Council, had found full support from the Chairman, and thus the crisis has reached a dangerous level where it is liable to explode.

Intentions of taking illegal and unnecessary action are being hinted, but these problems cannot be solved except through peaceful, democratic and legal discussion and understanding. As such, even now it is still necessary to convene emergency meetings of the Central and National Councils, and the following issues should be discussed and action taken on them:

1. Legislative branches should perform their proper function and confirm their oversight responsibility over the Executive branch;

2. Meetings of legislative branches should be held at regular times and whenever emergency meetings are requested;

3. The seven year experience of the PFDJ and the Government need to be evaluated objectively to become starting points for the front's congress and the constitutional government to be established after elections; conditions and forums for open and free discussions should be created, and committees that are accountable to the Central and National Councils should be established to conduct the discussions.

4. Draft legislation for elections and political parties, as permitted by law, need to be provided for discussion by the people. The respective appointed committees should gather opinions on them, and the finalized drafts brought to the National Council for ratification.

Appendices

5. Elections for the front congress and the constitutional government must be free and fair. Guarantees that the Election Commission shall be impartial must be provided.

6. In order to respect human rights and freedom of expression, the Special Courts, as well as the "Investigation Committee" illegally formed by the President, must be dismantled. The letter and spirit of the Press Law must be respected; the independence of the judiciary confirmed, and the government must operate under a declared and open annual budget.

If this is not done, we shall officially declare that we are unable to properly perform the duty entrusted to us by the members of PFDJ and the people, and we shall be obliged to decide not continue being tools of this incorrect administration.

Annex 7

The President

Date 29.03.2001

From: P/ Isaias
To: Sherifo
Hour: 10:50
N. I.: A290301.RTF

– I have, this morning, received and seen the letter you sent, dated 28/3/2001, in the name of those members of Central Council who had previously signed a request.

– I do not want to go into its false and baseless content and say anything.

– Because I have chosen to be tolerant, I will patiently avoid any invitation to an argument.

– But if by continuous provocation, you want to escalate problems by exaggerating non-existent issues, it is your choice.

– Again I ask you to refrain from this mistaken path and come to your senses.

PFDJ Secretary Highlights Defeatist Stand of a Few Central Council Members

Eritrea Profile, August 18, 2001

In an interview he gave to *Hadas Eritrea* newspaper on 8 August 2001, the Secretary of the People's Front for Democracy and Justice (PFDJ), Mr. Alamin Mohammed Said, underlined the destructive nature of the ongoing campaign by a few members of the Central Council of the PFDJ. Mr. Alamin noted that this campaign originates from the defeatist stand of the group during the third round TPLF offensive. Excerpts of the interview follow:

Why [did] the PFDJ and Government of Eritrea choose to remain silent in the wake of the open letter disseminated by 15 members of the Central Council in the past few months and the series of interview campaigns they conducted that subsequently gave rise to concern and discussion among the ranks of the general public:

Our wish and efforts regarding this issue has been to resolve it with patience and restraint, in line with the traditional work ethics of the People's Front. Soon after some members of the Central Council, in violation of this norm, said they would directly communicate what they had in mind to Council members and the public, claiming at the same time that they would not be held accountable for the consequences thereof, we not only indicated to them that they were embarking on a wrong course of action but also called on the group to come to their senses. Even after they proceeded to launch an open attack on the Front and the Government in rejection of this call, we were in no hurry to react. In the conviction that the public would grasp what lies behind their utterances and draw its own conclusions. We chose to remain silent apart from giving hints, here and there, so as to calm down the people's apprehensions. And this period of calm had its obvious benefits. Even during the present interview, it is not my intention to delve into the group's cover-up ploys and digressions. Rather, my purpose is to shed light on the fundamental frame of their thinking. Another thing I would like to point out from the outset is the fact that speaking of 15 members of the Central Council would portray a distorted picture. Although there are those who signed the open letter for different reasons of their own, it is only a few of them who are accountable for the damage inflicted on the nation and its people as well as the Front and the Government.

What is the damage they had inflicted?

In the first place, there is the question of the timing they chose. This is an issue the entire people are talking about. We have not yet been relieved of the danger posed by the TPLF; our borders have not yet been demarcated; our youths are still in the trenches; the families of our martyrs have not only yet been notified but also not given assistance to console them. At a time like this, it is incumbent on every individual, even the one claiming to have a cause of one type or the other, to give priority to the national cause and demonstrate patience, and thus refrain from any action likely to harm and weaken the nation or organization concerned. It is precisely out of this sense of high responsibility that our people continue to remain ever steadfast withstanding every imaginable inconvenience. It should be noted in this connection that some Eritrean families have deployed 4-5 sons or daughters to the war fronts in defense of the nation. On the contrary, it is both damaging and subject to accountability to see a few individuals who used to play a leadership role engaging, at this particular juncture, in a campaign that may undermine our united national resistance that should be no means be tempered with.

But members of the group claim that they are pursuing a right course of action, and that their campaign is designed to benefit the nation?

They could by no means convince the people that the current situation they have created would be beneficial to the nation. Certainly, it is damaging and destructive; it is not beneficial and constructive at all. Out of the many damages that the situation they have created might cause, three major ones could be singled out: One, it undermines the unwavering patriotic stance and united stand of our people that remains a firm guarantee to frustrate the aggressive ambitions of the TPLF. Secondly, it encourages the TPLF and all those harbouring enmity against this country to continue their conspiracies against Eritrea. The fact that the TPLF clique which failed to achieve its goal of subjugating Eritrea through war is even now striving hard to realize its wicked objectives by exploiting political and economic crisis that may emerge within our ranks bears this out. Thirdly, it negatively affects our relations of partnership with counterparts across the globe.

But what pushes them to engage in such action that harms the nation and offends the people? Are there political differences that justify this?

If we take a closer look at the utterances they have been making, it is quite obvious that there exist no fundamental political differences at all to justify any ground for launching a campaign that damages the nation and its people. For many years, these individuals used to occupy positions of leadership in the People's Front and the Government; each one of them was personally involved in the formulation of policies and programs; members of the public are aware that, until very recently, these same individuals were equally involved in activities of elaborating and reinforcing such policies and programs as well as explaining their anticipated outcome. It is inconceivable to hear them claiming all of a sudden that they were, after all, doing the wrong things. Moreover, other than the topics they are currently picking up, in an irresponsible manner that would hold them accountable, they are trying to incite various strata of society. The question of organizing meetings of the Front and the Government, improving and developing work efficiency, setting up and strengthening institutions, holding national elections and establishing political parties – all these have never been the subject of controversy and a cause for division as far as the People's Front is concerned. Ever since the Second and Unity Congress of the EPLF in 1987, there prevailed consensus regarding such matters and as such unremitting efforts were made to translate the set objectives into action using appropriate forums. The current talk claiming as if there existed political differences and pretending that one side is conservative while the other advocates change as well as pretending that one side is reactionary and the other democratic, that one side stands for elections and the other is anti-elections – all these are designed to mislead public opinion and a cover-up ploy or otherwise a mere political bluff.

What is the group trying to hide?

Firstly, and as is to be discerned from the interviews they had conducted, each one of them personally harbours certain things about which he entertains feelings of being restive. The second and main thing has to do with the stand they took regarding the issues of war and peace as well as during the third round TPLF offensive. Still at that time, they used to assert the firm stand of the people and the Government of Eritrea in favour of peace, our people's just and legitimate cause of defending the national freedom and sovereignty on the one hand, while condemning the TPLF's policy of war and aggression against Eritrea on the other. Furthermore, it is a matter of public knowledge that the group used to denounce the stand of the TPLF in various forums and enchant anti-TPLF slogans. Today, however, these same individuals are trying to portray Eritrea as if it were opposed to peace. And this at a time when, in sharp contrast to this country's abiding commitment to peace, the TPLF authorities have not only once again made it known that they mean to stick to their war agenda but are also visibly sabotaging the peace process to resolve the border conflict. The aforementioned stand of the few Central Council members constitutes a damaging act on the nation.

Such a stand openly surfaced during the third round TPLF offensive. During that decisive moment when the Eritrean people and their armed forces were putting up heroic struggle in defense of national unity and sovereignty, these individuals took a defeatist stand. Right after the Eritrean withdrawal from Barentu, these individuals argued that we could not stop the TPLF offensive. Besides, they claimed that since the TPLF authorities would not put an end to their offensive short of the ouster from office of President Isaias, they advocated the resignation of the President. The group further argued that in case the TPLF succeed to take control of the country, they would commit atrocities on the people, and hence we should appeal to the United Nations or the USA to assume control over the State of Eritrea. Members of the group were fully bent on implementing this plan due to the disarming stand they adopted. Taking a stand of this nature on the part of senior government officials, especially at extremely critical moment that might entail national disaster, is subject to accountability.

Certainly, the act is subject to accountability. But why were they not held accountable at that moment?

It is not the first time in the experience of the People's Front to be confronted with a grave situation that gives rise to instances here and there of extreme anxiety and defeatist attitude on the part of some people like the third round TPLF offensive. Our preoccupation then was wholly to mobilize the nation's resources towards frustrating the aggression of the enemy. Following the decisive victory over the aggressor, however, we entertained hope and did our best to induce the group to adopt a constructive attitude. The critical review made of the objective situation in the country in the political, military, diplomatic and information arenas last August/September during the 9th session of the Front's Central Council and the 13th session of the National Assembly that accompanied it, were part of these efforts. The 9th session of the PFDJ Central Council took note of the weak points manifested during the third round TPLF offensive, including the defeatist attitude on the part of some cadres and government official as well as some among the ranks of the public. The Central Council session stressed the need to immediately rectify these shortcomings. While there was no inclination on the part of the People's Front to look backwards, the few members of the Central Council, apparently worried that things would eventually come to the fore and in an attempt to cover up their misdeeds opted to blackmail the Front and Government, thereby doing harm to the nation.

A certain individual from amongst the group in one of the interviews he gave, even raised a point – without being asked – as follows: "In the same manner that President Nasser of Egypt was asked to resign in the wake of the Egyptian defeat by Israel, wasn't it correct to suggest President Isaias's resignation during the third round TPLF offensive?"

It is quite obvious that resorting to such a ploy amounts to trying to minimize the gravity of the issue. At a time when the nation was engaged in life-and-death struggle, it is not difficult to discern the fatal consequences that might ensue had the President declared: "We are defeated, I am quitting office." Hence, the damage committed by the few members of the Central Council.

It is also being talked about that the Berlin meeting of 13 Eritrean academicians and the anti-Front and anti-Government manifesto they issued was organized under the pressure of the group. Is that true?

Yes, it is true. Before going into details, it is pertinent to pose a number of questions: Who were those behind the convening of the meeting? How come that the participants who did not share, as they themselves put it, a common political view came to attend the meeting? Who covered the expenses of the meeting? And other related questions. These issues have been at the focus of public discussion and need to be explained.

Coming back to the main topic, the manifesto issued in the name of the 13 educated Eritreans and what the Central Council members are talking about are the same in content. It is to be recalled that the G-13 individuals claimed last October that unless the rift within the nation's leadership is quickly resolved, it may result in dire consequences. And this they asserted at a time when no one from amongst members of the public had the slightest idea about what these people were propagating. What the authors of the manifesto were keen to communicate in the process is quite obvious: let no action be taken against the senior government officials currently under discussion. These officials entertained hope that Eritreans abroad would voice support for the so-called Berlin Manifesto. There were even plans to hold enlarged meetings following the one that took place in Berlin, Germany. However, contrary to their expectations, the Eritrean people at home and abroad vehemently rejected the contents and message of the manifesto. Thus, the project failed.

Were similar attempts also made inside the country?

Yes, there were and still are. Attempts made, before the third round TPLF offensive and afterwards in particular to agitate cadres of the People's Front and Government on the basis of specific complaints they may have, ended up in fiasco. As indicated in the open letter, the few members of the Central Council argued as if they were pursuing the right course of action, while at the same time pleaded for reconciliation. This machination also failed in due course. What members of the group are presently engaged in is that of trying, through raising sensitive and delicate topics, to incite the public to stage protest action. One of these has to do with the questions of languages and balanced development. It should be stressed at this juncture that these attempts are not rooted in genuine concern and commitment. Still more, members of the group are claiming that the needs of the disabled are being ignored and that the assets of the Front should be given to them; so do they claim that the demobilized ex-fighters have been unfairly treated and that the Government does not want to demobilize those youths fulfilling their national service duties; they also argue that students should not be deployed for the Summer Campaign Program. And all these with the intention of inciting the respective social segments just referred to.

As the officials under discussion are launching the on-going campaign out of sheer personal motive and interest, and not out of concern for the nation and its people, their being engaged in anti-people and anti-state agitation and actions is not surprising. Nevertheless, these activities stand to be condemned and as such are subject to accountability.

Many members of the Front and Government who have been following up the group's utterances and actions ask why measures have not been taken against them. When and how would this burning issue be resolved?

Leaving aside legal issues to the pertinent institutions, it appears to me that two things are particularly interesting: the first has to do with the understanding of the public about the whole issue as well as its assessment and judgment. Secondly, and what is fundamental, is that of concentrating on the challenges currently facing the nation and devote national attention to those areas of over-riding concern to members of the public at large. Ensuring the nation's sovereignty – from the fulfillment of which the detractors are trying to dissuade us – occupies top position in our priorities. Then follows the task of rehabilitating our people and improving their standard of living. Likewise, we are presently engaged in efforts to develop the operational efficiency and strengthening of governmental institutions. Moreover, our efforts to enhance popular participation in public affairs are continuing with full force. These are areas the people are interested in above anything else.

In Lieu of Defamation, Better to Argue with Facts
Press Release Issued by the 15 Senior PFDJ Officials[1]

August 11, 2001

The interview in *Hadas Ertra* conducted with Mr. Alamin Mohammed Said on August 8, 2001, appeared on the Friday, August 10, 2001 issue (No. 211). The gist of the contents of the interview can be summarized as follows:

The 15 members of the Central [PFDJ, ruling party] and National Assemblies:

(1) have committed acts that are criminal and reprehensible;

(2) short of being driven by personal interests, they have no issues and philosophical differences [with the PFDJ leadership] that are of benefit to the people and that nation;

(3) whereas the people were calling for steps to be taken against them, and although the People's Front, consistent with its tradition and because it was too busy meeting the challenges and needs of the people, chose the route of patience and fortitude and would not make hasty decisions, some of the guilty parties will be called to task for their acts.

So explains the interview. These measures, which are based on bold-faced lies and as a pretext to justify taking illegal and punitive action, are part of a campaign of defamation that has been secretly in the works for nearly a year.

A – The So-Called "Reprehensible and Criminal Act"

1. Addressing the 15 members of the Central and National Assemblies collectively:

It [what Alamin] seems to accuse them for disseminating the "Open Letter" when their calls for a meeting were rejected.

---

[1] This is an unofficial translation of the press release issued by the G-15 in Asmara on Saturday, August 11, 2001. It was posted to the awate.com Web site on August 13.

Appendices

- In late January 2001, the Central Office of the PFDJ, without the knowledge and approval of the Central Council, the National Assembly, the executive council of the Front and the Government, had initiated a campaign whose contents troubled the people and defamed senior officials of the Front. Cognizant of the risks associated with the campaign, and with the understanding that the anxiety and worry that the campaign initiated could only be solved through a discussion at an emergency session, many members of the Central Council and the National Assembly saw the need and the urgency for an emergency session. On the suggestion that a written call should be made on the president to call for the session, not all the concerned members were in agreement: some signed the petition and withdrew their names; others wished not to continue with the process. Thus, the number of the petitioners was reduced to 15.

- To resolve the crisis created by the Central Office of the PFDJ and other differences in a session of the Central Council and the national Assembly via discussions and using legal and constitutional (transitional constitution) way, the 15 members repeatedly called for a session between February and May 2001. When their repeated requests were denied, they were forced to submit their request in an "Open Letter" in May 2001.

- The [call of the] Open Letter of May 2001 [was]:
  i. To correct the weaknesses and the work style of the Front and the Government;
  ii. To renew and rekindle the dwindling faith of the public on the Front and the Government;
  iii. To execute the goals and promises of the Front in an assured manner;
  iv. To ensure the welfare of the people and the nation;
  v. To initiate the open and free debate within the members of the Front and the masses so as to ensure an orderly, peaceful and democratic transition to a true, just and constitutional republic.

- Because our calls [for a meeting] were rejected, the only way to express our views was via an Open Letter. It was not based on personal interest and sentiments and does not hurt the nation and the people. Anyone can support or criticize it. Because the method used was appropriate and did not violate the constitution of the Front or the government, it is legal. It is not reprehensible nor can it establish culpability.

- In contrast, because both the Central Office of the PFDJ and Mr. Alamin Mohammed Said embarked on a defamation campaign that was neither confirmed nor approved by the legislative and executive arms of the Front and the Government and

206

because the President, as the Chairman of both Central Council and National Assembly, did not hold regular and scheduled sessions, they are, according to law, culpable.

2. That the opinions of some of the 15 members [of the Central and National Assemblies] make them culpable:

* Before and after the release of the Open Letter, senior officials of the Front and the Government, particularly the president and Mr. Alamin Mohammed Said, have been presenting their opinions via mass media inside and outside Eritrea even on issues where consensus had not been reached at the Central and National Assemblies. When presented with an opportunity, are the 15 members not allowed to give individual interviews to the mass media? Is it not legal and a right? Shouldn't the government-owned media outlets be held accountable for refusing to host the opinions of some? Isn't it the duty of those in authority to raise the consciousness of the people by exposing them to diverse viewpoints, which will broaden their horizons?

3. That, in matters of war and peace, and the stands they took during the Third Offensive, some of the 15 members committed wrongdoing:

(a) By stating that it was the Government of Eritrea that chose war and rejected peace, they [the Reformers] absolve the Woyane, who is well-known by the Eritrean people as their blood enemy, of all sins. This is a wrong that beautifies the enemy and harms the nation.

That the matter of war and peace with Woyane, before the ignition of war and to this very hour, is a furtive issue of much complication and one that is currently going through legal proceedings. And, in the interest and well being of the nation, it is best that it be handled sensitively.

Just as there is a post-war assessment of your and your enemy's strength and weaknesses, so should there be an assessment of the peace process. There can be differences in the assessment and conclusions drawn. If there is a difference in the assessment of your weakness and the enemy's strength, it cannot be said that it is a wrong committed trying to beautify the enemy and harm the nation.

Of the 15 individuals, there is no one who tried to absolve the enemy and place all the blame on the nation. On the issue of the Peace Process and the War with Woyane, two meetings were held at the Central Council and National Assembly level on July and September 2000. If there is an allegation that an attempt was made to absolve Woyane and place all the blame on the nation, bring the evidence and let the notes [minutes] of meetings be disclosed to the public. If the answer is, this has never been done and it shouldn't be disclosed to the public, we call for the formation of a National Committee of Elders who can be trusted with the information and the evidence.

As for the view that the Woyane should not be presented with a pretext to resume war, this is not one that was expressed in the past: it is a correct viewpoint that should be expressed now and the future.

The assessment of the war and the peace process that was presented by the Central Office [of PFDJ] to the Central Council and National Assembly on July and September 2000 was neither sufficient nor adequate and the resolution passed [by the two bodies] to follow up on the issue by a committee with broader participation ahs not been implemented to date. Even now, we call on the formation of a committee that will include all concerned and with input from the people to assess the war with Woyane and the Peace Process in greater detail and scrutiny.

(b) It [the accusation against us] alleges that, during the Third Woyane Offensive, we said: "We cannot foil and challenge the offensive, as long as the President is in power, the Woyane won't leave us alone and so the President should resign; if the Woyane advance and take over the entire country, they will embark on an oppressive campaign and we should call on the United Nations or the United States to be present." That the senior officers who harbored this extremely dangerous expression could have undermined the fighting spirit and brought about the downfall of the nation, and should be culpable.

Not a single individual from the 15 accused said anything like the above. If there is anyone who has evidence that states otherwise, we call on them to present their evidence.

Although the Third Offensive was foiled by the heroism and valor of the defense forces and the people, there are many failures of the leadership that the defense forces and the people inquire about. There was no member of the defense forces or the people that was demoralized. It is not acceptable to try to cover up your weaknesses by acts of reprisal and accusing others of defeatist attitude.

During the Third Offensive, particularly because of the withdrawal and the abruptness of the withdrawal from Barentu, it cannot be said that there was anybody who did not try to analyze the situation and present likely scenarios, alternatives and choices. Because most of the people were led to believe that after the first shot of the Third Offensive we were going to show miracles, the concern they had developed during the first days of the war turned into extreme anger and questioning the leadership of the war once we withdrew from Barentu. And because the war was being led by the president himself, it was natural that a great deal of the talk dealt about him.

Concurrent with the withdrawal from Barentu, wasn't there another extremely dangerous decision made and that a great deal of loss was averted due to lack of its execution?

The Central Council and the National Assembly, as the bodies that elect the President can – during times of peace and war – change or demote the President when they deem it necessary. Any member of the Assembly has the right to present the idea that the President should be removed and, if he gets the support of 2/3 of the members of the Assembly, can get his idea implemented.

The purpose of these two accusations is to scandalize the senior officials. In military matters, victory is owned by all and failure necessitates the search for a fall-guy. And if one is found, then it is he who is liable!

Although the 15 individuals expressed their opinions to one another, and to other colleagues, during the time of war, and during the peace process, they kept their views veiled from the people and the enemy until the very end. That they did all they could to carry out the missions they were given (and at times, of their own initiative) to strengthen the resolve of the people and to foil the goals of the Woyane is known by all and it is one that doesn't require witnesses or questioning. Just because you criticize the work of the leader or the leadership does not mean you should be considered the enemy of the people and the nation. A leader who works for the sake of the nation and the people should not only not fear criticism, he should encourage it.

(c) It alleges that, they are not driven by the national and popular interest and that other than their individual interests and sentiments, they have no differences of outlook [with the other government officials].

Other than the interest to correct and to introduce a constitutional way of work, these 15 individuals are not driven by individual interest and sentiments. If there are known individual interests and sentiments, why are they not presented? If the question is, "where were they until now?" it is better to start late than never.

Mr. Alamin [Mohammed Said] and whosoever is behind him accused us of not harboring national and popular interest. First of all, we did not embark on national and public service to please or displease them. We do not need their blessings and permission to serve the nation and the people. Our emphasis on exerting maximum effort to avoid conflict with Woyane and resolve it peacefully and, based on the post '98-'99 war assessment to attempt to avoid future wars, was not driven by individual interest and sentiment but for the sake of the nation and the people. [We should remember] that there were those who saw the '78-'79 retreat strategy of the Popular Front as driven by defeatist elements.

Appendices

The accusation that we absolved Woyane and accused Eritrea, that we were going to allow it to run Eritrea as it wished is not one that anyone will give an ear to. Whether before, during or after the war, none of our members held meetings with the Woyane. Since the fifteen of us have no ties with the Woyane or Ethiopia, we cannot possibly have a hidden task.

It is said that other than individual interest and sentiments, we have no differences in outlook. If there is no difference:

1. When we call for meetings of the assemblies, [why does] the President say no?

2. [Why does] the President curtail the work of committees established by the National Assembly?

3. Why aren't the constitutional duties and Assembly resolutions we itemized in our May 2001 Open Letter not implemented?

4. Doesn't our Open Letter of July 3 explain our differences?

5. It is said that we don't have differences of opinion and that all we try to do is exploit and amplify the issues raised by segments of the public. Isn't it a sacred duty to be aware of the issues and complaints of the people, to understand them, to advocate them and to try to come up with solutions for them? If there are issues raised and solutions proposed, does it then follow that the 15 individuals are always behind them? To believe so is to say that there are no problems the people are facing. To believe that, without a push from the 15, there are none that can, of their own initiative, move to resolve their problems is only an indication of derision.

(d) Our silence in the face of calls from people to take steps against them is only because we prioritize meeting the challenges and needs of the people; otherwise, their work is reprehensible and some of them will be answerable to charges.

Who are the ones calling for steps to be taken?

Are these the same individuals who, in the Central Office sessions of January 2001, thinking they won't be detected, attended several meetings and could not hide the fact that what they were saying was rehearsed and orchestrated?

Are they those who write under a pen name in Trgta [government newspaper] and think that their pen name hides their identity?

Are they the ones who, thinking their power is derived from heritage, accuse others at every seminar of harboring the view that they have an entitlement to power?

Are they the elected officials who earned power by paying their dues or are they those who piggybacked on power and without any accountability are attempting to be more Catholic than the Pope?

210

Or is it because they have a crisis of self-confidence and believe that if we disappear from the scene that their future opportunities will be enhanced and guaranteed?

Is the allegation that we have committed crimes that we are answerable for something that someone whispered in their ears? Or is it because they follow a philosophy of all are guilty until proven innocent?

Are the meetings of the Assemblies called for by the 15 individuals and the resolutions that should be implemented of interest to the public or not? Is the President not calling for meetings because he is absolutely lacking in time? Or is it because he considers it of lower priority than the other affairs he spends his time in? Although Independence Day and festivals should be celebrated, is the money, time and manpower spent on them something that should be given priority when compared to the needs of the people for money, time and energy?

Is it proper to delay, to create obstacles in implementing issues of national importance by using unacceptable threats and excuses such as "Not before mothers are notified about their martyred children," "not before those who are displaced are resettled," "not before the borders are demarcated"?

Couldn't the notification of the names of the martyrs to their families have been accomplished on Martyr's Day? Aren't those who have been displaced in need of rehabilitation on their return? And with regards to the border commission, regardless of how long that effort takes, isn't it certain that the process will be based on law?

Although both sides have agreed to be bound by the decision of the Border commission, to the question of "what if one side does not accept the results?" isn't the answer "peaceful efforts should be conducted to ensure that they accept the result" or is the answer necessarily war and conflict? It is possible that even if the border issue is settled, other pretexts can be found to spark a conflict? In these situations, one tries to identify potential causes of conflict and tries to solve them peacefully; if not, even the demarcation of the border will not preclude future conflicts and displacements. Thus, the reason given of "not before the border is demarcated" is simply a delaying excuse.

Will the meetings and implementation of resolutions called for by the 15 individuals be an obstacle to the announcement of the names of the martyred, the demobilization of the recruits, the demarcation of the border, the agendas of rehabilitation, and the defense of national sovereignty? No. In fact, it gives shape and order to the work. And these 15 individuals are, as ever, ready to enlist for any duty including the defense of sovereignty.

The assertion of "we chose to be quiet and not act in haste" is a joke. Who initiated the crisis and the defamation campaign in February 2001? Are the interviews and seminars that followed it, the three retreats in Embatkala, the July 6, 2001 meeting of senior officials at the Central Office of the PFDJ, are all these indications of "being quiet"?

As for the assertion that they wouldn't "act in haste," as Mr. Alamin [Mohammed Said] indicated in his interview, his claim that there are some who are and some who aren't accountable for crimes, and the underground efforts to break us apart, is it because they need time to intimidate and separate us and, having separated us, to make it easier to attack us?

Although they have attempted many campaigns to defame us, we are not from one region or one religion. Who we are and what preparations are being conducted to crush us won't be a secret to the people for long.

If anyone, including the President, is culpable, his crime and his accuser should be presented openly; he should have access to a lawyer, his rights should be respected and the case made in an independent court. Any step taken outside this context is illegal and will have repercussions.